T0369912

GHOSTS OF
NEW ORLEANS

*We at Trafford believe that it is the responsibility of us all, as both individuals
and corporations, to make choices that are environmentally and socially sound.
You, in turn, are supporting this responsible conduct each time you purchase a
Trafford book, or make use of our publishing services. To find out how you are
helping, please visit www.trafford.com/responsiblepublishing.html*

*Our mission is to efficiently provide the world's finest, most comprehensive
book publishing service, enabling every author to experience success.
To find out how to publish your book, your way, and have it available
worldwide, visit us online at www.trafford.com/10510*

www.trafford.com

North America & international
toll-free: 1 888 232 4444 (USA & Canada)
phone: 250 383 6864 ✦ fax: 250 383 6804
email: info@trafford.com

The United Kingdom & Europe
phone: +44 (0)1865 722 113 ✦ local rate: 0845 230 9601
facsimile: +44 (0)1865 722 868 ✦ email: info.uk@trafford.com

10 9 8 7 6 5 4 3

Madame X (Madame Pierre Gautreau)

John Singer Sargent, 1856–1925, American, 1883–84

Oil on canvas, 82 1/8 x 43 1/4 in. (208.6 x 109.9 cm)

The Metropolitan Museum of Art, Arthur Hoppock Hearn Fund, 1916 (16.53)

Image © The Metropolitan Museum of Art

Book Design: Karen Engelmann | www.karenengelmann.com

PLAYS BY
ROSARY HARTEL O'NEILL
VOLUME 2

GHOSTS OF
NEW ORLEANS

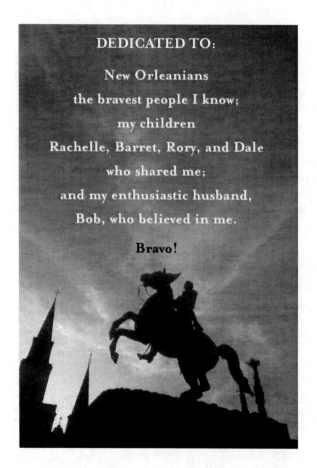

DEDICATED TO:

New Orleanians
the bravest people I know;
my children
Rachelle, Barret, Rory, and Dale
who shared me;
and my enthusiastic husband,
Bob, who believed in me.

Bravo!

ROSARY HARTEL O'NEILL

TABLE OF CONTENTS

THE PLAYS

FOREWORD

Rosary O'Neill is a playwright of enormous talent and range who deservedly has a large audience. We have known this true Southern Belle for many years and have showcased her multiple prize-winning plays at The National Arts Club. Dr. O'Neill has a fertile mind that can conjure unique fictional characters with real flesh and blood. The dialogue is always memorable, and the plots are singular and magnetic. We have always been enriched by O'Neill Plays and look forward to many, many more.

ALDON JAMES
President
National Arts Club, New York

DIRECTOR'S NOTES

I met Rosary through Susan Sandler the playwright and screenwriter of CROSSING DELANCY, who was also a supporter of Rosary's work. I directed the reading of two scenes from Rosary's WHITE SUITS IN SUMMER and THE AWAKENING OF KATE CHOPIN at the Uta Hagen/Herbert Berghof Playwright's Theater. Rosary's work is fascinating because it is variously romantic, historic and dramatic—reminiscent of the works of Flaubert, Chekhov, Tolstoy and Tennessee Williams. A variable trinity of dramatic spices, I've read and directed almost all of Rosary's plays, many several times, and they are complex and fulfilling and you discover new treasures every time through. Rosary's plays are a tremendous pleasure to see and work on, offering wonderful opportunities for the director, actor and designer.

TOM THORNTON
Director, New York

INTRODUCTION/VOL 2

Volume Two contains historical plays, mostly Victorian, with characters driven by stratified society and tradition. My interest in historical drama was triggered by my love of Chekhov, Tennessee Williams, and New Orleans architecture. Living in New Orleans, one finds constant reminders of a lost world: Creole cottages on the streetcar line, camelback houses facing the zoo, neoclassical mansions in the Garden District, plantations on the river. All New Orleanians have some fantasy house they want to restore or reclaim.

It is impossible to live in New Orleans and not have an interest in the past. New Orleans was not damaged by the Civil War. Most mansions, Creole cottages, and shotgun houses were spared because basically the war did not move that far South. So when you drive down and see these gracious manors in the Garden District, you think: Who lived in that house? Why? Who stays there now? You walk along the Mississippi River, you wonder: What ships are docked there? Who came to town or left?

My parents and grandmothers used to talk about New Orleans and New York being equally important ports and centers of culture before the Civil War. I couldn't believe this, given how little legitimate theatre remained in New Orleans. There was a hard-working Opera using rental space, a destitute symphony, and a few community theatres struggling for money. After the war, my folks said schools and theatres were stricken; only street music

ROSARY HARTEL O'NEILL

survived. The theatre world, which had been so vibrant, never truly recovered.

Fascinated by this disparity, I studied New Orleans theatre history at UCLA and wrote my PhD dissertation on New Orleans Carnival Organizations Theatre of Prestige, a study stratifying New Orleans society based on membership in carnival organizations. I visited different communities in the city and saw how generations clustered in the same neighborhood, married the same kind of people and were buried in the same cemetery. Similar birth-to-death experiences made each group feel safe. It also made for the bad parts of a stratified society.

There is a huge emphasis on beauty in New Orleans, on the past, on glamour. After the Civil War the Carnival balls and parades proliferated, encouraging extravagance and foolhardiness at Mardi Gras. Bands, flambeaux carriers, masked costumed riders with kings and queens, created the illusion that grandeur would return. People saved up all year to wear luxurious costumes and dance in ballrooms or with masked Indians on the street.

My family was totally involved in carnival organizations, with parades, balls, and dancing breakfasts till 4 am. From earliest post-war times, money has been squandered in New Orleans on lavishness. The queen's gown alone, which resembles a renaissance monarch—hand-beaded and scrolled with velvet—costs a minimum of $10,000. My grandma liked to drive her Cadillac to the questionable parts of town and have her chauffeur hand out beers from the trunk and then watch the men costumed as Indians in feathers and beads from head to foot dance around the car. Not politically correct for sure.

It was very difficult when I ran Southern Rep Theatre in New Orleans to raise money for plays, because New Orleanians' excess resources were all spent on Mardi Gras and themselves.

New Orleans was a city where people didn't leave. Ways of behavior were inherited, and a sense of family, of tradition, of culture, prevailed. New Orleanians are European by nature; they love to cook, to eat, to sit and talk endlessly after dinner. They enjoy being friendly because practically everyone they know went to high school with them or somebody else in the family or neighborhood.

Also, among the upper classes, certain old patterns continue: people sitting around the table telling ghost stories, grandmothers passing on anecdotes about who did what, people playing games like charades, cards, hide and seek. People wearing costumes and sneaking around and surprising family members. This sense of carnival and having fun glued life together there.

Knowledge of New Orleans history made me want to adapt Uncle Vanya. Carson McCullers, the famous Southern novelist, once wrote an article comparing the fall of plantation life in 1900 Louisiana to the collapse of the aristocratic culture in the Russia of Vanya. I loved the play but felt its details were too Russian to be understood by Americans. I took the bones of <u>Vanya</u> and put it on a plantation called Waverly, the last sugarcane plantation in Louisiana, and called my play <u>Uncle Victor</u>.

That play won a number of awards and hooked me on historical drama. I decided every week to visit a famous site in New Orleans to inspire my writing. I went to the Degas house on Esplanade, now a bed and breakfast, but the only existing house where Degas lived in the world. At that time, all 24 paintings Degas had done in the house were being displayed for the first time in the New Orleans Museum of Art, and I was allowed to live and write at the Degas House, provided I moved my garbage bag of clothes from room to room as specific ones were booked.

I wrote a nine-cast show, so struck was I by all Degas' relatives who had lived with him in 1872. Degas had tried to save his Uncle's failing cotton business and create new roots in the city of his mother. He fell prey to scandal and decadence. Often the more important the character, the more critical the problems. This works well in drama, where the playwright's job is to torture the hero.

Historical plays offer audiences a perspective on the human condition, the chance to see what is the same and what different over the years. Clothing and manners may change, but the desire to be somebody and give back to the community doesn't. The historical play may provide audiences with more spectacle, gorgeous people framed in a luminous place. It's like Carnival in New Orleans: we have kings, queens, maids, pomp, circumstance, and glamour onstage again. Certainly, one delight of historical drama may be the beautiful sets and costumes required.

My plays are historically accurate. Obviously, you take a scenario and expand the story but the main facts: the births, deaths, relationships are all to the best of my knowledge correct.

Places in New Orleans are so connected, full of history, full of pain. Some say they are still troubled by the ghosts that would like to come back and be celebrated again.

I visited a haunted sugar cane plantation, with its co-owner, a lead actor, and his blind dog. I and the cast of our then current show at Southern Rep (the company I founded in New Orleans) were served dinner and a fabulous cheese grits breakfast in the main dining room, by a kitchen staff still on call, who pointed out which of our bedrooms would probably have ghostly visitors.

I spent days visiting Kate Chopin's house in Cloutierville, La., the bathroom of which was said to be so haunted; though I was offered quarters in the house for research, I was afraid to spend the night. I interviewed descendents of Chopin's lover Albert Sanpite and town members about the scandals of her life. I read all available material on Chopin and talked with the leading experts on her (Barbara Ewell and Emily Toth). I researched in French and English all the books on Degas, both at the Tulane archives and at the Louvre in Paris. I did similar research in New York and Paris for <u>Beckett at Greystones Bay</u> and <u>John Singer Sargent and Madame X</u>, my newest plays, loosely tied to New Orleans.

The Degas House, New Orleans
Photo by Millicent Hand

We rehearsed and performed the <u>Degas</u> play both at the New Orleans Museum of Art (where I met Degas' two great-nieces, and the play was declared the official play on Degas) and at the Degas House, where interested actors were encouraged to spend the night. One of the most interesting experiences we had at Southern Rep was performing <u>Degas</u> in that Degas House on Esplanade. We used the side parlors to stage the scenes where Degas must have painted, eaten or danced. We used the hall staircases for the actors to come down from bedrooms where the characters had lived.

Often the actors felt like ghosts reliving situations that had haunted the house. They were being compelled by the house to do certain things they weren't even aware of. When it rained, the actors entered through the front gallery, ducking through the big windows dripping with rain and complaining about their fear the levee was breaking.

A major theme in my work is the struggle of the artist, the sacrifices made to maintain sanity. Degas' father wanted him to be an attorney.

We are glad Degas did go back to Paris and paint and didn't succumb to the temptations of New Orleans. We are pleased Sargent refused to change his scorned portrait of Madame X and that Kate Chopin forged a way to raise her six children and still write.

Often, I focus on the Victorian period, one play leading to another, creating a tapestry of artists working simultaneously in New Orleans. Kate Chopin's husband was friendly with the Degas family, and his cotton office was next door to theirs. She is less known, although a very important American novelist. I wanted to know what it was like to be a woman artist in the same post Civil-War period. Apparently Chopin and Degas are rumored to have walked the streets together at night.

There are many antidotes in New Orleans, and people believe them more than facts, saying that the homes of the famous will remain haunted till a family member moves back in and lives there.

I have never been in a town where people liked to plume up more like peacocks. Used to be more ball gowns were sold in New Orleans than in any other city in the world. All that comes from the amazing sense of fantasy about carnival and about life, where people want to present themselves in a striking way. Of course before television, Internet and email, the idea of sitting in a parlor, presenting yourself, talking about something interesting was a big part of what life was about…that human interaction, that connection to family. My grandma, for instance, used to receive nephews, nieces, and friends on certain holidays like Thanksgiving and January first. Her mansion on the streetcar line was open for specified hours. During Mardi Gras, many New Orleanians have open houses several days a week.

Carnival was at the heart of locals' hope: fantasy renewed belief that the good life would return. Prior to Katrina there was a ball or parade for fifty nights before Mardi Gras in every community. After the hurricane there was only one week. But without those few days of pleasure—eating, drinking, and celebrating—New Orleanians would have fallen apart.

Carnival creates that sense of suspended animation, the feeling that a marvelous, beautiful time will come back because all the glorious architecture, though distressed, is there waiting for the people to inhabit it, and traditions go on like the parade.

Now, with parts of the city destroyed, only certain areas will be able to sustain that legacy that created the melting pot, which New Orleans is.

One can only hope that the new composition of New Orleans will be as interesting as the old. Now with history jeopardized, New Orleans could become just another American city

On the downside, there was a great deal of poverty, crime, and illiteracy before Katrina, an increasing division between the haves and the haves nots. Louisiana was one of the poorest states in funding education and culture. Let's hope the recent devastation may lead to an infusion of talent, money, and vision that brings New Orleans forward as one of the premier cities of the south. These plays are dedicated to the blossoming of New Orleans.

ROSARY HARTEL O'NEILL
NEW YORK, NEW YORK

Degas in
New Orleans

A PLAY IN TWO ACTS

First performed in June 2002
at the Degas House, New Orleans

CAST OF CHARACTERS

EDGAR DEGAS, 38, French painter

RENE DEGAS, 27, brother of Degas

MICHEL MUSSON, 60, their uncle

DESIREE (DIDI) MUSSON, 34, their unmarried cousin

MATHILDE MUSSON BELL, 31, their married cousin

ESTELLE (TELL) MUSSON BALFOUR DEGAS, 29,
their blind cousin, Rene's wife

JOSEPHINE (JO) BALFOUR, 10, Tell's little girl from
her first marriage

EMILY CUCKOW RILLIEUX, 45, free woman of color,
Degas' second cousin

AMERICA DURRIVE OLIVIER, 24, Rene's mistress

WILL BELL (*offstage*), husband of Mathilde—never appears

SETTING

A two-story rental house at 2306 Esplanade Avenue, New
Orleans, Louisiana. It is 1872. A double parlor with the
remnants of grandeur: a glittering chandelier, an elegant
tattered sofa, a mahogany desk, and a high-back chair. To
the right, two floor-to-ceiling windows open onto a galley;
to the left, a door to the pantry. Upstage two matching
parlor doors lead offstage to an unseen, staircased grand
hallway that connects the upstairs, and the front and rear
of the house. Outside we hear the clanging of a random,
mule-drawn streetcar. Throughout the play, Degas' paintings or the rapturous colors within them are projected
onto the rear wall, lending their transparent blues, pinks,
and violets to the bleak setting.

ROSARY HARTEL O'NEILL

PROLOGUE: EDGAR

(Music playing softly. EDGAR stands facing the audience. As he mentions his cousins and brother, they enter the scene and pose in a tableau of beautiful young people in the countryside.)

EDGAR: I have a picture in my mind of the best painting I never painted: three women and two men in untouched expectation. It's October, 1863. I'm in the French countryside with my cousins, unclaimed jewels from New Orleans riding out the Civil War in France. My brother Rene is there, the bloom of youth on his cheek. I'm twenty-nine. He is only eighteen. We're dining in the forest, our enthusiasm buoyed by the smell of red wine, fresh bread, and the lightness of each other. Mathilde with her husky voice talking at full speed about Italian plums and Van Dyke. Didi with her notes on Flaubert and Tell, beautiful Tell, just twenty and already a Civil War widow. And oh, the sunlight and the, God knows why, laughter. We were in our twenties and life seemed good, forever a future. *(Music fades out)*

That was before thirty thousand Parisians were killed in the Commune, six hundred thousand boys died in the American Civil War. I was copying Delacroix at the Louvre and hurrying to the French country to relax. Nine years later when I visited New Orleans, our worlds had changed.

Slides—Degas' face and then the Degas house on Esplanade Avenue in New Orleans. Throughout the play we hear ragtime music like the compositions of Louis Moreau Gottschalk

BLACKOUT

ACT 1

(October 25, 1872—5:30 a.m. Gottschalk music and slides of the Degas House at the same time. JO BALFOUR, 10, is asleep on the floor, in a pink tutu and ballet slippers, her hair caught in a ribboned ponytail like Degas' statue of La Fille de Quartorze Ans. Jo rises dreamily and begins to dance. SHE lies back on the floor, returning to her sleeping state. TELL DEGAS, 29, a blind woman, feels her way across the stage, counting the steps from the door to a sofa. SHE is exquisite, fragile with a porcelain beauty. Now and then SHE stumbles but stabilizes herself with a little moan and moves ahead with even more fervor.)

SOUND: *Music fades, slides out, lights up.*

TELL: One, two, three, four . . .
(Bumps into a table)
Five, six, seven, eight.
(Stumbles on a suitcase)
Who put that there? Whose suitcase? Edgar's?
(Smiles affectionately)
Edgar's coat? What a wonderful smell.
(Her manner drifts to a shy girl as she wraps herself in it)
It's far too long. I must look like a scarecrow.
(Feels another coat and flask with a worried look)
Rene's coat. He'll sleep till noon.
(Turns, trips on her daughter's legs, and cries distraught)
Jo. You're supposed to be on the sofa.

JO: *(Gets up restlessly)* Oh Mommy. I dreamed I was a bird and could fly high, but I flew into a clothesline and my wings got caught. What's that mean?

TELL: You're just excited because Uncle Edgar's coming to visit.

JO: I don't want you to love him more than me.

TELL: Don't be foolish, Josephine.

JO: I told you I want to be called Jo after Papa.

(TELL goes to fold the sheets, trips on a puppet and cries disgustedly)

4

TELL: You can't leave these puppets out!

JO: I don't want to give my room to Uncle Edgar.

TELL: You must. This house is so crowded. If anything is out of place I'm going to fall.

JO: Use your cane.

TELL: I don't want Edgar to know I use it.

JO: Why?

(Turning, TELL stumbles into the table. She gives JO a sharp warning look)

TELL: Lord, Jo, did you touch this table?

JO: I didn't.

TELL: You can't do that.

JO: Why do I have to give my room to Uncle Edgar?

TELL: Fold up your sheets.

JO: I need my own place.

TELL: Painters are sensitive to their environment.

JO: Maybe he'll be my friend. Then they'll never send me away.

TELL: Are you listening to me?

JO: (SHE pauses, looking away—then with an undercurrent of lonely yearning) Buy me a little painting. Please.

(TELL turns to comfort her daughter, collides into the suitcase again and cries with nervous exasperation)

TELL: My God. I almost slipped again.

JO: *(Hugs her mother and her face lights up with a charming, shy embarrassment)* I want Uncle to paint you, Mama. You're so beautiful. If he would have painted Papa, he'd have been with me always. I don't know what he looked like. If Uncle paints you, you'll be with me forever.

(TELL smiles, puts an arm around JO's shoulder—coaxingly)

TELL: Come with me.

(A burst of laughter comes from the hallway. They hurry out. MATHILDE, 31, an elegant but frazzled woman, walks in through the pantry with a tray with coffee pot, cups, and saucers. Pours her coffee expectantly and sits on the sofa. UNCLE MICHEL, 60, dressed in a Confederate Army uniform, barges in from the front hallway followed by DIDI, 34, an intense pretty lady with soft features. All move quickly, full of eager anticipation to greet EDGAR first.)

UNCLE MICHEL: No matter how early I get up, it's never early enough. *(Goes to the back parlor doorway and calls)* Out, Jo, out.

DIDI: *(Shocked but giggling)* Shush, Papa. Take off that uniform. Someone's going to shoot you.

UNCLE MICHEL: I need to greet my nephew in style.

MATHILDE: *(SHE comes to him, laughing, and pats his shoulder playfully)* Go back to sleep, Papa.

UNCLE MICHEL: I want to have a quiet cup of coffee alone.

DIDI: I just wanted to have a quiet cup of coffee alone.

UNCLE MICHEL: *(With indignant appeal)* Jo, out. *(Grumbling)* The dressing room is always occupied in this house. God, I've got a headache.

JO: *(From the rear hallway shouts)* One minute.

MATHILDE: *(Gives him a sharp warning look, but HE doesn't see it)* You should stop drinking.

UNCLE MICHEL: Babies screaming through the night.

DIDI: Put some sherry on their lips.

UNCLE MICHEL: Or let me strangle one of them. *(Calls toward the back parlor doorway)* Jo. Get out. *(Regards DIDI with a shrug of his shoulders)* Mathilde, I want you to help Didi fix up. Didi needs a husband. Edgar is her last chance. I wouldn't have picked him, but the pickings are slim. A girl's life is like a ship. When she's sixteen, you've got to launch her, deck her with flags and ribbons, sail her out. At twenty-three, the ship turns and starts back to port. Didi is at the dock.

MATHILDE: Good morning to you too.

UNCLE MICHEL: *(Turns to DIDI, in a merry tone that is a bit forced)* Who's going to care for you when I keel over? Your sisters' husbands? The church? Remember what your mother said about those spinsters, who spied on their married neighbor. They'd snicker when they heard her husband beating her or when they saw bruises on her arm. One day, that wife charged out of her house and screamed, "You can laugh and you can hiss but on my tombstone won't be 'Miss.' On my tombstone won't be 'Miss.'"

MATHILDE: Just let us enjoy Edgar's company as we did in Paris.

UNCLE MICHEL: *(With humorous exaggeration)* Keep away from Edgar. You've got a husband.

JO *(Shouts from the hallway)* Finished.

(TELL comes in from the back hallway)

UNCLE MICHEL: Excuse me, girls. *(He leans over, kisses TELL's cheek impulsively, then turning back, adds with a constrained air)* Mathilde, do Didi's hair like yours. She looks like a gargoyle.

TELL: *(Once her father has gone, TELL speaks with girlish gravity)* Will didn't come home last night? I didn't hear him.

DIDI: Oh, you were awake; you didn't come down. Mathilde, your husband was drunk as usual.

MATHILDE: Edgar can help Will turn his life around.

TELL: How did Edgar look?

MATHILDE: It was so late and they were exhausted so we just greeted each other. *(SHE chuckles—then with a pleased, relieved air)* Uncertain, tentative, as if he had some secret. He was all dressed the part of the painter/poet—so kind and so subdued. You know how young bachelors do.

TELL: It's sad. They're not going to get drawn into matrimony, but they practice in case the real thing—

(From the hallway, JO and UNCLE MICHEL's voices are heard)

DIDI: *(Hastily)* Have you told your husband about the new item?

MATHILDE: Didi!

TELL: *(Too vehemently)* Not yet. Don't say anything. Y'all promised.

(UNCLE MICHEL and JO dash in, enthusiastically fencing with canes. HE laughs, and SHE laughs with him. There is an old boyish charm to his gestures.)

JO: Mommy.

TELL: Stop, Jo.

DIDI: Not with Tell's cane.

UNCLE MICHEL: En garde.

DIDI: It's not her, it's him.

UNCLE MICHEL: Move back the furniture.

TELL: You're messing things up.

MATHILDE: Stop him.

DIDI: *(Jokingly but with an undercurrent of resentment)* It's not my turn to watch him.

(UNCLE MICHEL and JO go out into the front hallway, still fencing.

ROSARY HARTEL O'NEILL

MATHILDE talks to DIDI with nervous irritation.)

MATHILDE: Didi, take Tell; I'll straighten up.

TELL: Yes, but if the furniture is off—

MATHILDE: By an inch, I know.

(DIDI hurries TELL off through the back parlor doorway. MATHILDE gets some coffee, sits, and drinks contentedly. EDGAR pokes through a gallery window. SHE stops abruptly, catching EDGAR's eyes regarding her with an uneasy, prob-ing look. SHE is overcome by a fit of acute self-consciousness.

MATHILDE: *(Cont.)* Edgar? Oh Lord. You scared me. You mustn't glance about, till we're—

EDGAR: *(With an awkward tenderness)* You look wonderful. I told you last night.

MATHILDE: I was tired. Why are you looking at me like that? I know I've changed. Will's business is doing poorly. I can't get rid of these dark circles. Once my husband talks to you...

EDGAR: *(A strange obstinacy to his face)* I'm not here to do business.

MATHILDE: We're depending on you for prosperity. *(EDGAR moves hasti-ly to the desk, his eyes are drawn to a picture.)* Tell's wedding portrait. To Joe Balfour. She was sixteen.

EDGAR: She looks like a pouty child.

MATHILDE: Not with those breasts. She got the family collection. Look, Edgar's blushing. Tell always did that to him.

EDGAR: No, it's you—you're trying to embarrass me. *(HE smiles now with teasing affection)*

MATHILDE: You have to know us to paint us.

(UNCLE MICHEL'S and JO'S voices are heard in the hallway. THEY enter in a flurry.)

UNCLE MICHEL: There you are. Welcome, Edgar.

JO: Oh, Uncle Edgar.

EDGAR: *(Takes her hands and gently lifts them up)* Can't be Jo. Such a big girl.

JO: Will you stay with us forever—

(DIDI comes in from the back parlor.)

DIDI: Edgar, oh no. Edgar. You're up already. I still can't believe you're here.

EDGAR: You've a different hair-do.

DIDI: You noticed. *(SHE smiles, her face lighting up, and hugs him gratefully. HE turns, sees TELL standing quietly in the front parlor doorway. HE speaks almost gently)*

EDGAR: Tell, is that you?

TELL: Hello, Edgar.

EDGAR: You're even more beautiful.

TELL: *(Embarrassed and pleased)* You think so.

EDGAR: *(Catches himself)* All the Musson sisters…beautiful

(DIDI, MATHILDE, and JO surround EDGAR.)

ALL GIRLS TOGETHER: Come talk to us. Tell us about Paris. Sit by me. No, me. Over here.

UNCLE MICHEL: Down, girls. Let's leave Didi with Edgar.

TELL: Fine.

(With a knowing nod to DIDI, UNCLE MICHEL, MATHILDE, JO, and TELL slip out. DIDI paces, speaks quickly, unable to tame her excitement.)

DIDI: I made a list of things we can discuss. I jotted down novels you might like, and borrowed those I could. We can't always get the latest books, it's not Paris. But I did find Madame Bovary, some Dumas père and Baudelaire.

EDGAR: I haven't read poetry for a long time.

DIDI: I got Alfred de Musset and George Sand. Are you following...the controversy about her novel, <u>She and He</u>?

EDGAR: Not yet. (*HE smiles, and SHE smiles with him. Then SHE changes to a brisk businesslike air*)

DIDI: The two principal figures are both artists...I suppose you've read <u>The Son of Titian</u>, whose hero is endowed with his father's talent but is so overwhelmed in love that he renounces his art.

EDGAR: (*Impressed—mollifyingly*) Are you still reading a book a week?

DIDI: (*With hearty confidence now*) No, but now that you're here I'll do more. I'm going to copy you. Whenever you paint, I'll write. I'm writing a novel.

EDGAR: The three Musson sisters, always together. (*Hesitates*) How's Tell?

DIDI: Fine. (*Her hands flutter up to her hair*) Did you get my letters? You didn't respond much.

EDGAR: (*Evasively*) Most painters aren't good with words. That is why we draw pictures.

DIDI: I don't like people who talk all the time but say nothing. I like your new signature. One word like Delacroix, not De la Croix. "Degas," not the two words "de Gas" that implies aristocracy. Your brothers were furious. They paid for that false coat of arms, and the name change. They don't want people to know the family goes back to a bunch of bakers. What I admire most about you is your awareness of the smallest element of art, even one so peripheral and personal as the signature. I've studied the signature and there are similarities between the D in Daumier, the e in Delacroix and the final S in Ingres. I need to find a distinctive professional signature for my writing and a male name like George Sand. With a woman's name you can't become successful. Don't you agree?

EDGAR: Sorry. I wouldn't know. *(HE stiffens, looks at her awkwardly, but SHE flounders on)*

DIDI: I amuse myself with letter writing. I used to so look forward to sealing that envelope, placing a stamp on it, knowing your hand would touch it. I'd reread each letter several times before I sent it. Most were not up to my standards, a misspelling, a clumsy adjective. Some I rewrote four or five times to get them perfect. Want to see? *(Goes restlessly to the desk, takes out letters with a frightened, protective tenderness)* These are the ones I never sent. Next to the ones I received. Silly, but I like to reread them both. My way of being in Paris with you. *(Compulsively, as if talking to herself)* I love your stationery and bright blue ink. The paper is so smooth and every letter signed boldly. "Degas." Just like your paintings. I've a special folder for each letter. You can count on me to guard every aspect of your history.

(EDGAR is sleeping on the sofa. DIDI tiptoes closer to him, baffled. Rebuffed and hurt, SHE minces toward the door, peers back at EDGAR, then slips out. TELL enters, with practical authority. SHE is silent, keeping her chin up, her hands stretched delicately in front of her. SHE bumps into the sofa, and with a tiny sigh recovers, moves forward. Carefully EDGAR stirs. SHE turns her head that way. Her smile vanishes.)

TELL: Edgar? Edgar. *(Worriedly)* Good. He's gone.

(EDGAR stretches. SHE turns back, stops abruptly, then moves again, her hands reaching for the table top. Slowly EDGAR wakes up. HE watches TELL, shocked—his expression becomes somber as HE stares at her with a growing dread. Suddenly SHE is self-consciously aware that someone is staring fixedly at her.)

TELL: *(Cont.)* Edgar?

EDGAR: *(Hesitates, then bursts out guiltily)* Tell, what's wrong? Can't you see me?

TELL: I wasn't paying attention.

EDGAR: I've been watching you. *(Gets up worriedly and touches her arm)* I don't know what to say.

TELL: *(Quickly)* Don't say anything.

EDGAR: You can't see me? *(A defensive uneasiness comes into his voice)* God, you can't see me.

TELL: I see a little.

EDGAR: *(Strickenly)* How long...

TELL: What?

EDGAR: Have you been this way?

TELL: A year.

EDGAR: That long? What...happened?

TELL: An infection.

(EDGAR stares at her, ignoring the explanations)

EDGAR: Go on.

TELL: Another operation—

EDGAR: *(Takes her hand with deep seriousness)* You don't have to be embarrassed.

TELL: *(Her voice is suddenly moved by deep feeling)* I want you to remember me the way I was.

EDGAR: I do.

TELL: For instance?

EDGAR: You used to run with such splendor. *(Struggling for words)* Always the first, way out in front of the others.

TELL: And what else?

EDGAR: In the country, how you loved to try out different paths, searching for new trees, flowers . . .*(Awkward pause where THEY smile at each other affectionately. Then a strange undercurrent of revengefulness comes into his voice)* All those letters—Didi said nothing. Why didn't Rene tell me? I'd have come.

TELL: I'd have thrown you out . . .

EDGAR: I wouldn't let you.

TELL: I don't want to fall in love with you again.

EDGAR: Yes. *(Genuinely concerned)* Perhaps in Paris the specialists can help. But…What can I do?

TELL: Ask me what I need and I'll tell you. If I'm walking towards a chair and you bring it to me I'll probably trip.

EDGAR: You see nothing? *(Stares at her—then looks away—after a pause)* Nothing at all?

TELL: I see blurs.

EDGAR: How do you cope?

TELL: *(With a brave air of weary acceptance)* You never get over it, you get used to it.

EDGAR: Do you?

TELL: I get by working with contrasts.

EDGAR: Is that so?

TELL: Analyzing the whole moving environment.

EDGAR: Oh.

TELL: Move and I'll find you. *(HE hesitates)* Go on.

EDGAR: *(Touched, his love for her coming out)* I can't…I'm so…I just can't imagine…

TELL: Do it for me.

EDGAR: *(Reluctantly, HE moves away)* All right. Should I talk?

TELL: *(Laughs, a lilt comes into her voice)* No, that would make it too easy. Go on. *(HE moves away; she walks in the wrong direction; HE steps into her path.)*

TELL: There! I found you. See?

EDGAR: I should have come sooner. *(His voice grows husky and trembles a little)* I could have helped you. If only you'd—

TELL: *(Changing the subject)* Do you look different?

EDGAR: *(Jokingly but with an undercurrent of passion)* I have a few gray hairs, but they say my shoulders are stronger.

TELL: Oh, my. I'm trying to imagine you—I'm so excited. I can't. *(Timidly)* Can I touch your face? *(Her hands glide lovingly over his features. HE squeezes her hands)* You haven't changed much. What's this scar?

EDGAR: A ricochet wound. *(HE is suddenly shamefaced)* I went through some ugly things fighting in the Commune.

TELL: Did you?

EDGAR: I've staggered through blood baths, watched my friends dying. Anybody in any way connected to the Commune or in the wrong place at the time was shot.

TELL: But you survived.

EDGAR: *(Looks away guiltily)* I escaped because I was mistaken for a corpse. All the friends I had in Paris are unhappy or dead. *(Grins at her provocatively)* I'm here to make a new life in New Orleans.

RENE: *(Scowling from the front hallway)* Tell, Tell.

EDGAR: *(Tactfully)* There's your husband.

TELL: I'm in here.

(RENE saunters in, enthusiasm covering his hangover.)

RENE: Morning.

EDGAR: Morning.

(EDGAR disappears to a chair on the gallery. RENE looks after him annoyed, then hugs TELL reprovingly.)

RENE: I reached for you in bed but you'd gone. I missed you.

TELL: I have a surprise for you. My heart is racing.

RENE: *(Putting an arm around her with a playful squeeze)* If you're happy that's all that counts.

TELL: I'm so distracted with the thrill of it. I don't want to disappoint you. I'm afraid I'm going to now.

RENE: *(Smiling, glances at mail)* You can't hurt me, Sugar.

TELL: I know what I'm going to say has to be approached delicately so everything can start in the best way…I know I look the same but I'm not. I want you to appreciate my change. *(Walks to him, giddy, and bumps into the sofa)* I can get around well by myself. I'm prepared for spontaneity. The children are happy. They see me as this person who does things in this magical blind world. Oh, Rene, we're going to have a baby.

(RENE stops short—then smiles broadly, with a painful effort to be a good sport.)

RENE: You're serious? It's settled? Another child? Oh my God. *(Hugs her, unable to conceal an almost furtive uneasiness)* You said you couldn't get pregnant…A…A third child. We agreed two were enough.

TELL: True, but a baby!

RENE: Last time someone had to walk you about. *(A look of contemptuous hostility flashes across his face)* Didn't the doctor forbid this? The other children aren't even three. One a year. Don't you remember how we had to walk the floor! Always some infection, the earaches, sore throats, the colic.

TELL: *(Ashamed)* You won't have to do anything.

RENE: Your father keeps prodding me about making money, about my place as head of the house. I turn around and you're having another baby. Can nothing be done? How did this occur? I thought you were nursing.

TELL: Yes…it's a miracle. God wants this for us, Rene. There are nights I feel something is happening inside me, despite me, I can't get over it. Please be happy for us.

RENE: The doctor says you're a high risk. Let's wait to tell the others till you're further along.

Stung, TELL disappears out the front parlor. HE watches her condemningly, swigging from the flask in his pocket. MATHILDE comes through the pantry, her face worried. SHE is reassured to find RENE alone. RENE turns, adjusts his jacket.

MATHILDE: Good morning.

RENE: Good morning.

MATHILDE: Coffee? It's wonderful to have you home. *(Winks with a kidding grin)* Did you have a grand time with Edgar in Paris? I like your new suit.

RENE: *(Nervously buffing his sleeves)* I've got to give the impression I'm successful, to make money in the future.

MATHILDE: You seem bitter.

RENE: That's what I sound like when I'm amused.

MATHILDE: Soon as you settle in, we must talk about the loan I made you. *(SHE looks at him—lovingly)* You promised to get Edgar to invest in Will's business.

RENE: Can this wait until later? I've such a headache.

MATHILDE: *(In a light tone that is a bit forced)* Will's creditors won't wait.

(UNCLE MICHEL and JO explode through the back parlor door, fencing with canes.)

JO: Parry.

MATHILDE: We need Edgar's help.

UNCLE MICHEL: Out of my way.

MATHILDE: Papa, please…

(UNCLE MICHEL and JO go out the front parlor door. RENE turns on him reproachfully.)

RENE: The man doesn't see I'm here. He's my father-in-law.

MATHILDE: You said Edgar would repay us.

RENE: *(Yells, in UNCLE MICHEL's direction)* And he can't say hello. Why is that?

MATHILDE: Is that a yes for the money?

RENE: Yes, but not today. *(MATHILDE lifts up the coffee tray with bitter resentment)* Leave the coffee.

MATHILDE: *(Turns on him sharply, goes out through the pantry)* This has to last the week.

Light focus changes to gallery.

(RENE stares at his flask with fascinated disgust, slinks in a chair, drinks. EDGAR goes to him with a stubborn, bitterly resentful look.)

EDGAR: She's blind. You couldn't tell me?

RENE: *(HE flounders guiltily)* The woman swore me to secrecy. She didn't want to see you. And now…*(HE laughs, then scowls)*

EDGAR: What's wrong?

RENE: Tell's…pregnant…I never get sandbagged by men, just women. I've pretty much decided my life is over for the next few years…

EDGAR: She wasn't supposed to have children?

RENE: Right. *(Evading his eyes)* We need money for—for doctors, medicines…

EDGAR: Here. *(Unfolding bills from a stack in his pocket)*

RENE: That's too much.

EDGAR: You're my favorite brother.

RENE: Soon as we go to the cotton office, you can help me collect on our accounts.

EDGAR: I'm not here for that. *(Stiffens)* I've got to paint.

RENE: *(Jovially passes him the flask)* Have some.

EDGAR: So early?

RENE: *(Puts an arm around EDGAR, with false confidence, gives him a boyish hug and steers him back into the parlor)* I'm celebrating your arrival New Orleans style. The thing about Louisiana is nobody's trying to get ahead. You meet amazing people who are not looking for money. They go to parties given by their best friends, that's all. I believe in New Orleans and her possibilities. No place has the flamboyance, the charm this city has. And I don't want us to sell cotton unless selling it makes our lives every day so much richer.

UNCLE MICHEL: *(Comes in from back parlor. HE gives a quick suspicious glance from RENE to EDGAR)* Edgar…Welcome. Good you came. *(With a concerned tone)* I need to talk to you about…Didi.

EDGAR: Why, is something wrong with her?

UNCLE MICHEL: No, no, she is fine. All right, we will talk about her later. *(His expression turns solemn)* First things first…Business.

EDGAR: Rene is doing well in the cotton business.

UNCLE MICHEL: Hasn't Rene told you?

EDGAR: No.

UNCLE MICHEL: *(With a resentful glance at RENE)* Rene is not in the cotton but in the manufacturing business. He manufactures unhappiness.

EDGAR: You are always joking.

UNCLE MICHEL: I won't talk about what it used to be like—when I ran things—because that would involve adverse comparisons.

EDGAR: I know Rene is doing his...

UNCLE MICHEL: Don't defend him. The man gives his best energy to traveling and drinking, activities that are clearly not lucrative.

RENE: *(HE flounders guiltily)* That's not fair.

UNCLE MICHEL: Did you do any business in Paris or did you just have fun?

RENE: I negotiated business with my father and I met with Edgar and I spoke to...

UNCLE MICHEL: Rene never said the word I. Then he married Tell...that word became his new toy. He can say I want financing for a new venture. I want tickets to Europe. That's all right. I can afford another child.

RENE: *(Wincing—his lips quivering)* I had my associates collate all my invoices and I will go over them personally...

UNCLE MICHEL: Now he pretends he handles things but he runs off or takes a nap.

RENE: You misunderstand.

EDGAR: Can I help in some way?

UNCLE MICHEL: *(Miserably)* See if Rene paid the rent, will you, and any of the bills? *(Yanks out some mail. Sourly, but with a trace of curiosity)* Oh, Edgar, the mail came. You got a letter...From the wrong side of the blanket. Cousin Norbert. I hope you're not getting involved with him. You should avoid confusion with these *gens de colour*. Everyone is free now so free men of color like him, they are the same as other colored; no, they are worse, they are angry and they are a lot smarter. Am I right, Rene?

RENE: Yes.

EDGAR: *(Attempts a light, amused tone)* He's a relative. I let him know I was coming. I'm very interested in his inventions.

UNCLE MICHEL: *(Ignoring this—spitefully)* Keep your distance. We don't want a family hanging.

EDGAR: I want to meet with him and hear about his vision of the future. *(Abruptly turns to leave)*

UNCLE MICHEL: Don't walk away while I am talking to you. *(Without conviction)* I'm fond of Norbert. We played together as boys. It's him I'm protecting. He's the one liable to get lynched. Stay away from these *gens de colour.*

(EDGAR is about to make a sneering remark to UNCLE MICHEL but HE shrugs his shoulders and goes out on the gallery as AMERICA slips in from the pantry. SHE lingers by the doorway as UNCLE MICHEL hands a bill to RENE and testily growls) Invoices with no checks. Both used to come in one envelope.

(UNCLE MICHEL sighs, goes out the front parlor. Once he is gone AMERICA lifts her head, laughs with a relieved air and runs and throws her arms around RENE. With a warning glance HE breaks away and nervously checks the doors and windows for eavesdroppers. HE hurries back to her and THEY kiss madly.)

AMERICA: Rene, finally we're alone. I missed you. Sixty days without you is so long. Every day I tell myself, one more day without Rene.

RENE: I can't talk now.

AMERICA: Tonight, usual place?

RENE: We've got to postpone our plans.

AMERICA: *(Stares at him puzzledly)* I don't want to wait any longer.

RENE: I can't leave Tell with the children alone.

AMERICA: *(SHE controls her anger defensively)* I care about her children, about the whole household more than she does.

RENE: Tell's…pregnant.

AMERICA: She's…You got her pregnant? You…slept with her while I'm waiting?

RENE: She said she couldn't get…

AMERICA: *(Dumbfounded, her voice rising)* You've…I thought you weren't intimate.

RENE: *(Moves to her restlessly, motioning for her to keep her voice down)* Ah, sugar. I'm just as upset…

AMERICA: What does that mean? Ah, sugar. Don't touch me. My husband gets angrier every day, looking for that money I loaned you.

RENE: I know. I can't let our cotton business go under. Now Edgar's here, we'll repay you. *(Takes her hands and gently wraps them around him. Kisses her)* Can't we talk later?

AMERICA: My husband's going to kill me if I don't give him that money right away. When he discovered it was missing, he tore up the house look-ing for it. At night he rolls over and makes awful grunting sounds, cursing under his breath. We've got to leave tonight…run off as soon as we can. Money and retaliation, that's all the judge cares about. One nod from him, and I'm in prison or a mental hospital. If he finds out I stole that money…

(A burst of laughter comes from the pantry. JO, shouting "Surprise" offstage, comes in carrying a birthday cake, prodded by MATHILDE. EDGAR walks in from the gallery.)

JO: Surprise. It's a birthday surprise.

MATHILDE: *(Gathering them around the cake)* Everybody get ready to sing to Didi when she arrives.

RENE: Edgar, come here. This is America Olivier.

AMERICA: *(Teasingly)* My goal is to move to your exotic Paris.

RENE: She reads to Tell and helps the children with their music.

EDGAR: How kind.

AMERICA: *(With a touch of pride)* Rene wants to move back, too. You must teach us how to do that.

(Happy voices in the hallway. DIDI comes in the front parlor door coaxed by TELL, her face lit up expectantly.)

ALL: SURPRISE!!

DIDI: *(Worried, glancing at EDGAR)* I don't like surprises. I said I'm not celebrating.

JO: It's just three candles.

DIDI: *(Embarrassed)* No.

MATHILDE: *(Lighting the candles with satisfaction)* You are still on the sunny side of thirty.

UNCLE MICHEL: From now on you should freeze. Your mother was forty for years.

(DIDI, half-reassured, blows out the candles. JO lightens the mood by getting all to applaud, then chasing DIDI around the table.)

JO: Round the table you must go. You must go. Must go...it's your birth-day.

UNCLE MICHEL: *(HE winks at DIDI, with an encouraging glance at EDGAR)* Let's give Didi a kiss.

EDGAR: *(With awkward enthusiasm)* I've missed you all.

BLACKOUT

(UNCLE MICHEL sits boredly; behind him JO crouches with her puppets, singing, putting warring puppets on his shoulders. MATHILDE and DIDI sit restlessly, sewing on the sofa, now and then glancing at EDGAR painting TELL on the gallery.)

JO: *"Frere Jacques, frere Jacques, dormez-vous? Dormez-vous? Sonnez les matines. Sonnez les matines. Ding. Dang. Dong. Ding. Dang. Dong."*

MATHILDE: If I were single, I'd marry Edgar. I would surely. Yes indeed. Last night I dreamed I was by Will's casket. I whispered, "Thanks for freeing me." And off I went to Paris. Does that mean my husband will get shot? It's awful.

DIDI: *(Embroidering diligently)* You've three children.

MATHILDE: I'm tired of living just for them.

UNCLE MICHEL: *(Affectionately reprimanding)* Come watch our puppet show. Someone needs to give Jo attention. Call all the children out.

MATHILDE: No. Not now.

UNCLE MICHEL: *(A trifle acidly)* You don't want to see your children?

MATHILDE: I need some time with Edgar. Desiree will later.

DIDI: *(Stung)* No, I won't. *(With a baffled shrug of his shoulders UNCLE MICHEL leaves through the rear parlor door with JO. DIDI puts her sewing down, takes her sister's hand with deep seriousness)* I'm waiting to read my writings to Edgar. Literature has always deeply interested him. There is the writer in him in addition to the artist. He quotes Racine and Saint-Simeon. We've much in common. Many of Edgar's paintings are based on his reading in Biblical, Classical and Romantic literature. Did you know that?

MATHILDE: So he'll be proposing soon?

DIDI: Our discussions are purely intellectual.

MATHILDE: Really. How disappointing.

DIDI: *(Quickly)* Who knows? He admires women writers and protagonists. He reads repeatedly Madame Bovary, no doubt discovering in it a solace for his loneliness.

(Focus swings to the gallery, EDGAR painting TELL with an awkward uneasy tenderness.)

SOUND: Something like Louis Moreau Gottschalk's ragtime music.

EDGAR: It's amazing. You have these moments of terrific intensity and utter passiveness. I can't wrap my mind around it. I work better from memory rather than reality.

TELL: I used to watch you painting at the Louvre for hours.

EDGAR: I sensed you watching me.

TELL: You didn't.

EDGAR: That's where the extra red came from in my Daughters of Japheth. I was blushing.

TELL: Really.

EDGAR: I wanted to paint your face on every female torso.

TELL: I never knew…

EDGAR: People are animals. We feel these things

TELL: It was a crush.

EDGAR: More like an affliction. I was observing you even when you didn't know it.

TELL: I felt you, observing me.

EDGAR: I felt you…feeling me observing you. *(Laughs)* That's what painters do. *(Hesitates—then slowly)* Still there was something inexplicable—sacred in the way we connected.

TELL: *(Her hands flutter shyly to her face)* You were lonely.

EDGAR: Don't diminish what I'm saying. You felt it.

TELL: Yes.

EDGAR: I wasn't prepared for how that would stay with me.

TELL: I wish I could see your painting.

EDGAR: You might not like it. *(Kiddingly)* No. You probably would. You're a good liar. *(Music fades out)* I always felt I had to paint but after you left I wasn't sure. *(Reluctantly)* There was this hole in my heart and I didn't know what side it was on. I had to proceed unattached. What else could I do but wait? *(Ashamed)* Even painting seemed senseless. I'd scattered interest in my art but I had to face it. No one believed in me like you had. I was no young prodigy.

TELL: Says who?

EDGAR: What talent I have has come through merciless work, experiment and deliberation.

TELL: You're a great painter.

EDGAR: That's not enough. *(With sudden tenseness)* The problem is, what kind of art to make and why.

TELL: It'll come to you.

EDGAR: When? Papa wants me to go to law school and follow a more solid profession.

TELL: Nothing's certain except your talent.

EDGAR: Maybe he's right. I admire my friends Edouard Manet, Henri Roualt. *(Dryly)* They're working along more daring lines.

TELL: Listen to your heart and you will know.

EDGAR: I don't trust my heart. I'm thirty-eight. I've wasted too much time. *(Turns on her—resentfully)* I didn't come this far to mince words. I'm not the man you knew. When you're in a crisis, there's no time to pretend. After you left, I volunteered for the National Guard hoping I'd get shot. Ran into shell fire, chose the scariest lot. Instead, I found myself searching for friends in mounds of blood, a rag to my nose so I could stand the smell. Something was going wrong with my eyes. I refused to admit it at first. I was weakly defiant. Then—*(HE frowns and shakes his head mechanically)* I promised myself if I made it through the war I'd see you once more. I dreamt about it . . .

TELL: We are not responsible for our dreams.

EDGAR: God was talking to me.

TELL: Warning you.

EDGAR: To confront reality. . . Turn. That's beautiful, Raphaelite. Hold it.

TELL: It's best not to eulogize distant friendships—

EDGAR: If you hadn't left, I wouldn't need to. *(HE stares at her sheepishly, his voice drifting deeper and deeper into himself)* When you touched my face earlier, I said nothing. But there's those intricacies of feeling even I can't understand.

(RENE walks in with nervous exasperation.)

RENE: Estelle. You think it's right to ignore the children? *(Babies crying comes from the rear hallway. TELL turns her head, stung, jumps up, and starts out. HE reaches for her arm guiltily, but she stiffens and keeps going past.)* Take the cane. You're going to kill yourself, swear to God. I can't raise these monsters alone. *(SHE stiffens. HE stares after her with scared defiance. To EDGAR, with amused dismay.)* My God, what's happening to me? I used to love children but I can't stand the sight of them. *(Lights in the parlor rise as she enters. RENE calls out worriedly)* Didi, help Tell with the…*(HE stops abruptly, drinks nervously from his flask.)*

EDGAR: You were the one with the vision of family life.

RENE: *(With a false heartiness)* I've no vision. My creditors have it but I don't. *(Puts an arm around EDGAR and hugs him appreciatively. THEY go inside the parlor)* You've no idea of the hardship conditions here. You can't just go out and find clients. There is always someone who can get there before you. *(Taking a swig from his flask)* Country traders bartering cotton. God knows who they are. Negotiating is getting ugly. Hell, I'd like nothing more than to get away from here as soon as possible. *(Drinking more)* When are you coming to the office?

EDGAR: I'm here to paint.

RENE: You can do that at night…

EDGAR: Don't start.

RENE: Hey…I need you at the office…

EDGAR: I never promised that.

RENE: What business have you done?

EDGAR: Huh?

RENE: Well…Have you asked Papa for another loan?

EDGAR: I just gave you money…look…Cousin Norbert is here.

RENE: I can't work with him.

EDGAR: Why not? He could help you with his new inventions.

RENE: It's not that simple. He couldn't do it without facing threats.

EDGAR: From whom?

RENE: Members of the White League. *(Glances uneasily to the entranceways with a change of tone)* They fight against the rising tide of colored people. Names like the Ku Klux Klan, the White Brotherhood, Camellias of Louisiana, mean anything to you? Uncle runs one white group. Our brother-in-law runs another.

EDGAR: *(His face hardens)* And you?

RENE: *(HE smiles strangely, his voice wavering)* I'm involved also…I have to be.

EDGAR: This is what your Confederacy has given you?

RENE: You don't understand how it works here.

EDGAR: *(HE turns on his brother accusingly)* I fought for a dream. I joined the Commune because I believed all citizens were brothers.

RENE: *(Smiles—cynically)* Nice theory.

ROSARY HARTEL O'NEILL

EDGAR: I still believe it. (*HE walks away, his face darkening with rage*) We admitted all foreigners to the honor of dying for our cause. The Commune numbered eighty-one members, mostly in their twenties. All lacked political experience. Each time a barricade fell the defenders were put up against a wall and shot. Three hundred died in La Madeleine Church, one hundred twenty women were massacred at one barricade. Citizens stabbing off the enemy with makeshift weapons. Bodies carried off. Pieces of men. You weren't there. The White League is the opposite of everything the Commune fought and died for...

RENE: (*Knows HE is lying...vaguely*) This is another world.

EDGAR: Then it's not mine.

(*EDGAR's face clouds over. HE keeps his eyes averted from RENE, goes out the front parlor and can be heard stamping noisily upstairs. AMERICA slumps against the pantry doorway, then seeing SHE and RENE are alone rushes over and kisses RENE with excited desperation.*)

AMERICA: Rene, when are you going to tell your wife?

RENE: (*Holding her in his arms, with quiet intensity*) Right now, I can't. Tell is very fragile.

AMERICA: And me? What will happen to me?

(*RENE grins at her provocatively, and takes a ring from his pocket.*)

AMERICA: (*Shocked but pleased*) A silver ring? I want you, I want a future, not a silver ring.

RENE: This isn't silver. It's platinum. Handmade in France. The jeweler was so snobbish I could barely talk to him. (*JO eavesdrops at the gallery window*) Later. Believe me, we'll talk later.

(*RENE looks at AMERICA with an understanding sympathy, kisses her and then slips out into the front hallway. AMERICA goes to the window, looking at the ring in dismay. SHE hears JO, looks up annoyed.*)

AMERICA: What do you want, anything?

GHOSTS OF NEW ORLEANS

JO: No.

BLACKOUT

(Slide then lights for street scene with another slide and music)

SCENE 2
EMILY AND EDGAR—STREET SCENE

(EMILY, a pretty middle-aged woman of color sneaks in panting, nervous. SHE spots EDGAR by a street lamp, touches his shoulder, and draws him into the shadows.)

EMILY: Edgar? You don't recognize me? Of course not. I am Norbert's wife, your cousin Emily.

EDGAR: *(Concerned)* I didn't think you were coming. Where is he?

EMILY: He doesn't know I'm here. I'm out of breath. I took all the back routes. Who'd have thought I'd be sneaking about? Any Negro is a target. Don't matter if you are free.

SOUND: Music fades out.

EDGAR: Why are people staring at me?

EMILY: Three reasons: your shirt, your hat—but the main reason is me. *(Whispers)* There was a lynching last night. Mob sounded like thunder. You could smell the fear. Boy barely fourteen, they strung him up. He died slow and terrible because he was so young and strong. They dug a trench, tossed him in it.

EDGAR: My brother didn't say that you and Norbert were in danger. He's an important man in Louisiana. I was hoping he and Norbert could work together.

EMILY: *(Looks at him, aghast)* Rene's like your uncle. Norbert's the best engineer in the South and his own cousins won't have him to the house. Don't matter he knows more. *(Shudders. Wraps her shawl tightly about her)* My legs are so cold walking through that dampness. Don't look like New Orleans is ever going to dry out. Does it rain in Paris?

EDGAR: Nothing like here.

EMILY: Do Negroes keep apart there like here?

EDGAR: No. Negroes live by whites.

EMILY: You kidding. Nobody try to lynch them there? My dream been always to go somewhere my skin isn't a source for punishment. To live in a safe place where I can walk the streets at night. *(Takes a deep breath)* Norbert deals with it better. He spends time in thought. While he invents I worry. They're killing strangers here. *(Swallows hard)* It's been seven years since the war, and it seems like the hatred got worse. How long does it take? God knocked Paul from his horse, but how many men get thrown down and start to see. Norbert says, "Lift them up, lift them up." He says a new age coming with shining kind people. Then the inventions will multiply. Carriages gonna go by themselves. Streetcars gonna run on tracks. He sees the bright future; I don't. He closes his eyes, I can't. He wants to leave for Paris; I want to stay.

EDGAR: The French love scientific progress, intellectual achievement. He'd be better off there.

EMILY: I know; he knows also. Norbert says that once we cross that ocean, we won't be coming back. *(With bitter stubborn persistence)* I don't want to leave. I say, Emily, you closing the book on one life to open the book on another. I'll sit by the river one last time, then I won't think. I'll just go. I fear I want something a woman can't have. But finally we are leaving. When are you going? I'll feel safer if we travel with you.

EDGAR: There are people I can't say goodbye to.

EMILY: Course you can. I know it's hard. Inside me I just want to scream. I got a sister and mother, all from here. When that ship pulls off and I hear that horn blow and see them waving, I know the tears going to burst me apart. I tell myself, serve as an example of a woman who got out. *(Holding back tears)* What you think God want me to do?

EDGAR: I don't know.

EMILY: You should. You wrote us there was Revolution there. What were y'all fighting for?

EDGAR: Freedom and equality.

EMILY: And what was the end?

EDGAR: Women and children massacred.

EMILY: That is always the end. (*Her face grows hard*) Terrible thunder! Looks like Satan's afoot. Oh Lord. We being watched. By that fellow over there and there. I better go.

EDGAR: They can't harm you. I'll make Uncle receive you—

EMILY: Don't go getting yourself shot. You dealing with some mean men. Yanks and the Freedman Bureau can't stop their rally. (*With bitter irony*) You haven't seen your Uncle's getup? He and Will are planning a battle. They are so mad they can't carry a gun and vote. (*Her voice trembling with rage*) They'll kill any Negro that try to stand up and any white man that help him.

EDGAR: Yes, I know. My brother also. (*HE reaches out shamefaced and takes her hand, but SHE drops it immediately*)

EMILY: Colored politicians can't save no one. You watch out.

EDGAR: (*Impressed and at the same time disgusted*) Christmas is coming and so much bloody news.

EMILY: Wars don't stop on a holiday. Run from here.

EDGAR: I'll escort you home.

EMILY: (*Glances about fearfully*) No, it's best I go alone. (*SHE turns with dignity and disappears through the shadows*)

(*Slide fades out.*)

BLACKOUT

SCENE 3
LATER AT THE HOUSE

(RENE sits at the desk, struggling with bills. JO, lying on the sofa, makes one of her puppets beat another.)

PUPPET—JO: I've had enough of her. I'm going to do something to her. *(RENE shushes her)* I'm not going to kill her, but she's got to suffer.

AMERICA: *(from the pantry, calls out)* Jo! *(JO hides behind the sofa. Strolling in, a basket of clothes on her hip, speaks with mounting peevishness)* Come practice piano. She is always hiding somewhere. *(In a detached, reminiscent tone)* Oh, Rene. I went looking for you upstairs.

RENE: This place is turning into a nursery. I had to come down. I'm going to pay for my children to grow up, then I'm going to Paris and stay drunk.

AMERICA: *(Inches behind him, puts her hand down his shirt, and kisses him deeply)* How long can I be expected to take all this? Have you talked to Edgar about leaving for Paris?

RENE: *(Runs his fingers through her hair)* I can't yet. Look...You're married too.

AMERICA: *(SHE laughs...a hopeless depressed laugh)* What kind of marriage do I have with that judge? *(Coquettishly)* At least before the war he never worried about money, because there was always more, more. Now he counts every penny. *(SHE gives a little nervous knowing chuckle.)* My grandma used to say, what would you rather be, an old man's darling or a young man's bride? I settled for the old man's darling, but now I'm not even that. The judge thinks because I worked in the kitchen before, I should be grateful for any crumb I've got. *(Sits on RENE'S lap, throws her arms around his neck, excitedly)* I'm young. I want to travel. He never expected me to want that. I'm so bored. When he talks, it's only to repeat himself or say something ugly. He hates everybody I like, and one day all his meanness will come out at me. When it does, I'm a dead woman. *(Passionately)* We've got to leave. When will you talk to Edgar?

RENE: *(Placating)* How can I leave when the pregnancy is in trouble?

AMERICA: Edgar can run the business! You've done your share here. I can't wait. My husband will put me in prison if—

RENE: *(Lowering his voice reassuringly)* I'll pay you as soon as the first check comes in. Don't worry. I'm going to ask Edgar for another loan from Papa. Used to be we talked about…us. You could enjoy life. We are the same.

AMERICA: *(sharply)* No, you're worse. I'm taking the risk for you.

RENE: *(There is a silence in which RENE moves away awkwardly. A strange aloofness comes over him as if he were speaking impersonally of strangers)* What time do the guests arrive?

AMERICA: They're not.

RENE: *(Goes on as if he hadn't heard)* I'm supposed to introduce Edgar to…new clients.

AMERICA: I canceled the party.

RENE: *(HE stares at her, stunned)* What?

AMERICA: I won't be one of those big-bellied women carrying around the memory of a fiery night.

RENE: You were supposed to help me and Edgar. Use the judge?

AMERICA: His friends have no money. They're looking for money from you.

RENE: *(Exasperated)* Everybody cannot be broke. Some people have inherited money.

AMERICA: Yeah, but the rich really love their money. They'll turn from you.

RENE: *(An undercurrent of rage comes into his voice)* So you're calling off the Christmas party?

AMERICA: *(Her manner becoming more and more distant)* To which I'm barely invited, although it's at my house. I'm the servant who happens to own the house. I don't act like one of y'all. But Tell's the angel mother. If I've to hear once more about her first husband being nephew to Jefferson Davis—

RENE: *(Jeeringly)* You said the judge would lend money, if Edgar approached him.

AMERICA: Yes, but we haven't had relations in eight months.

RENE: *(Stiffens defensively, his voice cracking)* You think it's fair to punish me? You know I'd love to run off with you. Never look at this wanting house again. How can I act dishonorably? So many people are depending on me. Every night when I go to bed I imagine you alongside me. Every other second I think of you. When I'm shaving, combing my hair, stepping off the gallery, hopping on the streetcar, opening the office door, picking up the mail. *(He gives a little despairing laugh)* There's hardly an action I do without daydreaming about you. That's my personal torture.

(AMERICA avoids his eyes, folding clothes, rigid, unyielding. JO sneaks out onto the gallery, frowning, leaving a puppet behind. AMERICA watches her, irritated, then picks up the puppet and throws it on the sofa, and walks out the front parlor. Outside it thunders, and rain begins to fall. Moments later, MATHILDE and JO come in from the gallery, MATHILDE with a vase of red gladioli.)

JO: *(JO hides her face in MATHILDE's skirt, sobbing)* It's true, I did see Mr. Rene and America kissing here. They're gone but they were here, kissing.

MATHILDE: My. They are just good friends.

JO: Good friends don't kiss so long. *(Gives her aunt a glance of concern)* Is she going to have a baby?

MATHILDE: *(Soothingly, arranging the flowers)* Heavens, no. It's Christmas time. People are drinking, full of friendliness. That kiss doesn't mean anything.

JO: *(Then worriedly)* Why are Mr. Rene and America always kissing—if it doesn't mean anything? *(JO tries to look in her aunt's eyes, but SHE keeps them averted, arranging the flowers)*

MATHILDE: Some things you can't understand until you grow up. *(Trying to speak naturally)* Now don't talk about this to your mama.

JO: Why not?

MATHILDE: Because—

JO: Because what?

MATHILDE: *(Protesting uneasily)* Josephine, that's enough. Now let's get you dressed for the Christmas party.

(MATHILDE coaxes JO out to the front hallway as TELL comes in the rear parlor dressed in splendid velvet and satin, her pregnancy heightening her voluptuous sensuality. On hearing the rain and thunder, SHE adjusts her sleeves with a forlorn gentleness.)

JO: *(Turning at the doorway)* Mama? *(Her curiosity recedes into helplessness and she leaves)*

TELL: Merry Christmas.

SOUND: *Christmas music plays, something like "Oh Holy Night."*

(TELL moves to the desk and smells the vase of red gladioli.

LIGHTS: *Lights dim and a slide is displayed briefly.*

(EDGAR comes in from the back parlor. A pause. His expression becomes thoughtful, almost as if he's seeing the painting, "Portrait of Estelle"

TELL: *(Hesitantly)* Edgar. I know it's you.

EDGAR: How's that?

TELL: I know very close friends by their footsteps.

EDGAR: Is that it?

TELL: Well, there's actually an energy.

EDGAR: That's better. *(HE stops short, overcome by his acute attraction.)* Can you sense what I'm doing?

TELL: It feels like you're watching me. *(HE observes her with growing pleasure.)* It's rude to stare.

EDGAR: *(With awkward uneasy tenderness)* I'm taking in the whole picture.

TELL: Can I get you something?

EDGAR: Just your company.

TELL: *(A defensiveness comes into her voice)* We should have champagne.

EDGAR: *(Fighting the effect of her beauty and trying to be flatly conversational)* You're all dressed in a rose-colored gown.

TELL: I mostly wear black.

EDGAR: Let me see.

TELL: *(SHE adds smilingly)* I've clothes I've never worn simply because I don't know what they look like anymore. *(SHE gives a little laugh of affectionate amusement)* For tonight I tried on every gown in my armoire.

EDGAR: I love fine fabrics, the softness on the skin, like being touched.

TELL: *(SHE raises her hands flirtatiously)* Don't muss me up.

EDGAR: Let's sit here.

TELL: *(Moves away automatically and bumps into the sofa, with a sigh. SHE recovers and sits)* I'm so nervous.

(EDGAR looks at her, impressed.)

EDGAR: Why?

TELL: I want to...please you.

EDGAR: And me you. I wish there was some way I could help.
(HE pauses, struggling with himself. Outside it thunders and rain drops down)
Could you tell me how the blindness first began?

TELL: I'd rather not . . .

EDGAR: I won't tell anyone.

TELL: I don't want people to know or remember. I began knocking glasses of water off the table. I couldn't tell where the ends of things were—tables, steps, and sidewalks. Two weeks ago, I lost a little more sight. Everything changed. Just that little fraction, I'm bumping into things. I've bruised my arms from walking about.

EDGAR: What did you do…at first?

TELL: I did what anybody would do. I denied it. I went to the Gulf Coast and knocked myself unconscious by walking into a tree.

EDGAR: Oh, my God. That's so awful, terrible.

TELL: No…Nothing is so good or so bad as you think it is going to be.

EDGAR: *(His face tenses)* I've never spoken about this to anyone, afraid to acknowledge it and make it stronger. I've been plagued with headaches. At first, I thought it was an empathetic response. I was suffering with you. Then I blamed the weather. It's unusually hot. Temperatures in December, I thought you had in June. I've had a sudden drop in vision. The less light in the room, the less I can distinguish. Colors and detail blur. My right eye is mostly worthless. They say you don't know what you have unless you lose it. Well, painters know our eyes are important. There is always that fear, so when it happens it's traumatic.

TELL: Maybe you should see a doctor.

EDGAR: Doctors know everything and nothing. What if I can't paint anymore? What if—if I lose the other eye? My God, no. You just woke up one morning, blind? I couldn't face it.

TELL: After two operations, when they put a sharp object in the eye…well, the results can be…*(Her voice trembles)*

EDGAR: Weren't you angry?

TELL: In a rage…But then acceptance set in. Now…Sometimes I think I sense more than when I had my eyesight. *(HE remains hopelessly silent. SHE adds sadly)* You've two options: don't paint or work with your limitations.

EDGAR: What choice is that?

TELL: A hard one, but I think you see from inside.

ROSARY HARTEL O'NEILL

EDGAR: You would.

TELL: Painting comes from there.

EDGAR: But if my eyes go and I can't see the colors, the tones, what can I do?

TELL: You'll find out.

EDGAR: How?

TELL: *(SHE smiles strangely)* You'll use all your senses, your hearing, your touch. I think I see you more clearly, now, than ever before.

EDGAR: That's what I miss the most—your optimistic attitude. After you left, I was dazed. I rode past places we used to haunt: parks, restaurants, and imagined you there. It was comforting trying to recall what you wore: the colors, the flowers on the table, the tone of the conversation. Sometimes I felt the places calling to me as if they missed you too. A silent partnership between me and an empty table. Other times I advised myself—don't think about her, imagine her dead. I counted off days in my journal, then weeks, months. I told myself my need for you would lessen as time passed, but the images of you got stronger, not vaguer. I said that wasn't the real you...You were harsh, conniving, cruel. There was a side of you I hadn't seen, a side that made you prefer a flashier life, a life with Rene, not me. I bargained with God. I'd give up drinking if you'd write me one letter. My painting suffered. I couldn't focus. I cursed your intelligence, humor, sensitivity. I lay in bed assuring myself God would send me someone better than you if I just concentrated on my work. I told myself: just do your work and get through the day. She's not thinking about you, remembering you. Then you had one baby, then two. And still despite all the evidence, my heart would-n't let go of you...(*HE reaches out and clasps her hands...sadly. Outside the rain intensifies. AMERICA comes in from the pantry, flounders*)

AMERICA: I'm sorry. Edgar, we must talk about that trip to Paris—

(From the hallway, we hear uncanny, gay singing. MATHILDE, DIDI and JO walk in through the front parlor doors, singing "Oh Holy Night," letting them-selves go now and then, bellowing with delight.)

AMERICA: *(Looks at TELL with focused repulsion)* The plan for a party won't work now—I've canceled it. *(Everyone freezes, shocked. Staring at AMERICA. SHE stammers)* What with the rain, the heat…Every few seconds this nasty thunder.

DIDI: I counted on this evening. One night I wouldn't have to be the household nun.

MATHILDE: What about the guests?

AMERICA: *(Self-righteously)* I told the servants to send them away.

DIDI: I guess I won't recite the Baudelaire I had planned.

MATHILDE: *(Encouragingly)* No, recite it for the family.

DIDI: *(Minces a bit waveringly to the center of the room. Recites dully with flat, empty gestures)* "Woman…for the artist…is the object of keenest admiration and curiosity that the picture of life can offer its contemplator. No doubt woman is sometimes a light, a glance, an invitation to happiness, sometimes just a word; but above all she is a general harmony, not only in her bearing and the way in which she moves and walks, but also in the muslin, the gauzes…in which she envelopes herself…"

(AMERICA rises, guiltily, avoiding their faces. SHE looks remotely in RENE'S direction.)

AMERICA: Who will walk me home?

RENE: I'll walk you home. A terrible storm's coming. I didn't expect it. It hasn't rained in weeks. *(Pats TELL's cheek in dismissal, huskily, forcing a smile)* Don't wait up. *(Follows AMERICA out)*

JO: *(Trails and taunts them with her puppets)* Kiss me, kiss me.

MATHILDE: Put those up. Come with me.

JO: No, I want to stay.

TELL: Let her stay.

MATHILDE: *(Attempts to catch her niece's eye)* Where's Will with the little tree? He's promised to decorate it with Edgar. If only he can spark Will's confidence.

(MATHILDE turns away with a tense laugh and goes out the rear parlor. TELL walks somberly to the sofa. JO tiptoes behind her.)

JO: Can I comb your hair, Mama?

TELL: *(Her lips quiver and she keeps her head held high)* Yes, there is a brush on the desk.

JO: Mama. *(Pauses, staring at the floor, her face set in a defensive expression)*

TELL: Yes?

JO: Never mind. *(With a probing look)* What was Papa like?

TELL: I've told you this before, Jo. Your father was good-looking, dashing. I picked him from a circle of carefree southern boys, now mostly dead.

JO: Do you miss Papa now you've a second husband?

TELL: That was a long time ago. We were children then.

JO: What's it like being married? Do you kiss a lot?

TELL: *(Unable to hide a furtive uneasiness)* Sometimes.

JO: Do you need to be married to kiss?

TELL: No.

JO: *(Losing all caution)* Do married people kiss other people too?

TELL: *(A spasm of pain crosses her face)* Sometimes. Yes, but differently. *(Injuredly)* So many questions.

JO: Why did you have to marry again? Who do you love most? Papa or Mr. Rene?

TELL: I love you most; that's all you have to worry about.

JO: I miss my real Papa. I keep thinking about what it'd be like to have him here. I'd sit on his knee, play horsey. Why did you bring Mr. Rene into our

GHOSTS OF NEW ORLEANS

lives and not Uncle Edgar?

TELL: Be thankful you have Mr. Rene.

JO: I want a real Papa, not a pretend Papa. *(SHE reaches out and grasps TELL's arm)* Send Mr. Rene back to Paris and marry Uncle Edgar.

TELL: And the babies? Don't they need their real Papa?

JO: I never thought about them. *(SHE gives a little sad sigh)* Does it hurt having babies?

TELL: Sometimes. Babies don't care about their mama. They don't know where they're going so they kick and scream. You arrived fighting, your face red.

JO: My face was red?

TELL: Your uncle, Jefferson Davis, sent me a diamond pin, a swan with green eyes, but I hocked it way back when.

JO: Why did you marry Mr. Rene and not Uncle Edgar?

TELL: *(Smiles with ironic amusement)* Rene played the part of the successful young banker. So handsome and so smart. He'd been to his tailor and bought the costume. Suntan suits in summer, a scarf thrown over his shoulder to give the impression he was rushing. He flitted around the edge of single ladies, not knowing he'd get caught in the web of a blind woman.

JO: That's not true. *(Stares at her, puzzled)* You like being married?

TELL: The best part is anticipation. Hearing a man's footsteps at your door.

(MATHILDE comes in from the rear parlor door, frowns admonishingly.)

MATHILDE: This isn't talk for a child.

TELL: *(Pats JO's cheek)* She's mine. Besides, she understands everything.

JO: I do. *(Bell jingles)* That's Uncle Will. *(Bursts out excitedly)* He promised he'd bring the tree trim with Uncle Edgar. *(JO runs off into the hallway)*

ROSARY HARTEL O'NEILL

MATHILDE: *(Trying to shake off her hopeless stupor)* No party.

TELL: I feel so unhappy.

(DIDI walks in with prim politeness through the front parlor, hands a note to MATHILDE.)

DIDI: A message for you. I didn't open it.

(SHE leaves curtly. A loose smile twists MATHILDE's face as she reads.)

MATHILDE: There'll be no tree.

TELL: Will won't be home tonight? Is he with…

MATHILDE: *(With a tough, tortured laugh)* Don't mention her name. *(Walks toward the vase of gladioli on the desk, yanks off leaves)* All men cheat. When Will went to the altar, instead of saying "I do," he should have said, "I'll try." Certain women become the strange attractors.

TELL: Why do men think they can get away with these heartless episodes?

MATHILDE: Because they can.

TELL: *(SHE smiles strangely)* How do you handle it? How can you accept it?

MATHILDE: *(Sliding into intense detachment—quotes casually)* There is a sense of relief when you know, but you never admit it. I light a candle, recall my licentious thoughts. It's good for wives to reflect in silence. If we can't save ourselves, perhaps we can save our children.

TELL: I couldn't cope…

MATHILDE: *(Brokenly)* Men are hunters. They aren't capable of loving a woman, much less of telling her they do, or of doing anything about it.

TELL: *(SHE talks excitedly)* That's not true. There are men who value how their actions affect others, men who listen.

MATHILDE: *(Disdainfully)* Edgar, again?

TELL: I didn't say that.

MATHILDE: Aren't you tired of standing at the door, wringing your hands, asking your husband to talk to you till your voice sounds like thunder?

TELL: I'm just lonely.

MATHILDE: I've suffered loneliness for sure but I've lots of tasks done for me so I can keep my shine. Wives have to look good, so as our husbands age, we can replace their mistresses and become their mothers, perfecting the technique of living with them while they're ignoring us. The home should be a wife's sanctuary. I try to shift the routine by putting breezy sur- prises into every day, a Christmas ornament. *(Her hands fly up nervously to fix her hair)* An Easter bouquet. Nothing unpleasant. I dare not mention the loan to Rene.

TELL: *(With stubborn naiveté)* He's repaid you, hasn't he?

MATHILDE: No, and now I find out...he hasn't paid the bills for six months, nor has he spoken to Edgar about a loan.

TELL:For God's sake...take this. *(TELL yanks off her ring)*

MATHILDE: Not your diamond. *(With bitter sadness)* Anyway, it's nothing. A drop in the ocean.

(MATHILDE goes out quickly through the pantry doors. Thunder intensifies. Moments later, EDGAR enters, carefully watches TELL for a few moments. HE walks slowly to where she sits. She looks tired, miserably sad.)

EDGAR: It's Edgar. Are you all right?

TELL: I'm fine. I'm in alone time. It's necessary, it's difficult, but it's here. See me in the morning, and I'll have a little repartee with you.

EDGAR: *(Moved in spite of himself)* You're one of the solitaries of the world. *(With fond solicitude)* We'll celebrate tomorrow.

TELL: *(Bluntly)* Stop trying to make things right, to understand, to help so much!

EDGAR: Sorry.

TELL: *(Rebukingly)* You should know better.

EDGAR: It's been a long time since I've had family.

TELL: Start one of your own.

EDGAR: Maybe I should.

TELL: *(With dull anger)* You've got a ruined Christmas.

EDGAR: I can handle it.

TELL: Will's drunk and not coming with the tree.

EDGAR: That's all right.

TELL: The Christmas party is canceled.

EDGAR: There'll be others.

TELL: *(Cynically brutal)* Why are you so…so complacent?

EDGAR: Because you…make me happy.

TELL: I don't know why.

EDGAR: I don't either.

TELL: You annoy me. *(SHE avoids looking in his direction. There is condemnation in her smile mixed with a new violent attraction)*

EDGAR: *(HE tries to copy her coolness but is unable to get over his heartsickness. There is a pause of icy silence. HE goes to the window, watches the rain as if HE were talking aloud to himself)* Such a cold moon night. A brittle moon, stone blue. Like your wedding night. The hard darkness of the Cathedral almost gobbles up your bright gown as you come down the aisle. I imagine you are walking to me. I get there an hour before the others just so…I can be ready…for what I don't know. *(From the window, without turning around)* Why'd you—marry Rene?

TELL: He made me…the right offer.

EDGAR: *(Turning abruptly)* What is that crap!

TELL: I'd a small child…He was willing to live in America.

EDGAR: Off your Papa's money…When Rene told me he'd marry you, I accepted it. I adored him, so why shouldn't he have you?

TELL: You were upset?

EDGAR: Crazed…Up to the last minute, I thought, prayed you might cancel.

TELL: You never came over.

EDGAR: Why bother? Rene was always there by you. I had to get through him to see you.

TELL: You acted aloof.

EDGAR: *(With a maudlin laugh)* What in the hell did you expect? The most difficult thing was to say congratulations. Because till I said that you weren't really married.

TELL: You never spoke—

EDGAR: Hearing you say, "I do," I…I…My body felt like stone. I was cold quiet. But you knew. You knew. It was there all over me, in my eyes, my awkwardness.

TELL: People said you were ill.

EDGAR: *(Wincing his lips, quivering, pitifully)* I blamed it on a fever, yes.

TELL: You left early.

EDGAR: I told myself I'd get through it if I didn't see you. To stay away at all costs. Don't write. Don't—

TELL: We thought you were off painting.

EDGAR: But I was so down, painting became unimportant. *(Shrugs his shoulders—thickly)* And when I went back to painting, my perspectives were off. I've said about all I can say without—

TELL: *(Protests penitently)* I thought your role was to paint, that's why I chose Rene. I was a widow tired of crying, hungry for life. *(With sharp irritation)* You never proposed. I waited…and waited.

EDGAR: *(Wrathfully)* Admit it. You preferred him.

TELL: *(With sudden tenderness)* Rene was carefree with a childish grandiosity. True. *(Wryly)* And you sat in the corner with your paintings, quiet, unpredictable, even defiant.

EDGAR: *(Breathes deeply and looks away)* I couldn't look at you and speak at the same time. And after you left, I kept in motion, traveling about—Rome, London, Madrid—even their visual splendor couldn't keep my eyes from turning inward. Each day I wrote you a letter and each night I tore it up. And no word from you.

TELL: Didn't Didi write?

EDGAR: Yes, but she hardly mentioned you. I combed her letters for clues. Were you happy, sick…(*HE takes her hand with deep caring*) I wish I could have been there with you when you lost your sight.

TELL: Me too.

EDGAR: *(His voice grows husky and trembles)* I would have been your eyes. You could have counted on me.

TELL: *(Half-reassured, but frightened)* How—with you somewhere off…Look. I'm married. I can't talk from my heart.

EDGAR: Oh, don't be prim. Not with me. We're two broken souls so . . let's have one thing complete between us. An intimacy. "In to Me See."

TELL: *(Clutches her stomach in pain. Startled, EDGAR looks about nervously and helps her to the sofa. SHE looks up at him, pleading frighteningly)* All right, I'm going to the end of this…or as close to the truth as I can possibly stand. *(Stricken with a cramp, SHE stiffens, patting his hand, trying to act normal)*

EDGAR: Let me call someone.

TELL: No. Now that I've got you here alone, stay with me. Closer. Be with me. Bless me, Father, for I have sinned. For so long I've dreamed of having you here like this, your face by mine. Your hand here. *(A spasm of pain crosses her face. SHE squeezes his hand in hers)*

EDGAR: Let me call Mathilde.

TELL: No. And since you came, I can't sleep. I barely eat and I feel full. I sat before you while you painted, heard the brush on the canvas, smelled the oils, felt your voice all around me and I was totally happy. I wanted to sit there forever, bask in your radiance, feel your eyes on me. That just having you in the same room could make me so delighted. I ordered my fingers to hold on to the chair for fear I'd lift off. You're here leaning over me.

EDGAR: Don't talk.

TELL: *(For the moment SHE loses all caution)* I feel like I must have died and gone to heaven. That I could have you beside me to myself. And you could tell me you've been loving me all along. That it's your hand on mine, your eyes looking at me. Your body bending so close. I don't want to move or wake up for fear you'll be gone. I want to live here in this dream.

EDGAR: Let me call your sisters.

TELL: No…stay with me. One more moment. *(Another intense cramp)* OH, MY GOD. OH NO. OH, MY GOD.

BLACKOUT

ACT 2

(Slide up of the Degas house, then ragtime music like the composition of Louis Moreau Gottschalk and lights at the same time, slide out.)

(JO is on the floor dancing in her dreams, Rene sits wearily at his desk, rises, walks slowly out like an old man. Sounds of flooding rain. JO crawls onto the sofa like a scared little girl. DIDI and MATHILDE come in from the rear hallway, DIDI whispering roughly to hide her tense nerves.)

DIDI: I can't sleep.

MATHILDE: *(Dully)* Me neither. America's hatred level spikes at night. How did she take over the house?

DIDI: She runs Rene. The woman who runs the man, runs the house. *(DIDI stops, looking through the front parlor toward the window where the rain pours)* If only Edgar would take me to Paris.

MATHILDE: Bring me and Will too. *(With a confused strange smile)* How did everything go wrong? I was a joyful person. Remember? Then life turned sour. When did we take the wrong turn? Maybe Edgar can figure it out.

DIDI: You've been hit too many times. I'm so disappointed. If I could just understand. We were happy once. All of us in this house. How did we come to this? I can't talk to anyone anymore, and we used to chat into the night. Now if I say anything to Will or Papa, it erupts into a fight.

MATHILDE: *(Weakly defiant)* What happened to my marriage? My family? Edgar's the only nice one—

DIDI: You've got to stand up for yourself. Papa schooled us for a better life. We were raised in a family where men took care of women. Men were generally mean, but they took care of us. Now, they don't care for us, and they're mean.

MATHILDE: *(With a bitter laugh)* Who knows which way is better, with or without a husband.

DIDI: *(Lowering her voice—hurriedly)* Come in my room when he's violent. You suffer more than Mama did.

MATHILDE: Papa didn't beat her.

DIDI: *(Pats her hand consolingly)* No. But their marriage was based on her obedience. Show those bruises to Papa.

MATHILDE: *(Her vanity piqued—testily)* Will would deny it or blame Edgar. He shames anyone who won't join the White League. *(SHE turns her head away)* I keep hoping Will will get shot in a skirmish. Collapse with a heart attack. Bless me, Father, for I have sinned. *(AMERICA comes in with an irritated glance around the front parlor. With a hard obstinant face, SHE walks over to JO, and yanks her sheets off)*

AMERICA: Jo, get up. Get up, I need your help.

JO: *(Her eyes half-open, SHE scrunches into the sofa)* I'm sleepy.

AMERICA: *(Maliciously)* We've got beggars all over the house. Your grandpa keeps letting them in because of the flood.

JO: Go away.

AMERICA: Get up, I'm telling you. We've got homeless everywhere. There's a break in the levee. Can't you be useful while we're exhausting ourselves?

DIDI: *(With a quick calculating glance at AMERICA)* She's just a child. She's—

AMERICA: *(Ignoring, DIDI—resentfully)* A bully. Bully, bully!

DIDI: Go away. I'll take over. *(Quickly)* Shush. Tell needs her rest; she's still hemorrhaging.

AMERICA: Jo sleeps way too much. Nobody helps me. Jo's the one who should assist me. She waits for me to do everything. *(Turning to DIDI)* And you and Edgar encourage this laziness, when you should demand that she help out. Jo's so lazy, lazy, lazy!

JO: *(With sudden exasperation)* I'm not!

AMERICA: The girl's totally spoilt, mentally unstable.

JO: *(Shouting)* I'm not!

AMERICA: She should be off on her uncle's grand plantation, playing.

DIDI: *(SHE laughs—then scowls abruptly)* Filled with war veterans, amputees, victims of malaria.

AMERICA: I'm trying to hold things together. Jo can't live in the nursery.

Yesterday she threw a pair of scissors at Gaston, then she punched little Will.

JO: Little Will punched me and Gaston threw...my puppets out the window...Ask Uncle Edgar.

AMERICA: *(Stung to sneering jealousy)* I've a headache, which she has given me. I've had one for two days now.

JO:Uncle Edgar says you should go home.

AMERICA: And leave this house unattended? Who can take care of it but me? Tell's health is precarious. Jo just irritates her. She should leave before things get worse. *(In a burst of resentful anger)* I know what's best. *(UNCLE MICHEL approaches—swaying in the front parlor doorway—in a loud voice)*

UNCLE MICHEL: What's going on here? Will's drunk and the children are running around. *(Chuckles tipsily to DIDI)* You should be with Edgar.

DIDI: Go to bed, Papa.

AMERICA: Mathilde's husband gambles and drinks. Edgar couldn't straighten him out. *(They watch UNCLE MICHEL's wavering progress through the front parlor. HE goes out)* That old man's a drunk too.

DIDI: *(Her rage still smoldering)* Please show my father some respect.

(DIDI and JO go out the front parlor door, and AMERICA stomps off through the rear parlor door. RENE, clutching a baby, enters from the gallery, turns, watching the rain. Sips from his flask. Moments later MATHILDE slips in from the pantry with a bassinet.)

MATHILDE: *(Whispers, alarmed)* Did you get the doctor?

RENE: *(Sarcastically)* In whose boat? There's six feet of water out there.

MATHILDE: You've been drinking.

RENE: I've got to have a few drinks to start the day. How's Tell?

MATHILDE: Her bleeding's slowed. But the baby is worse.

RENE: I know. (*Moved despite himself—helplessly*) Doctor doesn't want Tell to get too attached, because it's a matter of time. They sent me here to get the baby.

MATHILDE: Take it quick before she comes back.

RENE: (*With a hurt, bitter look, blinking back tears*) How tiny, how warm. Poor little creature can't survive long. Struggling to breathe. Oh my God. I'd like to help it—comfort Tell, but—I never wanted this baby, and she knew it. Her name's Jeanne, but she's no fighter. She hardly opens her eyes. When I put my finger in her fist, she barely squeezes. I rub her stomach, but she scarcely notices. (*A look of terror comes into his eyes*) If only I'd acted enthusiastic, gotten more loans through Edgar, things would have turned out all right—

MATHILDE: (*Wisely*) Maybe not.

RENE: (*HE winces—all life seeming to drain from his face*) They say with Jeanne's pneumonia it'll be a sweet painless end. It'll get harder for her to breathe until she stops. I hope I don't have to see it.

MATHILDE: Does Tell know?

RENE: (*HE stammers wearily*) No. I had to fake some slight hope for her.

MATHILDE: (*Her eyes are on him, condemningly*) You gave her hope?

RENE: What else could I do? The woman keeps waiting for good news. (*Uneasy now—with alcoholic talkativeness*) How did this happen? Yesterday I was a banker's son in Paris. Women sparkled about me, sent me perfumed notes, anonymous flowers. I thought I'd come to Louisiana, and Tell's father would make me a southern planter. Louisiana was the New World. Where you could be a success by age thirty. Yesterday I was a superficial dreamer. That was the real me.

MATHILDE: Let's prepare the baby.

RENE: (*HE sighs—gloomily and resentfully*) I tried, swear to God. What did I find when I got here? Lazy people too lost to help me. Mosquitoes, moths and caterpillars dropping from trees. A bitter humidity, thousand-leg spiders, termites gobbling all they see. Prehistoric roaches. A stifling heat. A

ROSARY HARTEL O'NEILL

river waiting to burst its banks full of alligators and moccasins, and water rats fleeing up the oak trees. Children dropping with yellow fever, scarlet fever, typhoid. Unnamed infections. Hurricanes, floods, and infants struggling to breathe.

MATHILDE: *(SHE puts her arm around him soothingly and gives him an affectionate hug)* Go on, cry. Let your heart break like everyone else's. *(Firmly)* But do what you have to do.

RENE: *(In a changed tone—repentantly)* I suppose I'll order a little casket.

MATHILDE: Yes, you must.

RENE: *(Gulps from a flask, grins wryly)* Thank God for alcohol. Things seem pinker, calmer. A strange quiet soothes your ears, making you able to hear anything, accept anything. Soon in a room of death you are peacefully apart.

MATHILDE: Is that what you want?

RENE: *(With drunken melancholy)* In this house you can't be by yourself. People coming and going. I want to be alone.

MATHILDE: No, you don't. You want to be with someone else.

(RENE holds up a hand, then walks out heavily. SHE stares after him with mingled worry and irritated disapproval. Seconds later, UNCLE MICHEL blusters into the room, his eyes glassy.)

UNCLE MICHEL: I can't sleep.

MATHILDE: My God, Papa, go back to bed.

UNCLE MICHEL: *(HE starts as he hears heavy footsteps on the stairs—with suspicion)* Where's Rene going? We have a White League meeting today. He's supposed to bring Edgar.

MATHILDE: Leave Rene alone.

UNCLE MICHEL: He's probably going back to sleep. He works from a part of his brain which is least developed. *(For a second HE looks miserable and frightened)* Oh well, maybe he's a good fighter; that's his last hope.

MATHILDE: *(Commanding)* Leave him alone.

(DIDI hurries in through the front parlor doors. She pauses, wrinkling her brow.)

DIDI: Where's Rene? Did he take the baby? *(MATHILDE leaves discreetly with the baby through the pantry as EDGAR enters quietly through the rear parlor doors. DIDI spots him, lowering her voice to a delighted tone of whispered confidence)*

DIDI: There you are. Papa is already drinking this morning. Will has smoked up all the cigars…*(With intentional impertinence)* I'll have to declare myself sick to get rest. Is it still raining?

EDGAR: Steadily. *(Smiles with detached tenderness)* I'll be leaving soon.

DIDI: *(Alarmed)* How soon is soon?

EDGAR: Next week.

DIDI: Couldn't you stay a little longer?

EDGAR: It's time.

DIDI: *(Coaxingly affectionate)* Could I ask you something? *(UNCLE MICHEL rises, fighting a tipsy drowsiness. With a remote amusing smile HE goes to leave them alone)* It's about this novel that I am writing. *(Intrigued, UNCLE MICHEL grins a bit drunkenly and sits again)* I want to check certain details. The story's about a woman who wants to be a writer, live in Paris. Is this possible, for a woman…to have her own Bohemian garret?

EDGAR: Yes, but artists' studios are small, unheated, with a horrifying amount of dust and dirt.

DIDI: *(SHE gives a little exalted, shy laugh)* Yes, I know, I know. So she lives in this poor garret, but she joins the Paris café society, and finds artist friends who are challenging and supportive.

EDGAR: Let's not forget jealous. That café crowd, everyone is in competition with everyone else.

DIDI: *(With stubborn blankness)* Yes, I know. Despite the envy she causes,

ROSARY HARTEL O'NEILL

she enjoys evenings spent in the salon, musical soirees. She does public lectures sponsored by friends whose estates she visits in Normandy.

EDGAR: How did she learn to maneuver so well in a—

DIDI: *(Her tone has become more and more rapturous)* She had a taste of this as a young girl. Exhilarating afternoons spent with her cousin at the Café Guerbois and the Nouvelle-Athenes where ideas for a new painting were debated. *(With an elaborately offhand casual manner)* Well, it was here that she became stronger and stronger. Her sense of purpose became clearer and clearer. She met a man, a painter who fought in the Commune.

UNCLE MICHEL: *(Rises dazed as if this were something SHE shouldn't talk about)* What nonsense, Didi!

(UNCLE MICHEL goes out on the gallery. Suddenly DIDI'S whole manner changes. SHE becomes pathetically relieved and eager.)

DIDI: She falls in love with this man...and they marry.

EDGAR: *(With a feeble attempt at teasing)* I was in love with all the Musson sisters.

DIDI: And we with you—

EDGAR: *(HE doesn't appear to hear her. HE adds pleasantly)* I couldn't get enough of you all, Mathilde, you and Tell. Beautiful Tell, so young and already a mother and a war widow. I used to study her from afar.

DIDI: You studied her?

EDGAR: *(Obsessed with the memory)* Such a stricken face, the tightness of the lips, the untidy strands of hair. Her eyes, deeply shadowed, downcast, always wet as if bleeding for that young captain sent to slaughter. I couldn't look at her without thinking that face filled the eyes of a dying man.

DIDI: *(Backs into a chair)* You couldn't forget her face?

EDGAR: I had no concept of what loss could be till I saw this vision. No matter what I brought to captivate her, bon-bons, marrons glaces, she found no consolation. No comfort. Even now weak and suffering.

DIDI: *(Stammering)* So she's the one...Bravery?

EDGAR: You're right. She's the brave one. I'm the coward. *(Kneels by DIDI, takes her hand in a comforting gesture)* I made a mistake. I never should have let Rene have Tell. Although she's blind and sick, I'm still in love with her.

DIDI: *(Crestfallen)* You're in love with her?

(UNCLE MICHEL comes in through a gallery window. EDGAR is on his knee in front of DIDI. Triumphant, fighting the effect of his last drink, UNCLE MICHEL blushes and bursts out.)

UNCLE MICHEL: Didi, why don't you get downstairs. Baby's screaming. I'd like to offer some sherry in celebration, but our liquor supply is shot.

EDGAR: We had wine in the cupboard.

UNCLE MICHEL: *(Joshing)* No more, it's drunk up. About the wedding...

(JO runs in from the gallery. She turns impulsively to her aunt, grabs her arm.)

JO: Aunt Didi. Gaston's thrown all my puppets out the window into the water. Aunt Didi...Gaston's...

DIDI: *(Drops her hands from her face, with a loose, twisted smile)* All right. I'm coming.

(JO pulls her off onto the gallery. UNCLE MICHEL stares after them with bleary affection, looks suspiciously at EDGAR, goes out the front parlor door, baffled. Moments later, with a growing dread, TELL rushes in from the pantry. SHE feels about the room. Tense with a hopeful, fearful expectancy.)

TELL: Edgar, is that you?

EDGAR: Yes.

TELL: Oh, my God. I can't find my baby. Where is she? Did she die? Where did they put her?

EDGAR: Mathilde is watching her.

TELL: Why did they move her?

EDGAR: *(HE stops her—gesturing upstairs—lowering his voice sincerely)* Mathilde just took her to the sick room.

TELL: *(With frightened resentment)* But she needs me to hold her. How can they take her from me without asking?

EDGAR: You were sleeping.

TELL: Jeanne needs me. If she misses me too much, she may lose heart. Has her fever gone up? *(SHE moves about worriedly, speaking with a tone of concern, burying her face in her hands miserably. EDGAR stares at her sheepishly and shakes his head)*

EDGAR: They wanted to spare you. Come here.

TELL: Spare me. They've taken her off to die.

EDGAR: No one would do that.

TELL: Is her breathing worse? Did the doctor ever get here?

EDGAR: He's on his way.

TELL: Damn floods. No one can get in or out.

EDGAR: *(With awkward tenderness)* Come. Sit. Get hold of yourself.

TELL: I don't want to. *(Hesitates, then blurts out guiltily)* You're the only one who talks to me. Rene hasn't said a word since Jeanne was born. I don't think he's seen her. God, he can't visit me? Not for ten minutes? I can't face this alone.

EDGAR: Jeanne's…just in the sick room.

TELL: *(SHE stiffens, with a terrified defiance)* Isolation, that's the first step. I've spoken to other mothers. She'll stop eating. Without me, she won't eat.

EDGAR: But you're weak.

TELL: I know. My milk is bad. I'm an unfit mother. I fed the others.

EDGAR: Nothing's wrong.

TELL: I cried without stopping since my baby was born. Now I can't even feed her. *(Her expression becomes somber)* I called her Jeanne, after the Maid of Orleans, because I wanted her to be strong. But I've got to face it. She's not. *(TELL speaks quickly, with a superstitious dread)* What will I do if she passes? My babies keep me going, holding them, skin on skin.

EDGAR: She's a little better.

TELL: Don't lie. Not you too. Not you too.

EDGAR: *(HE takes her hands and gently seats her by him. Puts his arm around her, HE draws her against him)* Here, sit back.

TELL: *(Her fear receding into resigned composure)* I want my girlhood back. The Paris Opera, the ballet, the racetrack. I want to see dancers turning in white tutus…*(Wistfully)* Arabian stallions, you drew so well.

(Light changes.)

EDGAR: *(Touched, leans in closer)* If you move to Paris, I'll buy you a stallion and we'll ride it. *(Music and slides of Paris during his speech)* I'll take you to the opera, the ballet, the popular theater, and the absurd Café Chantant, past the Rue de Rivoli, the Champs Elysees, the Arc de Triomphe.

SOUND: *Music and slides out when SHE sits up.*

TELL: *(Grins, at her ease again)* That's what I miss. Nonsense and seeing your work.

EDGAR: *(His manner becomes tenderly solicitous)* I'll take you to my studio, show you my modeling in wax. I'll put each piece in your hands. Do you remember the "Walking Horse" I made once? You could feel the muscles, the shadows. I'll teach you. We can forget conformity, gentility and even the need to remember. *(His voice is suddenly moved by profound feeling)* I've been holding your words close. They've been driving me, whispering to me, filling my thoughts with hope. I've had to face a lot of emotions I've been painting about obliquely for a long time. I tell my mind to stop, but it goes to you anyway. I blink, and you're in my thoughts. I'm fantasizing about you, fighting a slow idolatry. When I'm with you, I look for the unspoken— the nod in my direction.

TELL: Don't give me hope for something that's never going to happen.

EDGAR: It's hard to confess but I have to…And you?

TELL: I know what I feel is inconsequential. *(SHE looks away with a helpless far-off quality in her gaze)* If I go away, I'll never see my children again. Rene's—not the person you knew. He's confused. But he's my husband.

EDGAR:…and my little brother.

(EDGAR goes slowly out the front parlor door, a blank, hard expression on his face. Moments later, DIDI comes in from the back parlor. Worried, SHE speaks in a placating tone.)

DIDI: Tell…are you all right?

TELL: Yes, I'm fine. *(SHE becomes restless, sensing DIDI'S devotion, and struggling to keep down her emotion)* Didi, I've got to tell you something. I know it's wrong. There's no excusing it. But I always tell the truth, which endears me to no one.

DIDI: *(Cynically)* It's about Edgar.

TELL: Yes. First I…*(Pauses, ashamed)* I admired his persistence…His commitment to painting contemporary life. What ferments in his head is breathtaking. I'm scared of it, and awed by it at the same time.

DIDI: *(With a wry sadness)* Yes. I am too.

TELL: Then I loved his…his humility. *(SHE gives a little laugh of affectionate amusement)* He's uncertain about the quality of his earlier works. Astonishing paintings of ballet rehearsals and horse races as I recall them. Then I appreciated his loneliness, assessing in middle age what he wants to do with his life. With him it's visceral—it goes beyond language—it's crazy, it's wonderful, that at my age, with my difficulties, Edgar loves me and I love him.

DIDI: *(Appalled)* You've already had two husbands, it's not fair.

TELL: I...I never encouraged him. I'd forgotten what it's like to feel valued.

DIDI: *(Starts and stares at her sister with bitter hostility—thickly)* So you have to steal Edgar. You...you seduced him. You know how to fix yourself up—how to flirt—There are no men left since the war...You knew I wanted Edgar. How could you?

TELL: I said I'm sorry.

DIDI: *(Her mood changes to arrogant disdain)* Don't excuse it. Maybe it isn't your fault. I can't wash away the unwanted birthdays. Men say they want intelligent, independent women, but they don't, not really. *(SHE puts a hand to her face, holding back a sob)* Edgar and I are perfect for each other. The same artistic ambitions. I'd be happy just living with him, writing my stories. But with you flaunting yourself, he doesn't see me.

TELL: *(Looks down, guiltily)* Didi, calm down.

DIDI: I will not calm down, not this time. You're blind not only with your eyes but with your heart. *(In a burst of rage, SHE grabs her sister by the arm and twists it till TELL falls backwards)* Your own husband's having an affair with America, and you don't see. Yesterday I walked in on them in the back hall. But no, no matter what Rene does, you won't see. You lie there, doing nothing, feeling sorry for this baby you should never have had. The doctors warned you, but no, you had to put us through this misery. *(Her voice trembling with suppressed fury)* Where do you think that sickly baby is? In my room. I'm the one who's got to watch it die. You're a saint, while I'm just a woman without a husband. No matter I sit up nights writing. Nobody ever asks to read my work. My eyes burn while you lie there in your lace and satin, flaunting those new nightgowns Rene bought you. And you know that he did it out of guilt because he's seeing America. I take care of a dying baby so that Rene can sleep with America and Edgar can drool over you. *(Emotion raging through her)* I've been dreaming of him, praying he'd come for me, but he never stopped loving you. *(Guilty with the shocked realization of what she's said)* There is a bridge between our past and our present. Somehow when he arrived, like lightning you and he were connected all over again. *(DIDI chokes huskily, sobs overcoming her, as SHE barrels out to the front hallway. MATHILDE, who is coming in, shrinks back, then calls to DIDI uneasily)*

MATHILDE: Didi, what happened? *(Turns to TELL in a confused panic)* Are you feeling worse again?

ROSARY HARTEL O'NEILL

TELL: I don't want to talk about it.

MATHILDE: You can tell me.

TELL: *(Her face tensing)* No, I don't want to talk about it. Leave me alone.

(MATHILDE goes out into the hallway, yelling indignantly.)

MATHILDE: Desiree, Desiree?!

TELL: *(TELL stiffens, turns toward the doorway with frightened defiance, then hollers)* Rene! Rene! Rene!

(Moments later, RENE dashes down the stairs, hurries to the front parlor door, anxious.)

RENE: Yeah. What's wrong? The baby's fine. She's with me. Sit, you all right?

TELL: *(Bursts out with a look of accusing hate)* I've just had a terrible shock. I learned something that I…I can't believe.

RENE: From whom? Edgar.

TELL: No. Now tell me the truth. Don't lie to me.

RENE: *(With guilty vehemence)* I won't. You all right?

TELL: Someone came to me.

RENE: Edgar?

TELL: *(Staring condemningly at him)* And told me you're having relations with America. Is it true?

RENE: Who told you that?

TELL: Never mind.

RENE: Someone is talking behind my back? *(With vague exasperation, HE forces a casual tone. He comes to her, embracing her with a quick measuring look. SHE breaks away)*

TELL: Is it true?

RENE: We're friends.

TELL: *(Hysterically)* Did you make love to her?

RENE: How could you believe such…gossip.

TELL: Did you touch her?

RENE: America is…loyal.

TELL: Kiss her?

RENE: I would never do…*(Keeping his eyes averted)* How can you think that? You're making up vicious stories.

TELL: *(Turns on him, wounded, broken)* Liar! Liar! Liar!

(MATHILDE runs in the front parlor door. She sees RENE moving to the rear parlor door and lingering there. SHE regards him with dislike, comes round in back of TELL, touches her shoulder tenderly.)

MATHILDE: Tell?

TELL: *(Shattered, her eyes fixed downward)* I thought that America was a fine person…*(Strangely, as if talking aloud to herself)* Sometimes I felt queasy when she was overly solicitous of Rene…Still, I told myself, don't be small-minded because she is so good with the children. *(Pause of dead silence)* Now I've got to accept the fact that while I was being nice, she was sleeping with my husband. Or so Didi says. Rene denies it.

(RENE scowls, signaling to MATHILDE to lie for him. Without turning from RENE, MATHILDE says sharply.)

MATHILDE: He's a coward.

(RENE looks after MATHILDE angrily, shrugs, and goes and slouches by the rear parlor door.)

TELL: *(To MATHILDE, disgustedly)* You knew? You knew, and you didn't tell me? You were protecting Rene. God. I'm your sister. You and Didi have been covering for him.

MATHILDE: For God's sake. Everyone knew about it but you...and maybe Edgar.

TELL: Tell him too! Inform the world.

UNCLE MICHEL: *(Comes in from the pantry, letting the door slam behind him)* What is happening in my house? In the old days women knew how to behave.

MATHILDE: Papa, go to bed.

(MATHILDE and TELL go out the front parlor doors, with UNCLE MICHEL grumbling. Once they have gone, HE strolls maliciously up to RENE as if he will hit him. RENE moves quickly away from the doorway, feigning concern about an envelope on the desk. UNCLE MICHEL goes out, slamming the door behind him. Seconds later EDGAR comes in, reviewing some bills. HE looks at RENE with a quick calculating glance. Walks over to RENE at the desk. EDGAR's hands jerk nervously as he shows RENE a bill. RENE gives him a strained, almost contemptuous glance.)

EDGAR: Tell me if I'm wrong, but it doesn't look like you've paid back any of Papa's loans.

RENE: I can't talk about anything else today.

EDGAR: I've got to make some sense out of these records.

RENE: *(Tensely, moves away toward the window)* As I explained, Papa stopped keeping books for the planters. The old field hands are getting credit from shopkeepers. Railroads and the telegraph are diverting cotton to inland markets and drying up the power base on the river.

EDGAR: Still, we've been selling cotton without exacting a commission?

RENE: *(Ignoring this resentfully)* I contacted our creditors. I did everything short of sending a drawing with a gun to my temple saying "Pay this or I'll kill myself." I didn't create the financial panic. I've had a short and sorry business life. I don't speak the language, I don't get the nuances of these cotton people. I just want to leave. *(Abruptly his tone changes to exasperated contrition)* If it wasn't for Tell, I'd have left Louisiana. I don't know a single person who wouldn't leave if the means were at hand. The French Quarter is the end of New Orleans, which is the end of Louisiana, which is the end of the world. We're standing at the end of the end.

EDGAR: I'm trying to get some clarity.

RENE: So you can report to Papa what you did right and I've done wrong.

(RENE drinks restlessly, sensing EDGAR's struggle to make sense of the invoices)

EDGAR: I'm the one who influenced Papa and our sisters and brother to invest in cotton, but you've the control over all his property. That's what Papa wanted; I'm not questioning it.

RENE: Did I run away when Uncle went bankrupt, sold the big house and moved into this wretched rental property? I'd to get Papa's power of attorney to keep us from starving.

EDGAR: *(Looking down, trying to ignore RENE's tirade)* But self-dealing will put you in jail.

RENE: True, Papa loaned me too much money. *(Suddenly pointing a finger at EDGAR, his voice trembling)* But he also financed the girls' marriages, your never-ending studies, not to mention the Confederacy. *(Moving a step back, defensively, his face growing hard)* Papa wanted to turn to you, but trusting me was all he had. Our grandfathers were the geniuses, not him. They made the fortunes in Louisiana cotton and Italian investments. He just inherited their nest egg.

EDGAR: Poor fellow trusted you. You came home raving about Louisiana and telling us all we had to do was give you money for the shears and you'd cut the golden fleece. *(HE stares at RENE with increasing enmity, removes a letter)* Do you know what Papa wrote to me? "I was counting on Rene, who has sent me nothing. Is he going to let our bank, that was held up with so much effort, tumble down? If the creditors put my back against the wall, they'll take me to jail."

(RENE crouches on the sofa, picks up his flask listlessly.)

RENE: Papa's been using the bank to loan himself money. That's why his bank is in trouble.

EDGAR: Fine. Even if I sell a painting a week I can't make enough to stop them from—

RENE: *(HE glances away, miserably dogged, drinks.)* American-style business wiped Papa out. I worked hard.

EDGAR: For which you charged us substantial fees. God, we can't have a conversation with you without getting billed. *(Confronting him with the charges)* Look at this: conversations with Michel Musson, your own uncle, whose house you live *in gratis*, ten hours. And this, bank deposits for Uncle, conversations with Didi, Mathilde, and Tell Musson. My God, you even billed us for talking to your own wife.

(RENE shrinks onto the floor, sitting sideways by the sofa, so HE cannot meet EDGAR's eyes)

RENE: I charged you a reduced fee.

EDGAR: You knew the cotton business was failing and you gouged funds. You were my favorite brother. God, I trusted you. You had it all, and you took it all.

RENE: *(HE jumps up, losing his temper, refusing to admit anything to his brother.)* I am appalled you think I'd do anything unethical. The authorization for my action was Papa's idea. In reference to your…accusation…about my fees. I and my assistants have spent many hours working…

EDGAR: *(Takes a threatening step toward him)* Such as?

RENE: *(Jeeringly, shoving EDGAR back)* You have benefited…directly from the money you have received…your gallery openings, your studies, your trips, as well as indirectly from Mama and Papa's generosity to you from monies they've received. It's not my fault the cotton business is failing. I am deeply hurt by your actions as my brother. *(His rage smoldering, HE pushes EDGAR violently into a chair)* If you chastised me for my relationship with America, that I could understand. I feel guilty about that.

EDGAR: *(EDGAR'S hand goes to his head in an aimless stunned way. HE stabilizes himself, looking straight at RENE now. There is a tense pause)* What is that you are saying? You are sleeping with America? I knew she was helping you with running the house, tending to the children, caring for Tell, but—

RENE: It's been more than that for some time.

EDGAR: You're not…You are. You're having relations with her. *(Sharply, letting his resentment come out)* Here?

RENE: *(With a detached, impersonal tone)* She understands me. Comforts me.

EDGAR: Your baby is dying, your wife is critically ill, and you're having an affair with her neighbor in her house?

RENE: It didn't start now. It started a year ago.

EDGAR: This is worse than the money. This is Biblical sin. *(Gives a hard, sneering little laugh)* I can't believe I gave Tell to you. I let you have her, court her first. And you wasted this possibility. You knew how much I cared. She commanded my attention, and she did so for a long time. *(With threatening anger)* You couldn't tell me about America all these months I've been here. We all have to deal with unbearable situations. But we don't bring our mistresses into our house.

RENE: I hate myself. But God, I'm bored. *(With broken weariness)* There's no defending it. I've become the men I knew. I wake up and see, like Papa and Uncle, I've a mistress and a wife. *(RENE goes to the window, glad of an excuse to turn his back)* I want it to end, but it's impossible. I'm too exhausted to break it off. Too disappointed. When we're alone, America's different. She lifts my spirits. *(From the window without turning around)* No one believes in monogamy anymore. We only choose it when we have no appealing alternatives. Sex is everywhere in the city, except in a husband's relationship with his wife. I say I love my wife, but I'm cold below the neck. I feel nothing. She's attractive to many men, but to me she's not, so I put on a false face. My life is a total lie. Wives dream of other husbands, husbands dream of other wives, and we both shut our eyes.

(A pause. The brothers avoid looking at each other.)

ROSARY HARTEL O'NEILL

EDGAR: Does Tell know about America?

RENE: I guess she suspects. *(RENE comes around in back of his brother, not looking at him, and grabs EDGAR's shoulder)* I don't want to lie, so I'm evasive. It takes so much energy. Believe me, being a liar is tiring.

Slides in, then a

BLACKOUT

SCENE 2
EMILY AND EDGAR: STREET SCENE

(EDGAR and EMILY walk cautiously down an alley. SHE pauses, a look of growing uneasiness comes over her face.)

EMILY: We leaving tomorrow morning. Four days on trains, three hours in New York, ten days at sea in an English ship. Goodbye, New Orleans. *(SHE stares before her, hopeless)* We got no choice. Look out there. Soldiers marching up and down the streets. People running. Mean-eyed police. Now free people of color don't mean anything. The whole city is in silence. Men are fighting everywhere. It's madness. *(Turns impulsively, grabs his arm, lowers her voice)* Last night four men in sheets broke in our house. They knocked Norbert down. Cause he spoke out. Because we feed these poor souls that come to our door. You don't read the paper. Go out? Coloreds are hit for no reason. And the poverty. Homeless every corner. It's getting worse. There's going to be a fight. Too many hungry people, and ones who got nothing but hate.

EDGAR: *(HE pats her arm with an awkward tenderness)* I need to leave. But I have unfinished business.

EMILY: You best go before a battle break. You don't want to be a foreigner in gunfire. *(Her voice begins to tremble)* I've seen things these past few days. Secret groups riding and killing more than ever now. Yanks pretend they want to help but they do nothing. Old masters want to stop coloreds from getting their rights. They watching people like Norbert. Next time it be worse.

EDGAR: *(HE frowns and shakes his head mechanically)* I can't leave Tell with no one to protect her. She can't count on Rene. He's never there.

EMILY: *(Suddenly it is too much for her and SHE breaks out and sobs)* Take your luggage and get out. Before they send a pack of dogs and madmen to get you. You have a mission in life. *(She throws her arms around him, hides her face in his shoulder, then runs out)* God bless you. Goodbye.

(Music and slides in as SHE is leaving.)

SCENE 3
LATER AT THE HOUSE.

(TELL sits on the porch. SHE has fallen deep into herself and finds relief for an instant in silence. JO comes in, dressed in a traveling cape and bonnet. With forced gladness, SHE taps her mother on the shoulder. TELL hugs JO to her breast; using remoteness to contain her sorrow.)

JO: I'm ready.

TELL: *(Squeezes her affectionately)* Your whole life you have been with me. Now, different cities, different houses.

JO: I'll come back for the Carnival balls.

TELL: And Papa will present you. I can't take it.

JO: Don't cry, Mama; I'm not afraid anymore. I want to leave.

TELL: No, do you really?

JO: I'm grown up. *(SHE pauses—then speaks in a flat, empty tone)* I can travel alone. I'm leaving all my puppets. I placed them in a row for little Jeanne so she can play with them when she gets better. I'm too old for puppets.

TELL: Well, won't you miss them?

JO: I packed a baby one in my bag, but don't tell anyone.

TELL: *(Smiles as if SHE hasn't heard it)* I won't. Are you sure you want to go? You don't have to if—

JO: Don't stop me.

TELL: *(With detached motherly solicitude)* Oh, I can't stand it.

JO: I want your life to be easier, Mama; you worry so. Trying to make everyone happy. I know how hard it is, because I see.

TELL: Oh, shush. I just need another hug.

(JO climbs on her lap, hides her face in her mother's shoulder.)

JO: I'm only going for a while. Then I'll be at the convent in Mobile. I'll come back a grown-up elegant lady. Everyone will like me. Now I just make trouble for you.

TELL: *(Her voice shifting far away)* How can not having you be better for me?

JO: You'll see. Things will be easier.

TELL: Don't talk that way.

(DIDI walks in wearily from the front hallway, sits tensely on the sofa staring before herself as if in a sad dream.)

JO: There are too many people here. When people are squished like that, it's hard for everyone to be nice. It'll be better for you if I leave.

TELL: *(Rocking her like a baby)* You don't know, you don't.

JO: *(Curling a finger through TELL's hair)* Don't feel sad. I'm happy, Mama.

MATHILDE: *(Walks in briskly from the rear hallway. SHE looks at DIDI matter-of-factly)* You're in one of your depressive moods.

DIDI: Jo's been mine since she was three weeks old.

MATHILDE: I thought you were fine with her going.

DIDI: *(SHE sighs gloomily)* I've enough other reasons to be bitter and sad.

MATHILDE: Oh, yes. Edgar is also leaving.

DIDI: *(Her face set in stubborn denial)* Don't talk. I don't want to fall apart.

(Reluctantly, JO leaves her mother and walks slowly to where her aunts stand waiting.)

JO: I'll go say goodbye.

DIDI: (*Grief-strickenly whispers to MATHILDE*) I won't survive this.

MATHILDE: Didi, I didn't think I'd survive the death of my baby boy. I made it, and you'll make it.

(*JO walks in, sees DIDI crying. JO looks at her aunts, bravely covering her helpless, hurt feelings. She feels their sad eyes on her and forces a smile.*)

JO: I would like to say goodbye to you, Tante Didi and Tante Mathilde.

DIDI: (*Stubbornly fixing a hat on JO's head*) Oh, no.

(*UNCLE MICHEL comes in from the back hallway—summoning his soldier's heartiness. Takes JO's hands, sits, and gives her a pony back ride on his knee. Feigning a laugh, HE clicks his heels and waves an imaginary whip.*)

UNCLE MICHEL: I'm proud of you, Jo. I'm glad your grandmother didn't live to see this day. I'll go with Jo. Soon we'll be galloping on horses in Pass Christian.

JO: You're too old, Grandpa.

UNCLE MICHEL: I never do things like old people. I feel like I'm three. I used to look around, and I was the youngest in the room, and now I'm the oldest. (*Another forced laugh*) I should leave also. After the fall of New Orleans, I refused to take the oath of allegiance to the Union, so they're not going to tell me what to do.

MATHILDE: You'd only get in the way, Papa.

UNCLE MICHEL: (*Importantly*) Jefferson Davis is writing a chronicle of the war. Now Jo's going, I can tell you for the past ten years I've been—

DIDI: Keeping a journal, we know.

UNCLE MICHEL: (*With painful effort to be jolly*) But Jo doesn't know the extent of the collection. I've been writing down each dream I've had along with every daily event and political occurrence. About fifteen hundred pages a year. For my heirs so they can know everything about me.

JO: (*Enthusiastically*) About me too?

UNCLE MICHEL: *(Glad for an excuse to keep talking)* Yes, I'm showing how the dream relates to the event and the routine. *(Tries to get his appeal started)* Well, what do y'all think? I've thousands of entries. Mr. Davis will find them interesting.

DIDI: Papa, she doesn't understand.

JO: Yes, I do!

MATHILDE: Shush. *(MATHILDE is about to make a sneering remark to her father, but SHE shrugs her shoulders and embraces JO)* You're such a big girl, so grown up, and you'll be even more so when you return from your Papa's people.

JO: I want to go with Uncle Edgar.

MATHILDE: Will and I are moving to Ocean Springs—that's not far from you. I'll visit. I'm only sorry Aunt Didi won't be with us.

DIDI: *(Grumbling)* Thank God I don't have to cope with Will anymore.

UNCLE MICHEL: One more hug. Rene can't make you go, if I say no.

JO: Don't worry about me, Grandpa.

MATHILDE: Don't blame Rene; we all agreed.

UNCLE MICHEL: *(HE growls)* I never.

DIDI: Papa, please.

UNCLE MICHEL: Write me like you promised. A page a day.

JO: Yes, sir. Have Uncle Edgar send me a little sketch of the family.

MATHILDE: *(Distracted, sad)* I almost forgot the lunch basket.

UNCLE MICHEL: *(Feigning a smile)* We'll wait for you outside, Jo.

(UNCLE MICHEL gives her a strange lost glance, disbelieving she can truly be leaving. UNCLE MICHEL blows his nose and goes out to the gallery.

ROSARY HARTEL O'NEILL

MATHILDE and DIDI give way to a flurry of guilty business and leave swiftly. While JO is silent, keeping a head turned toward their footsteps, EDGAR comes in with gifts for her. HE goes directly to JO, his face set in an expression of kind sympathy.)

EDGAR: Where's the little lady? I have a gift for you.

JO: What is it?

EDGAR: *(Puts a hand affectionately on her shoulder)* Open it.

JO: *(Embarrassed and pleased)* Are all these pencils for me? Oh my.

EDGAR: That's not all.

JO: A miniature of Mama! Oh, she's so beautiful. Thanks, Uncle Edgar. *(SHE smiles, her face lighting up, and kisses him gratefully)* Come with me to Mississippi. How will I learn to draw if you don't teach me?

EDGAR: Take my memorandum book.

JO: I couldn't.

EDGAR: All my life I've carried a notebook where I sketch images. *(With a touch of pride, HE gives her a shiny binder)* I took this one when boarding the Scotia, the last paddle steamer. See, I've sketches of the passengers. Here I've drawings of horses, a genre painting called "Pouting," and the "Orchestra of the Opera."

JO: I couldn't draw like that. I dance even in my dreams, but if I try to draw I cannot.

EDGAR: Neither could I at first. *(SHE laughs and HE laughs with her)* You must practice. That's how you learn. Study and paint, then come to Paris. I'll get you permission to copy inside the Louvre. Show you Ingres and Delacroix.

JO: What are those?

EDGAR: Great painters. Let's find your mother.

JO: *(SHE opens the book, smiles with humorous exaggeration)* Let me sign my name. Jo Balfour 1873. *(Reluctantly)* Must we go?

EDGAR: Sometimes we must go away even though we'd like to stay.

JO: I don't want anyone to know about the miniature. They might take it.

EDGAR: *(HE looks at her with understanding sympathy)* It's our secret.

SOUND: Music fades in slowly.

EDGAR takes JO's hand and THEY walk out bravely to the gallery. SHE smiles, controlling an impulse to cry, clutching the miniature. MATHILDE comes out to the gallery—uneasily—with a plate of sandwiches. All feign smiles and hug JO with elaborately casual airs and pathetic attempts at heartiness. TELL hugs her to herself—sobs brokenly. JO leaves slowly and her mother rushes back inside, bumping into RENE. Huskily trying to force a smile, RENE walks on to the gallery just as JO passes out of sight. HE waves feebly. Mournful sounds of a carriage are heard. Moments later, AMERICA marches out onto the gallery. SHE attempts to catch RENE'S eye, looking for sympathy, but HE walks back inside, staring at the floor. There is a dead silence. AMERICA follows RENE inside with guilty talkativeness.

AMERICA: Jo should have appreciated me more. She forgot to thank me. The girl's all right as people go, but one more child or less, in this house...what does it matter?

(MATHILDE and DIDI walk dully into the parlor. MATHILDE's expression changes as if she were deliberately giving way to hunger and seeking to hide behind food. SHE attempts a light, amused tone, and passes sandwiches to DIDI, RENE—loitering at the desk, and AMERICA.)

MATHILDE: These sandwiches look lovely on Mama's calendar plates with Monarch butterflies and roses.

DIDI: How can you talk of food when Jo's leaving?

MATHILDE: *(Gives her a quick apprehensive glance)* Edgar's going.

(AMERICA glares at the sisters with a hard accusing antagonism. Her face is stony and her tone icy.)

74

AMERICA; Food shouldn't be eaten in the parlor. You want rats? Yesterday I saw one leap from the banana tree. We'll have to shave it back, replace that rosebush with a cement slab. We must economize if Rene's going to get back to Paris. Isn't that right, Rene? *(HE doesn't respond and SHE leaves noisily through the pantry)*

MATHILDE: People usually behave better with food.

DIDI: *(Gloomily)* When exactly are you leaving?

MATHILDE pauses—then lowers her voice to a tone of whispered confidence.

MATHILDE: After Will's meeting at noon. Excuse me if I gloat. I woke up this morning and thought, "Praise God I'm finally leaving." I'll have my own big house and my own room, thick sheets and a satin quilt. Aren't you happy for me?

DIDI: I should be happy for you, but I'm not. Abandoning me with Tell and Papa. He won't come in, and she won't come out. *(SHE gives a little rebellious toss of the head)* Don't you need someone to read to the children?

MATHILDE: We'll get a nurse in Ocean Springs.

(The front parlor doorway opens and UNCLE MICHEL walks in, worriedly, with a quick sly glance at RENE. Children's voices are heard and UNCLE MICHEL walks to MATHILDE with a disconcerting laugh.)

UNCLE MICHEL: Mathilde, little Will needs you. He's bawling for Edgar.

MATHILDE: Thanks, Papa.

(Vaguely resentful, MATHILDE goes out into the front hallway.)

UNCLE MICHEL: *(Moves over to RENE—irritably)* It should be over by now.

DIDI: *(Looks about, tense)* I have a feeling something bad's happened. What is it?

RENE: Will's been in a duel.

DIDI: What? *(RENE pats her shoulder. SHE gives him an uneasy, almost frightened glance.)*

UNCLE MICHEL: Will was set on a challenge. They were shooting pistols at noon. Strange, since it's usually dawn.

DIDI: *(Looks at him sharply)* We should warn Mathilde.

UNCLE MICHEL: *(His face hard—grimly)* It's over by now. Anyway, it's not women's business.

DIDI: We should do something.

RENE: Calm down.

DIDI: *(SHE turns on her father accusingly)* But Papa—*(AMERICA comes in from the pantry. SHE is terribly annoyed again, as if the strain of the departure activities had been too much for her. SHE frowns at them suspiciously)*

AMERICA: Are you talking about me again? Every time I leave and return, I see these caught faces. The devil's going to punish you for talking about me. I won't have it.

RENE: *(Turning away, wryly)* We were discussing politics. A certain weariness in people getting their dream—

AMERICA: I know what I hear.

UNCLE MICHEL: *(HE shrugs his shoulders—cynically)* She'd be a good woman if someone held a gun to her head twenty-four hours a day.

AMERICA: How dare you insult me?

UNCLE MICHEL: I'll do what I want. I'm the head of this house. And the head doesn't take orders from the tail. *(HE takes a threatening step toward her, raising his cane)* Would you mind leaving?

AMERICA: Happily.

UNCLE MICHEL: I'm in a fighting mood. If I kill someone, it might as well be her. Nobody would miss her. *(HE stamps his foot, genuinely pleased and grateful for the explosion. HE goes out the front parlor—roughly—grazing past MATHILDE, who is coming back in. MATHILDE adjusts her hair in an aimless anxious way and walks to RENE, seated at the desk. Her hands drop distractedly to her dress)*

MATHILDE: Somehow I'm so nervous today. We're all packed, Will has to run off. I don't get it. If he knows we're leaving, couldn't he stay home? What could be so important? *(With forced casualness)* Sweet Jesus, don't let him get into trouble.

(AMERICA comes in through the front parlor, goes straight up to MATHILDE, who avoids her eyes. There is a cracking silence.)

AMERICA: Mathilde, Mathilde, Mathilde. It's such a disgrace. *(There is a tense pause, then she speaks jeeringly)* I just received word at the door; Will's been shot in a duel.

MATHILDE: Shot?

AMERICA: *(An undercurrent of revengefulness comes into her voice)* He never made it to any meeting.

MATHILDE: Is he dead?

AMERICA: Wounded, slightly.

MATHILDE: *(With a despairing laugh)* Will's always tilting against windmills.

AMERICA: This time he killed a police officer.

MATHILDE: *(Stunned)* He did what?

AMERICA: They've posted a bond and thrown him in jail. You'll have to use your travel funds to bail him out.

MATHILDE: *(Hastily—gruff)* Well, get my hat and coat!

(Her reaction has an automatic quality as if it did not penetrate to real emotion. Her face darkens—stung, and SHE goes out. With a scornful shrug of her shoulders, AMERICA snaps.)

AMERICA: Don't bring Will in the front door! We'll never outlive the humiliation. *(SHE starts for RENE and sighs grudgingly)* I suppose I'll have to clean up by myself. I want you to tell Didi and Mathilde to help around the house. I don't intend to keep getting used. If you're curious about what you can do to help out, I've got some suggestions. *(Guiltily explosive)* Are you listening to me?

RENE: *(Bored with her complaints)* I'm trying not to.

(RENE takes out his flask and drinks. AMERICA gives him a quick biting look and disappears through the back parlor. Moments later, EDGAR comes in the rear parlor doors, suitcase in hand. His manner is nervously apprehensive. HE stops abruptly, catching RENE'S eyes, regarding him with an uneasy hopeless look.)

RENE: I can't believe you're going to leave when we've so much trouble. I've been counting on you, looking up to you for twenty-five years. You can't leave with the baby ill and the cotton business bankrupt. I depended on your partnership. You were coming here to help us. What happened to that? *(HE is moved in spite of himself. His voice quivers)* In six months the cotton business could turn around. I can't have this end with us not talking. I did the best I could.

EDGAR: It's better for everybody if I go. Better for me and Tell.

RENE: What about me? I need you. I'm drowning here. I've no one to turn to.

EDGAR: Talk to your wife.

RENE: *(HE looks directly at EDGAR, a note of pleading in his voice)* You don't understand. I wanted to impress you. That's why I took this big chance. *(Putting on an eager heartiness)* Oh, don't give up on me. Stay. How could it be better with you miles away?

EDGAR: I'm stepping back for the second time. It's not healthy for me to be so close to your family. I start being overprotective...thinking I'm the father...the husband—

RENE: *(With a cynically appraising glance)* You're too fond of my wife?

EDGAR: *(Averting his eyes, suddenly overcome by guilty confusion—stammers)*

No...Yes. I must leave. Take this last chance and save your marriage.

(UNCLE MICHEL comes in hastily from the back parlor. Goes worriedly to EDGAR, puts his arm around him.)

UNCLE MICHEL: This house is always in the middle of disaster. Now I have to get Will out of jail. *(A shadow of vague delight crosses his face as HE hands EDGAR a magazine)* Something to amuse you on the ship. I think it's a sin to read these magazines. I read them anyway. So what. The problem with heaven is some awful people are going to be there, so I'd just as soon be in hell.

EDGAR: Well...Thanks...Uncle Michel.

UNCLE MICHEL: *(With a flash of apprehension)* It bothers me to hear my name. My name embarrasses me. Before I was Michel Musson. Now I don't know who I was five minutes ago, let alone next week. I'm sixty and I don't know anymore.

EDGAR: The whole world is changing. People want to breathe freely... Negroes, whites—everyone just wants to breathe.

UNCLE MICHEL: *(EDGAR goes to UNCLE MICHEL but HE cannot face him)* I don't understand your ideas about a New World. I want my old one back. You're leaving, Jo's gone, Mathilde's in trouble. Suppose I should be happy. Less mouths to feed, more room. *(Heroically covering his grief)* Still— I've to bludgeon myself to fake a smile, to put one foot before the other. My God, can't you stay? Your brother needs you. You're the strong one. We never got along, but I respect you. I don't know anything about painting, but I know people.

EDGAR: I'll miss you. I'll miss you all.

UNCLE MICHEL: Is that a fact? You're the strange one that's hard to tell. Money was what you came here for, wasn't it? *(EDGAR looks away, shrinking into himself)* You and Rene, prospecting in the New World. Take this for your trip. *(HE pulls out a small roll of bills from his pants pocket and carefully selects one. EDGAR refuses it)*

EDGAR: I'm fine.

UNCLE MICHEL: I'd liked to have given you more. Twenty years ago, I could have. It was a damn comfortable life. I hoped we'd have something in common...that you'd take an interest in the White League. *(EDGAR turns sharply, seized by guilt, fumbling with his pocket watch)* What's that frown for?

EDGAR: Shame overcomes me when you talk about this. I'm not from here. But oppressing the Negroes cannot be justified. People must learn to live together.

UNCLE MICHEL: Everyone oppresses someone! Right, Rene? *(RENE shrinks in the doorway; EDGAR stares at his watch without seeing it)* The Negroes are angry...there are conspiracies among them to murder the whites and outrage our women. The White League was formed to protect our rights. You want to see your cousins raped?

(EDGAR looks up with a start.)

EDGAR: This is the old ghostly fear.

UNCLE MICHEL: *(With rising anger)* I don't know what I did to offend you...I don't understand you. I welcomed you into my home. I treated you like the son I never had. *(Removes a gun from the desk, engages it, calls distract-edly to RENE)* Rene, we have a meeting to attend. *(EDGAR stops RENE with a punitive glance. For a second HE seems to have broken through to him. RENE shrugs guiltily, and skulks out the rear parlor door after his uncle. DIDI enters, breathless from the gallery. Seeing EDGAR, SHE blushes. Her voice flutters)*

DIDI: So, you're leaving. Can't you wait till summer? You haven't experi-enced anything till you've spent a day out in the boiling air and open sun. It's really refreshing. The heat just hangs there between the oak trees. I picked you a boutonniere. *(SHE pulls out a flower SHE'S been hiding behind her skirt, touches his lapel gently. HE draws away, smiling uncomfortably)*

EDGAR: *(His hands jerk nervously to his lapel)* I'll do it.

DIDI: *(With an excited obstinacy to her face)* Mama used to have a flower lady who came every week and taught me what to do. Hold still a minute.

EDGAR: I don't know if I can. *(Hesitates)* They like you to board early. I'll be returning on a French ship, traveling via Havana. Where did I put the ticket?

ROSARY HARTEL O'NEILL

DIDI: Your jacket? Check the front pocket. Where? Oh.

EDGAR: I hope I didn't pack it.

DIDI: (Soothingly) There it is.

EDGAR: (Grateful, steps back) You're so observant.

DIDI: That's what you said when I first visited Italy. You said I found more subtleties in your painting than anyone you knew. That's because I saw the suffering.

EDGAR: I don't have much time. (DIDI gives a quick suspicious glance to the entranceways, then kisses him passionately. HE backs off and turns her away from him with genuine concern) Wait. Forgive me if I've done anything to mislead you. You're like a sister to me.

DIDI: (Mumbles, a trifle acidly) Like a sister.

(SHE stiffens, with resigned helplessness, and backs out onto the gallery from the room. TELL comes in cautiously through the rear parlor doors with a hopeful, fearful expectancy of finding EDGAR.)

TELL: Edgar, are we alone? Good. I want to remember the feeling of you alone in the room with me.

EDGAR: It doesn't have to be a memory. (With awkward tenderness) I've said little in lots of time. Now I feel I must say lots in little time.

TELL: All this time I saw myself going with you. (SHE smiles rigidly, her voice beginning to tremble) My life wasn't touched by you; it was scalded. I, who had ruled out happiness in my life, suddenly had access to it. And now you're leaving. I didn't know it'd be this hard.

EDGAR: (HE walks her to the sofa, regarding her from somewhere far within himself, a place of bitter sadness) There were a lot of things I didn't know. The brutality of your sun. Can I tell you a secret? Before I go to sleep I imagine you beside me, a hair's-breadth away. Like in a painting, I imagine your neck, your body caressed by thick sheets, the quick-silver light falling on your thighs. I'm terminally romantic. I close my eyes and imagine you touching me on a wild and melancholy night.

TELL: *(With strange coquetry)* I know.

EDGAR: How many times when my soul fell into solemnness have I lain with you? Bodies merging, two wrongs becoming a right. *(Then with a teasing boyish laugh)* Now what use is my fantasy? I'll have my pencils, papers, paints. But here, I've been surrounded by little ones.

TELL: You're dancing with something bigger than family, your talent. There's an involuntary glory in that. You must hurry. Paint the paintings only you can paint. *(SHE seems not to notice the tears in her eyes)* One day you may lose your sight. Painting will be your legacy. Other artists, your family.

EDGAR: I'm wistful for a home of my own. *(Moved in spite of himself)* Come to Paris with me.

TELL: Nonsense.

EDGAR: Let nonsense become sense.

TELL: I'd be a burden.

EDGAR: You'd inspire me.

TELL: And the children?

EDGAR: More subjects to paint.

TELL: Rene would never let them go—

EDGAR: He'd have America.

TELL: You're brutal.

EDGAR: Honest.

TELL: Three children and a blind wife.

EDGAR: Finally, a family.

(SHE lets him take in the fantasy, hiding deep within herself. Her face looks amazingly youthful and innocent. Then SHE gives a forlorn toss of her head.)

TELL: You're crazy.

EDGAR: In love.

TELL: Go before you—

EDGAR: Do something impulsive: jump the fence, strip naked, swim the Mississippi. *(HE stares at her with the quality of a bewildered boy)* I can't bear the thought of life without you. Drifting into the day, meaninglessness setting in. You make me believe in myself, in my deep judgment.

TELL: *(SHE pauses with a bitter laugh)* I'm the latest in a long line of people who believe in you.

EDGAR: Not true. I can give myself to you without being consumed. After you left, I shut down my heart. My wounds were so deep I thought I might die if I made my heart vulnerable. I joined the ranks of the dispossessed. Became another mad soldier. I've let you reenter my heart and know my deep self. And now I can't leave without you. Return to that cynical place.

TELL: *(SHE smiles hopelessly)* You know if you really need me, I'm there for you. *(Her voice quivering)* Who knows, maybe we'll be together in another life.

EDGAR: I want you now, today. *(Bell chimes)* Run off with me. Leave. My best art was done like that, in a flash. A release of spirit, a concession to a greater power.

TELL: If I went...your paintings would suffer.

EDGAR: *(A trusting smile on his lips)* I have to step back and take care of bigger things than my painting, things that painting didn't take care of. There is an illusion with art that feels like it can save us. Dreams do not go away. They go to the grave with you. As you move toward a dream, the dream moves toward you. It meets you.

TELL: *(SHE winces—her lips quivering pitifully)* But how can we...I can't leave my children.

EDGAR: I'll take your arm, wrap it around mine, and we'll walk out of hell together. *(Sound of carriage bells)* God, it's time to go.

TELL: No, no, no.

(HE draws her to her feet, HE touches her face and SHE his forehead, eyes, mouth. SHE buries her face in his neck. HE draws her away, but SHE gets up and throws her arms around him—hiding her face in his shoulders sobbingly.)

EDGAR: *(Suddenly it is too much for him and HE breaks out)* I don't think we were meant never to see each other. I don't think I was never meant to hear your voice or the ripple of your laugh, or to see the dimple when you smile.

TELL: Don't forget.

(EDGAR breaks away and leaves quickly out the front parlor door. SHE does not respond at first, her hands fluttering to her eyes to wipe back the tears. Her two sisters join her, coming in hastily from the rear parlor. The three sisters rush after him, moving to the gallery window to wave farewell. DIDI, forcing a laugh, inches in front and waves the most. RENE walks in from the pantry with awkward, heavy steps. HE goes somberly to the window. HE nods in EDGAR's direction. Once EDGAR has gone, RENE steps back into the parlor and busies himself at the desk and speaks with a sad bitterness to TELL, who comes into the parlor, shaking her head helplessly.)

RENE: Tell, I wish there were something I could say. This is embarrassing, sugar. I won't ask any questions and you shouldn't ask any questions. Maybe this way we can live together. *(His eyes stare at the floor, his face set in an expression of defensive cynicism.)*

TELL: *(Rebuffed and hurt, shrugs her shoulders)* I hope so.

(MATHILDE comes in and walks TELL to the gallery for fresh air. They look in EDGAR's direction. MATHILDE sits on the arm of TELL's chair, her arm around her. DIDI joins them from the front parlor, standing behind TELL's chair.)

DIDI: *(With finality)* He's gone.

TELL: *(Wistfully)* Paris took him back. I wonder if anyone will know that Edgar came to New Orleans?

SOUND: *Music plays softly.*

EDGAR: *(Walks slowly to the ship's railing, slipping into reverie)* I stood on the deck watching New Orleans fade into light. It felt like peering through a looking glass, hallucinatory, the vast wild sky expanding into mirror-like water. I'd come to find the people to whom I belonged, to close up this hole in my soul. *(A blank, far-off quality in his voice)* The long way back made me face my own lie. I'd come for Tell. If only I'd captured her beauty in that painting in 1863. I recalled her home on Esplanade, the half-exposed body, the bare shiny arms, the wonderful warmness of the profanity of life. Broadly-stated limbs, outstretched arms with a vaguely underwater feeling, gossamer torsos caught up in light and shade. *(HE pauses—then longingly)* I'd found a raw reality for my paintings. A new direction I'd been avoiding in life and on canvas. And I would struggle to feel it deeper and deeper in explosions of color, people, soon called Impressionism. *(Nostalgically)* Years would pass. Great stretches of time, and like New Orleans, my cousins would fade in memory. Little Jo, Didi, Mathilde, and Tell. Sweet beautiful Tell. *(With strange, sad detachment)* And all the paintings in the world would never bring them back.

(HE leaves abruptly, 3 slides appear in incandescent, blues, violets, and scarlet, ending with something like "The Portrait of Estelle.")

(JO's ballet movements cross the stage. SHE twirls bravely, with a voracious delicacy reminding us of Degas' "Fille de Quatorze Ans." There is an uncanny, gay freedom in her manner as if in spirit SHE were released to live again.)

CURTAIN
BLACKOUT

BAYOU FOLK MUSEUM

The Awakening of
Kate Chopin
A PLAY IN TWO ACTS

CAST OF CHARACTERS

KATE CHOPIN—31, dark-haired Irish beauty, with waves and curls about her shoulders. SHE has direct eyes that look right at you and a captivating face with a frankness of expression.

OSCAR CHOPIN—39, her husband, an aristocratic cotton merchant recuperating from "malaria." Handsome eyes, a feverish glance. HE retreats into silence and brooding.

MARIA NORMAND DELOUCHE—26. Cuban vixen with broad smiling mouth, tip-tilted nose and full figure. SHE wears Spanish mantillas and flowers draped over her curly hair.

ALBERT SAMPITE—38, wealthy planter with charm and animalism. Devilishly good-looking, deep eyes with an insolent manner.

OFFSTAGE: KATE'S FOUR SONS ages 11 and under, and her INFANT GIRL.

SETTING

The Chopin plantation in Cloutierville, Louisiana, a one-street town blighted by the Civil War.

SCENE ONE: Six p.m. on a dreary Friday, December 5, 1882.

The sun sets on shabby genteel furniture in a gloomy parlor.

SCENE TWO: Later the same night, December 5, 1882, Albert Sampité enters.

SCENE THREE: Later the same night, December 5, 1882, Kate's parlor.

SCENE FOUR: 2:00 a.m in the wee hours of the morning, December 6, 1882.

SCENE FIVE: Same night, 2:30 a.m., December 6, 1882, continuous with previous scene.

SCENE SIX: Six days later, December 12, 1882, dusk.

SCENE SEVEN: Several hours later, December 12, 1882.

SCENE EIGHT: A week later, December 19, 1882, late afternoon.

SCENE NINE: Five months later, May 19, 1882, noon.

SCENE TEN: Several weeks later, June 10, 1882, suppertime.

SCENE ONE

(Six p.m. on a dreary Friday, December 5, 1884. The sun sets on shabby genteel furniture in a gloomy parlor. KATE CHOPIN enters in a glamorous robe; SHE turns up an oil lamp of clear glass with an amethyst tinge. Retrieving pencils and her manuscript from inside a walnut drawer, SHE makes sure SHE is alone, pours tea and prepares to write. Someone knocks at the door and hollers, "There's a beggar outside." KATE stuffs the manuscript under a cushion, hands money through the door, gets the manuscript and returns to writing. A jangle of carriage bells. Christmas carolers sing off-key. Then, a pounding at the door and a cry, "The tax collector is here." KATE writes so furiously SHE breaks a pencil point.)

KATE: "She was seeking herself and discovering herself. No. She was seeking herself and finding herself. *(Pause)* But the voices were not safe. Were not soothing. But the voices were not soothing that came to her *(Pause)* from the darkness…in the sky above and stars."

More incessant ringing of a service bell. Children's cries offstage. KATE hides the manuscript, but an end sticks out. SHE trips over a toy, unlocks the door, exits. Outside bells jangle as a carriage arrives. OSCAR CHOPIN enters the room. HE starts to change into a patched cashmere sweater, and is startled to see KATE's manuscript. HE scans the cover. A noise offstage. Oscar hides the manuscript. KATE reenters with books wrapped in gold paper singing.

KATE: "Oh Holy Night. The stars are brightly shining. It is—The night of our dear—"

OSCAR: "Savior's birth." *(OSCAR kisses her)*

KATE: We're not starting that.

OSCAR: Why not?

KATE: 'Cause.

OSCAR: 'Cause what?

KATE: 'Cause that leads to…your malaria could be contagious.

OSCAR: *(OSCAR looks at the gift books)* Karl Marx. "The Rise of the Working Class"—Friedrich Nietzsche?

KATE: They're for Christmas.

OSCAR: Darwin, the scientist who ate roaches?

KATE: They're controversial, but—

OSCAR: Radical.

KATE: Don't you want to stay current?

OSCAR: In Cloutierville (*pronounced "Clutchyvill"*), Louisiana? *Pas de tout.*

KATE: You said this respite was temporary. It's not even a town,

OSCAR and KATE: It's a place.

OSCAR: Look. I want to leave, too.

KATE: Living on one street with population three, I'm starting to talk to the birds.

OSCAR: I've several plots going to get us to—

KATE: When? I don't know how long I can maintain a jolly personality.

OSCAR: My brother and his wife want us to—

KATE: God-awful relatives conspiring against me. I want to talk about something besides—

OSCAR and KATE: Their children and cooking.

OSCAR: Me too. I'd like to take up my painting again.

KATE: In New Orleans…you could. We went to all the art openings, the symphony—

OSCAR: I'm not going to feel bad because we can't afford luxuries. That's what I get—

KATE: The children can't go past grade school here—

OSCAR: For letting you visit your mother—

KATE: You're starting to contract, repeating the same phrases. Quoting your brother, Lamy, the dullest man in Louisiana.

OSCAR: Unfortunately, I don't have any relatives with intelligence.

KATE: You used to paint, recite poetry. Read one book for our salon of two. Darwin.

OSCAR: Cotton merchants don't want to read that "We come from apes" or "God is dead. We've been to his funeral."

KATE: I've got to have someone or something I can learn from.

OSCAR: I miss my watercolors, but sacrifices must be—

KATE: You said—We'd do something cultural, at least once a month.

OSCAR: And we will...soon. I like to read, but I also like to touch your face, neck, your breasts. (OSCAR reaches for her.)

KATE: Don't tickle.

OSCAR: I'm checking your fatness factor. You always put on weight at your waist first.

KATE: My brain is shrinking, while my body expands. (OSCAR starts to undo her robe.)

OSCAR: If you don't like what I do, you can stop me quick enough. (KATE reaches for a cigar.) I did what you wanted. Took that god-awful cure, measured doses of quinine and hot mineral baths, treatments worse than malaria. I'm home three days, and you sneak out with your manuscript, that cigar in your mouth—up early! up late! Always weary.

KATE: I've had to take on your role. We lost three calves this morning. Everything needs repair.

OSCAR: What was done while I was gone? Nothing?

(OFFSTAGE CHILD'S VOICE: "There's someone outside.")

OSCAR: Send them off. Our store was popular today—

KATE: 'Cause you're lenient—

OSCAR: Tomorrow no more buying on credit. *(HE is suddenly nauseous)* Why is my body taking revenge on me? For defying the stock market crash—For believing in the infallibility of cotton.

(From offstage, we hear MARIA'S voice)

MARIA: Oscar, Kate.

OSCAR: That horrid woman with her wild stories.

KATE: She likes you.

OSCAR: Why not? I like myself. Everyone knows someone who's off. I wonder how off she is when I'm not there. Say I'm asleep.

KATE: Lie?

OSCAR: That bitch needs to be whelped. If her father-in-law wasn't my doctor—

KATE: She knows a lot about—

OSCAR: Then what's she doing living in a shack, telling fortunes. They won't let her in Church.

KATE: Still her medicines make you feel better. And no one can top her with that sewing machine.

OSCAR: Remember your social status.

KATE: Phooey! She taught me to ride bareback, walk alone at midnight, smoke a cigar . . .

OSCAR: Those are assets? *(OSCAR exits.)*

(MARIA NORMAND DELOUCHE rushes in with a large squashed dress box and a bag of medicines.)

MARIA: Hi. Your dress got squashed. For a seamstress that's a debauchery. Doc says limit quinine to once a day.

KATE: I did that, but he chases me.

MARIA: Good. Oscar's ordered you a walking costume. A high-feathered headdress.

KATE: Do my Tarot cards—

MARIA: Try this on. This isn't an ordinary gown, honey; it's an event.

KATE: I've no place for that!

MARIA: Wear the dress…and ask Oscar to hire me at your store.

KATE: Hasn't Sylvere found work?

MARIA: That skunk. I've aged five years for the one I've been married…

KATE: How can I function—all strung up? My breasts poke out every-where.

MARIA: Nice.

KATE: Naughty. Oscar wants relations. He's barely been up a day.

MARIA: You're blessed with the gift of Venus. You evoke the goddess.

KATE: You can really grow to hate a person who worships you.

MARIA: I need to ask a personal question. *(Pause.)* Does Oscar have a big— You know?

KATE: When we were first married he was so proud. I can't discuss this—

MARIA: I must tell you a story.

KATE: Keep it clean.

MARIA: A portrait artist came through town and I wanted him to paint me, but he was expensive. I made a deal for this grand portrait, to let him bed me. And when it was done we had to—Arthur was four foot eleven. His member was— Then, he had this device from a Paris smut shop that made it even bigger. I said, "Don't even think about that." *(Laughs)* Doc gave me a pill for Oscar for after the act. It reduces any fever caused by—

KATE: Whose idea was that?

MARIA: Accommodate Oscar. Once I'm in your store, I can —

KATE: Sex twice a day can irritate the malaria.

MARIA: Something my brother-in-law said— "Sometimes you have to feed the animal."

KATE: We've only done ten percent—of what Oscar....He's thrown out his smutty tabloids—

MARIA: Why didn't he sell them—? .

KATE: He says he'd have done better in cotton if he hadn't sedated himself with spirits and sex.

MARIA: Lord, I used to do that. What if he worked in his uncle's bank in Saint Louis?

KATE: He's scared to leave the plantation...Unfasten this dress.

MARIA: Wait. An ingredient's missing. *(MARIA lays down Tarot cards on a black cloth)* Nine of wands—means a battle. Marriage card is reversed. You don't feel bonded—

KATE: I want to surrender to Oscar.

MARIA: That won't happen because of— your growing awareness of your own needs.

KATE: My needs include Oscar's.

MARIA: No, the cards that represent you are mourning and disappointment.

KATE: I want someone to give me strength.

(*MARIA turns over the emperor card.*)

MARIA: The man of your dreams is you. You are the emperor. Cut me a card.

KATE: Ace of wands.

MARIA: Some people read it as a big phallus. It means a new enterprise. This one's on fire.

KATE: Should I bed Oscar?

MARIA: Act like a slot machine. It gets men back because it pays off. Irregularly. Once every ten times or so. Talk to Oscar about my job. Flatter him. And promise to put money in the slot machine.

(*KATE exits.*)

SCENE TWO

(*ALBERT SAMPITÉ enters, pauses, opens a ledger.*)

MARIA: Albert! How's it going?

ALBERT: I never know.

MARIA: I've been visiting Kate hoping to see you—

ALBERT: Visit less.

MARIA: Oh, there's dust on your sleeve. I'll get it. You smell so woodsy.

ALBERT: You're in my light.

MARIA: How's your wife?

ALBERT: She exists; she's at home.

MARIA: Rumor says you're leaving Loca?

ALBERT: I try to maintain grace in disgraceful situations.

MARIA: *(SHE takes out a tape measure.)* Fine shirt. Blue on blue, like the sea. Soft smooth cotton.

ALBERT: Don't measure me.

MARIA: My dream is to make you an armoire of clothes. Silk jackets, ties, scarves.

ALBERT: No closer.

MARIA: I see you in town and you say you'll give me thirty seconds.

ALBERT: Don't touch.

MARIA: How can I fit that white suit I promised you? You said, if I made that suit, you'd wear it.

ALBERT: Three years ago.

MARIA: *(SHE puts his ledger aside.)* I still wear your locket. The heart with your name Sanspite.

ALBERT: Sans pitie means without pity.

MARIA: A lover is a puppeteer. You control my whole body.

ALBERT: *(Pantomimes a scissors)* Snip. Snip.

MARIA: The only addiction I have left is excitement and you fuel it in a big way.

ALBERT: Quiet.

MARIA: Oh, Albert, I remember everything you've ever done. Your tiny goodbye kisses brushing my hairline, curling the bow of my lips. Your moustache bristling on my mouth. I waited for you Thanksgiving. Sat up, eyes sleeping wide. "I'll be by later." That's what you promised. I slept by the gallery—so I'd be sure to spot you when you rode by—But you never came. I went by your place. You were sitting on your porch, feet propped up. Later I spied that flask by your side, and I knew why you were so friendly.

ALBERT: I'm through with heavy drinking.

(MARIA exits. A few moments later, KATE enters in her red dress)

ALBERT: I looked for you at the landing. Good, you weren't in that.

KATE: I've got to get ready for—

ALBERT: You look ready.

KATE: Living with boys, I've lost my sense of fashion. I can talk about playing ball and blackjack.

ALBERT: Put rouge on in front of me; I'll be a rapt audience.

KATE: Can I get you something?

ALBERT: Just your company.

KATE: Part of my job is to charm people.

ALBERT: I've noticed. Actually I'm here to balance the books. *(Points to some boxes)* Your inventory is low. I'd a shipment coming. So, I added on— fabric, seeds...

KATE: Last week it was harnesses...The week before, boots, saddles.

ALBERT: It'll put a few zeros in the books. I know with women you have to feel right to accept money. Men, we're excessive.

KATE: Oscar's unaware of the inventory you've supplied.

ALBERT: Good. I like the lightning bolt flashes that go off in my brain when I spoil you. It makes me feel I've a purpose. Money is the last bastion of sovereignty in this world. *(Takes her hand)*

KATE: Please remove your hand. You have beautiful hands. *(There is a noise offstage)* Is that you, Oscar?

OSCAR: *(Offstage)* No.

KATE: *(SHE gets a roll of black fabric)* Your wife won't pick up the taffeta she ordered.

ALBERT: I don't see her. I live in the carriage house.

(ALBERT holds black fabric up opposite KATE's red dress.)

ALBERT: Gloomy fabric, next to red. Widow's weeds are all she wears.

KATE: I don't see why Loca wouldn't—

ALBERT: Appreciate me? I'm too blunt.

KATE: Coffee? Chocolates?

ALBERT: I put up with hopeless conversations, so I can visit the children.

KATE: Poor you.

ALBERT: I let her expound for five minutes and then I talk about something she can't relate to.

KATE: Why'd you marry her?

ALBERT: For a baby that later died. *(Pause)* I've a high need for freedom. *(Pause)* When the baby passed, I wouldn't let go of the dead thing. I got off my horse, crawled out on my land for hours and wept. A neighbor came along and thought I was dead....I still feel guilty I can't love her.

KATE: She's agreed to the divorce?

ALBERT: Sure. If I give her everything. "I want the house, its contents and all the money you've got." That what she said. "Take them," I replied. It's like she's got so much, there's nothing left. False gods....I'm just protecting the children. When I threaten to claim my half, she sets fire to the carriage house. Objects were never designed to replace the real anchors of life.

97

GHOSTS OF NEW ORLEANS

KATE: And what are they?

ALBERT: Friends like you. I'm happier about the divorce than I was about the marriage. What religion forbids divorce, if people are miserable and want to kill each other? We should torture our spouses for the Church? I've stayed married for two thousand years. Lived with a woman, blaming me for our dead children. She lost four out of six.

KATE: How did you get over it?

ALBERT: You never get over it. You get used to it. I spent too much time denying, clawing my way to sanity. Gave up warmth and companionship. Became a cowboy on the range; bucking and fighting...I rationalized cold-ness till it felt right to me. I work fifteen-hour days. Retreat here at night. I love my children, but I can't stay with her for them. Hour by hour a part of me dies.

KATE: You don't feel anything?

ALBERT: I do without. The servants say when I leave, Loca hums and sings.

KATE: But what do you want for your life?

ALBERT: To be selfish. When you're selfish you're true to yourself.

KATE: Is that all you want?

ALBERT: No, I want to be able to touch and hold someone. You've been in my dreams. The contents are blurry, but you're very real....You don't understand the rules, but I do. I don't like shabby women. I'm embarrassed to be with them. It's the whole woman that's seductive, the way she moves, handles herself. It's not just the body. It's what's underneath too, the soul.

(OSCAR enters)

OSCAR: Albert, you look wonderful. *(THEY shake hands) Magnifique.* You always dress so well when others dress so poorly. *(Sees boxes)* More supplies? Extraordinaire.

ALBERT: And a get well gift.

OSCAR: You're the old style of Louisiana with "Let me comfort you."

ALBERT: I may go to Colorado—to buy land.

KATE: And leave us stranded —

OSCAR: *(Opening his Champagne gift)* Veuve Cliquot—A French monk discovered this—so it's bound to lift the spirits.

ALBERT: Have you read the paper?

OSCAR: My doctor told me I can have three drinks a day. That's down from eight. *(ALBERT holds up a paper with the headlines: 1884 Cotton Prices Plunge. Railroads Destroy Markets.")*

OSCAR: Not before we eat. For supper I only want white oysters, white grapes, and champagne.

ALBERT: Paper says, "Spending on cotton is like—"

KATE AND OSCAR: "Feeding a corpse."

ALBERT: I'm trying to keep y'all afloat—voluntarily—Look at these bills: binding: $1,045—cotton bagging: $5,450—bales: $1,970. We need to make some daring changes..

OSCAR: Not to worry. I don't pay bills until the last day they're due. I've got envelopes marked Tuesday, Wednesday, Thursday, Friday—and a bill in each slot.

ALBERT: What kind of business is this?

KATE: It's the business most people have now.

OSCAR: *(To KATE)* But not Albert. He pays workers a pittance—fires them without pay and hires more for less money. Well, I can't let my workers starve. It could be me.

ALBERT: *(To OSCAR)* It's going to be you.

KATE: Perhaps we should hire Marie Normand.

OSCAR: Good God. A woman like that doesn't come up the highway; she comes up one of the canals.

(ALBERT and OSCAR laugh incessantly.)

ALBERT: *(To KATE)* What do you know about her—?

OSCAR: She's absolutely no self-doubt. Now, Albert. What do you know?

ALBERT: She seems like a sweet soul, but I wouldn't get too close; she bites.

OSCAR: Every man in town will tell you something different.

KATE: *(To OSCAR)* One thing I hate is when I try to help and you call my suggestions ridiculous!

OSCAR: I'm doing the best I can without taking big risks. *(Laughs again)*

KATE: Maybe you should be daring and less of a dope. I read the papers. The plantations that have survived have taken risks, followed radical procedures. Now Albert's leaving, we can't numb ourselves with champagne and pretend we're not drowning here.

OSCAR: *(To ALBERT)* Pardon. Kate has no idea of her place in the household. She's aggressive. *Comme un tigre.* Excuse us.

(ALBERT takes his ledger and goes outside.)

KATE: *(To OSCAR)* Was that a call or a summons?

OSCAR: *(OSCAR squeezes her cheeks hard).* Keep your mouth closed if you know what's good for you. *(KATE grabs a cigar)* Let's get this straight. This is my house, not yours. *(KATE blows at OSCAR)* I don't like you smoking! Keep it up, there will be consequences. No one understands why I put up with you. *(Shoves her)* Selfish bitch!

KATE: Certainly there'll come an age when women won't have to carry cigars to have an audience for their thoughts.

OSCAR: Look. I'm just a businessman who wants a good life for his chil-

dren and a happy wife. I'm not the enemy. *Je ne suis pas le diable.*
(HE exits.)

KATE: Maybe all wives should wear black.

SCENE THREE

(KATE's Parlor.)

KATE: "An indescribable oppression, which seemed to generate in some unfamiliar part of her consciousness, filled her whole being with a vague anguish. It was like a shadow, like a mist passing across her soul's summer day. It was strange and unfamiliar; it was a mood. She did not sit there inwardly upbraiding her husband, lamenting at Fate, which had directed her footsteps to the path which they had taken. She was just having a good cry all to herself." *(KATE swats a mosquito)* "The mosquitoes made merry over her, biting her firm, round arms and nipping at her bare insteps. "

(ALBERT returns.)

KATE: One day, I'll pull myself together and determine what character of woman I am.

ALBERT: Why bother when I can tell you who you are?

KATE: You should go.

ALBERT: Don't join the long list of wives done in by their husbands. Close this plantation store, diversify your crops, pay your debts.

KATE: The land's been in Oscar's family for years.

ALBERT: You feel by guarding these things you're holding on to your life. But you're not. When you die, the world goes through your house like a tornado.

KATE: I thought—once Oscar was home—

ALBERT: You have to be strong enough to live simply…I'm driving a vehicle most people would call an eyesore. What I could show you slowly and thoroughly—.

KATE: What would you want in return?

ALBERT: To be the one man you can count on. Don't you want your perspective to soften towards the world?

KATE: Perhaps—

ALBERT: *Entre nous*, every time I give money away, I give my blood away—

KATE: You've never been broke.

ALBERT: My whole life, if I wanted something I'd to earn it. Only a fine line separated me from death and that was money. Money to me is freedom. If you don't have money in America, you're dust.

KATE: All our overdue amounts are not in that ledger. Oscar forbids me to look at the others. (*KATE brings a box to ALBERT.*)

ALBERT: Good God. There are dozens of bills, going back...years.

KATE: What's that? What?

ALBERT: You've seven years of unpaid taxes. They're going to seize your land.

SOUND: *The dinner bell rings. KATE'S boys shout offstage, "Time to eat. Yea!!"*

ALBERT: I'll be back. We'll deal with this.

(*ALBERT leaves. Offstage, the boys scream after him. It starts to rain.*)

KATE: (*Reads*) "She liked the touch of Alcee's fingers on the page, and closed her eyes sensitively. She only looked at him and smiled. His eyes were very near. They continued silently to look into each other's eyes."

(*OSCAR "appears" in a mustard-green robe, enacting her thoughts.*)

OSCAR: Toys all over the house. Nurse is sleeping in a chair. I dare not inquire if you supervised cook. The roast is scorched, the vegetables poorly seasoned.

KATE: I don't mind a little scorched taste.

OSCAR: But when the children don't eat, trifles must be taken seriously. I spend money enough to procure one meal a day, with which a man could retain his importance.

(OSCAR "exits.")

KATE: "But the voices were not soothing that came to her…"

KATE: (as OSCAR) "The roast is in some way not to my fancy, and I do not like (Pause) the way—"

KATE: No, the manner: the manner in which the vegetables are served. No, his…self-respect. With which a man could retain his self-respect—

LIGHT: Lights Fade.

SCENE FOUR

(2:00 a.m. the same day. There is a knock at the door. KATE interrupts her writing and turns up the lamp.)

ALBERT: (Offstage) I sprained my ankle. Riding those muddy banks. (ALBERT limps in.) I exhaust myself so when I put my feet up, I'll pass out.

KATE: You can't do bills now. Oscar's in bed.

ALBERT: I tell my feet to leave but they freeze. See, I'm trying to go.

KATE: Right.

ALBERT: Why aren't you sleeping?

KATE: Sometimes I…get up too early and stay up too late…

ALBERT: To do what?

KATE: If something bothers me, I write. I stay with it till I'm numb, or the

GHOSTS OF NEW ORLEANS

quiet hushes me, or my body claims the night.

ALBERT: Why?

KATE: Writing is my way to grow. Sorry. I have this deep, dark, dying contessa thing.

ALBERT: You don't have to apologize. I know what it's like to be lonely. I wish I didn't. You don't have to be embarrassed.

KATE: I don't require many people to make me happy, just some. *(Pause)* I'll wrap your ankle.

ALBERT: I'm forced to work, but here you could become isolated totally.

KATE: I know. I fantasize a lot. I used to picture myself as an Indian goddess floating above a waterfall—And my lover would glide to me, and we'd make love in the grass by the creek. And the birds would sing. And I would write all these wonderful stories.

ALBERT: Inside your heart and mind, that's who you are.

KATE: I rarely speak like this—Usually Oscar and I discuss his childhood, his work, and his health problems.

ALBERT: What do you want to talk about?

KATE: What's ideal? The reasons for existence. Our behaviors.

ALBERT: Our behaviors? When I was twenty, I'd have admired you. I was a roamer. I rode 'round the country, a satchel on my back.

KATE: I'd have fallen for you, I bet.

ALBERT: I tripped because I was doing something I shouldn't: coming to your house.

KATE: Is that wrong?

ALBERT: I caused myself pain to dispel other thoughts which…aren't good either.

KATE: You're talking yourself out of your feelings?

ALBERT: Towards you? At least halfway. I need to occupy my mind with something besides our friendship. We're meeting every day but not getting together.

KATE: In the summer, these issues will get pushed aside.

ALBERT: *(Laughs)* Right. This wrap feels tight. Can you loosen it? That's better.

SOUND: Offstage noises are heard.

ALBERT: Tell me about your writing.

KATE: Women don't get published.

ALBERT: Pshaw! Find out what the men did and do that...

KATE: I want to tell the stories of people who are disenfranchised, and—to be a Southern writer is already to be discounted.

ALBERT: Some people create better from a position of exile.

KATE: Not me. I want to be read.

ALBERT: Then you will be. I spent my life asking questions of successful people.

KATE: What did you learn?

ALBERT: There are no guarantees other than do your best, and most of the time it works.

KATE: I threaten men.

ALBERT: Good. You walk the earth with a voice that needs to be let out. Read something—I want to hear the words when you say them.

KATE: *(Reads fast from "The Awakening".)* "He stood close to her, and the effrontery in his eyes repelled the old, vanishing—"

ALBERT: To me. Let me…get it all.

KATE: *(Reads slowly)* "He stood close to her, and the effrontery in his eyes repelled the old, vanishing self in her. Yet drew all her awakening sensuousness."

ALBERT: Go on!

KATE: "He saw enough in her face to impel him to take her hand—And hold it while he said his lingering good night."

ALBERT: That's first rate. Don't stop.

KATE: *(Reads; slides and microphone voices may augment the reading)* "The voices were not soothing that came to her: 'I don't like you.' She went on in a high, excited tone, attempting to draw away her hand. 'I'm sorry you don't like me,' Alcee said. 'I'm sorry I offended you. How have I offended you? What have I done? Can you forgive me?' And Alcee bent and pressed his lips upon her hand as if he wished never more to withdraw them."

(OSCAR, unobserved, appears in the doorway and observes them)

ALBERT: It's wonderful. Your words are romantic, human—And oh so radical. I hear you and—I live in a new realm—where you're very alive—

KATE: Please remove your—Your sweet rough fingers.

(ALBERT strokes KATE's cheek, leans over, kisses her, as OSCAR enters)

SCENE FIVE

(Same night, 2:30 a.m., December 6, 1884, continuous with previous scene.)

OSCAR: It's so discouraging, the wife I do everything for, values so little my dignity. *(ALBERT rises, adjusts his sleeves, bumping into a table as he moves away. KATE pins up her disheveled hair, moves to the sofa's edge. OSCAR turns up the amethyst lamp. Outside a drizzle falls.)*

OSCAR: I'd better close the curtains. Well, that explains the boxes filled with merchandise.

ALBERT: I tripped and hurt my ankle.

KATE: It was late. I was tired.

OSCAR: *(To KATE)* You vile, egotistical bitch.

ALBERT: Hold on.

OSCAR: *(To KATE)* My God, I could have you killed.

ALBERT: Easy.

OSCAR: *(To KATE)* You walk around in your robe.

KATE: Don't raise your voice.

OSCAR: If I want to, I'll scream. Damn it. You don't like the way I run things, leave— *(To ALBERT)* I should nail you to the wall. Where do you do it? Before the children? *(OSCAR takes a dueling pistol from a drawer)*

ALBERT: Give me the gun.

OSCAR: Yesterday, I saw you rest your hand on her arm— I excused it as friendship.

ALBERT: There are transgressions. This is not paradise.

OSCAR: *(Points gun at them both.)* I become emotionally tipsy, when things go radically wrong.

ALBERT: People fail.

OSCAR: Like seeing you here. That's radically wrong.

(ALBERT takes out a flask.)

OSCAR: I bought you that flask, had it engraved—I used to watch you work, insist you stay for dinner.

ALBERT: I was indifferent to the meal.

OSCAR: Till you saw my wife. Let's call the children. Let them see. *(OSCAR shoots at the ceiling, then aims at KATE. ALBERT grabs him, they wrestle. OSCAR retrieves the gun, backs off, pointing at his temple. HE pulls the trigger…nothing happens.)*

OSCAR: I'm discontinuing your services.

ALBERT: You can't fire a volunteer.

(OSCAR sits. ALBERT takes the gun, looks at KATE, exits.)

OSCAR: *(calling after ALBERT)* Careful on that ankle. *(OSCAR picks at a box of chocolates.)*

KATE: I was wrong.

OSCAR: Austrian chocolates from your mother. Incredibly priced—She can't give anything without flaunting the cost.

KATE: I fell prey to kindness.

OSCAR: No one's mistreating you.

KATE: I need to be cherished for some deeper self.

OSCAR: Well, behave better.

KATE: If you'd encourage me to open my heart.

OSCAR: That's not what you want.

KATE: We could narrow the gap between how we wish to live—

OSCAR: You want to humiliate me—

KATE: And how we're living. Don't you crave love that is more joyful?

OSCAR: You're incapable of that. *(OSCAR pulls up a box of family mementos.)* I look so gullible in this wedding portrait. And you with that virginal face.

KATE: That was Kate O'Flaherty's.

OSCAR: Albert's get-well card. It feels dirty. The children's picture—

KATE: With their…your mistress. How I've paced at night—To compensate for that blow of over-giving I experience with you. I made love with you after each episode to see if you could still perform. I'll bet that's how you got swamp fever—Frequenting mosquito-infested whore-houses. Swearing nothing's wrong with looking at nudes—if you don't do anything. Tell that to the betrayed wives who sleep alone.

OSCAR: You don't wish to be a good wife and mother. Fine.

KATE: I've been a good one for a dozen years. I may not be, for the next— I don't know who I am.

OSCAR: You're Kate Chopin. My wife.

KATE: Mama wanted me to be a scholar, now you desire a good wife and mother. When I state my beliefs, you say they're foolish. I have to find my soul. Be a mother, sister, spouse to myself.

OSCAR: (OSCAR picks up the manuscript) Spouse? There is nothing about me in this manuscript. It's consumed with Alcee. (Quotes) "The effrontery in Alcee's eyes drew all her awakening sensuousness." It's so humiliating. "Alcee or rather Albert took her hand and held it while he said his lingering good-night." (OSCAR tears pages)

KATE: Don't tear it!

OSCAR: Why write if it offends?

KATE: To save my mind…When—I see through ripped pages…bleeding mosaics of my life—And must face how little you value me.

OSCAR: Say every nasty thing you can. I loved you.

KATE: When I was young and flirtatious. But you dislike the mature me.

OSCAR: Believe what you want.

KATE: I haven't known what I wanted. I've been living in the confusion of others' needs. (SHE flattens out pages and inserts them in her manuscript) For twelve years, I put aside my writing whenever a child cried. And children cried all the time. I hoped finally to get a writing life started. Late but started. But, you've kept me pregnant—I didn't want this many children. Last time, I prayed God would spare the baby but kill the mother.

OSCAR: What a foul comment.

KATE: You've kept me moving. Magazine to Coliseum Street to Louisiana Avenue—

OSCAR: Each time to a more prestigious address—

KATE: With less money,

OSCAR: Such was my devotion.

KATE: Too much emphasis is placed on longevity as a sign of a good marriage. I have to feel you're heeding my needs.

OSCAR: You have six children—

KATE: I need to write. Darwin had ten children—and kept creating.

OSCAR: You're not Darwin.

KATE: Mama'll pay for extra help.

OSCAR: Females goading useless ambition—just because you excelled at the convent. *(Picks up a box)* Your mother sent this shrine of your medals—to remind me schools here are—inferior—

KATE: St. Louis has the best schools—

OSCAR: Next she'll tell the children I flunked college and spent the night in a brothel. *(HE tosses the box.)* Just because you're the only surviving child, doesn't mean you have to be everything, do everything, win everything. *(Pause)* You'll do what I say…*(OSCAR squeezes her face)* Quit this writing. Or I'll plow your brains out. *(HE throws her down.)*

KATE: Holy God!

OSCAR: And leave you for dead.

(OSCAR exits, lights fade.)

SCENE SIX

(Six days later, December 12, 1884, dusk. Thunder. Lightning. MARIA enters with a bag of medicines. Not seeing OSCAR in the room, SHE curses loudly in Spanish, yelling after some men who are chasing her, coughing as if SHE has inhaled smoke.)

OSCAR: Sometimes I'm not up to your blundering personality.

MARIA: How are you feeling?

OSCAR: All right.

MARIA: Only all right?

OSCAR: I don't want to brag. You come in like an animal. You don't close the door?

MARIA: There's a cyclone of catastrophe out there. You can't do enough to make up for it.

OSCAR: The whole town knows of the affair. Kate's locked in her room.

MARIA: Arsonists from the White League sit there, playing with smoke.

OSCAR: They have to be there to set the fire. That's what they'll do if Kate continues this—this—

MARIA: The townies won't let her get way with—

OSCAR: It's a childish love. A love without consummation.

MARIA: For now. You should take your children to your brother's—the ungrateful...whore!

OSCAR: I don't want those men to hurt her. I can hurt her but—

MARIA: Give her a taste of vinegar—instead of those long tears of compromise.

OSCAR: Shut up. I have multiple personalities and not one of them likes you.

(MARIA dances about seductively.)

MARIA: The most wonderful things are waiting on the other side.

OSCAR: I'm too old.

MARIA: *(Pats his tummy)* We all have these tummies. I look in the mirror and made my peace with it. Now I don't see it anymore.

OSCAR: You're what I need. You're one of the evil clique. You started stabbing your way up. Your husband just died. He was only 24. Of course you had to pretend you were sad. But inside you're saying "yes." *(Pause)* I'll never go back to your life. I'll throw everything away. Each of us has a ghost— worth escaping from. Last time you painted me in such a black corner, all I could do was cut my way out the back side.

MARIA: Nonsense. People are coming into your life daily to help you be decisive.

OSCAR: I'm not an indecisive person. I've made too many mistakes to be that.

MARIA: Kate needs a spiritual counselor. She's a nun *manqué'*. A nun without the habit. She's searching for—

OSCAR: Some ghost?

MARIA: When she comes to my house, I have to put all my religious objects out.

OSCAR: I don't trust people who are fanatics.

MARIA: You projected your own love on Kate and didn't see the signs—

OSCAR: I knew when my wife painted the bedroom blue, it was over.

MARIA: We are all afraid of being alone. For the right money, I could feign being beaten up and scare sense into Kate.

OSCAR: Do it. *(Hands her money. SHE puts bruises on her face while HE talks)* I wish you had known Kate before. There was no dying in her, just beautiful gentleness. She had not yet departed to some far away interior place. I used to spoil her with letters, occasional bunches of outrageous flowers. Our home was happy. There was the sense the house had seen things. It was a house that had eyes. She wasn't a mother. She was someone who had transformed to— *(Pause)* I've got to try not to care so much. I don't know how to function as a person who lives alone with meager belongings and bountiful fear. Over the years I have learned not to cry, but this time there will be good reason.

MARIA: Stop whining and destroy her writing. That'll fix her.

OSCAR: No. Not yet.

MARIA: *(Handing him the medicine as HE exits)* Herbs you sent for—. *(Calling to him)* Don't take too much quinine —(MARIA exposes "painted on" bruises on her neck as KATE enters)*

KATE: What's wrong with your neck? Answer me.

MARIA: Gash of violence.

KATE: The White League?

MARIA: They've surrounded the house. Keep near Oscar —away from Albert—They'll hurt you too. All over town, men are loading guns, blaspheming, frightening women.

KATE: Have you seen Albert?

MARIA: No. He's defying everybody, gambling, drinking, riding stripped to the waist. I enjoyed time with him before you came—

KATE: You —when—you were married?

MARIA: He ripped me open. But that didn't stop my desire to have him.— *(SHE lays Tarot cards on a black cloth)* Ask a question. Only one. Two confuses the cards.

KATE: Should I choose to be with Albert under these sorry conditions?

MARIA: Such persistence. *(Holds out the deck)* Think of Albert and cut with your left hand. Good. Choose a card. Another. Another. Few more. *(MARIA lays out cards)* The traveler card. Ladies' men run in the Sampites....the card of ruin. Albert rides at night to stop a plunging depression. He broods for days. See that blindfolded man by the sea? *(Points to a card)* Albert's sad because the screaming woman—There. She's lost her mind. See. He beats his wife.

KATE: He's divorcing.

MARIA: His second wife. Cut again. *(Lays out cards)* No union card. No marriage card. That's you. Solitaire—that means solace. But— you've got the money, the success, the jealousy card, and—oh, no. That devil in flames? It's a? Death card, and it's coming soon.

KATE: Oscar's dying?

MARIA: Portals are closing. With Albert.

(KATE crosses to her desk, and packs her writing supplies.)

KATE: I come from women who lived to their nineties, when most died in childbirth.

MARIA: Are you taking the children?

KATE: I've already buried my father and brothers— Great-great-grandma got the first legal separation, built an empire on the river. Great-grandma killed a Yank who assaulted me. Mama married a tyrant to save her siblings from starvation. She claimed her widowhood 'cause widows control their property and children, but wives do not.

MARIA: Don't go mad. Talking like a waterfall—With no one listening.

KATE: Wrap these toy soldiers.

MARIA: If you're going to your mother's—

KATE: Metal men break so easily.

MARIA: Make sure…it's without Albert.

KATE: I like riding bareback, climbing trees, recklessly high. What's the next step down from rural Louisiana? I don't know but I'm not taking it.

MARIA: Your children will miss their father.

KATE: I can't make Oscar the man he was—before I became myself—

MARIA: You said for better, for worse.

KATE: I'm giving the world the best I've got.

MARIA: For richer, for poorer, in sickness—

KATE: No one should stay in a bad marriage—

MARIA: It's good to be surrounded by love.

KATE: It's also good to be surrounded by yourself. It's not a matter of finding the right person; it's being the right person.

SOUND: *Horses' hooves, a neighing outside. ALBERT's voice, "Oscar."*

MARIA: I'm off.

LIGHTS: *Lights fade.*

SCENE SEVEN

(A bit later. ALBERT and OSCAR enter.)

ALBERT: Your keys and ledgers. I don't have to work sixteen hours a day anymore. I do, but I won't. Leaving. It's a triumph of will.

OSCAR: People disband.

ALBERT: For the amount of work you put in, there is usually some…

OSCAR: Speak up.

ALBERT: You took out the old French fort your papa gave you.

OSCAR: Just at Christmas. It wouldn't survive the year.

ALBERT: The infantry are missing.

OSCAR: Yes. You're right.

ALBERT: I suppose…well, have a fantastic life.

OSCAR: We've had an expansion of all these modifiers. You can't just have a nice day. You have to have a fantastic day. I'd like a nice day.

ALBERT: I should have left before. But I hoped to salvage something.

OSCAR: What, a twenty-year friendship? My wife—

ALBERT: Don't be sarcastic.

OSCAR: Sarcasm from the Greek to cut or tear out. *(Outside a drizzle falls)* Today, Kate and I will be married twelve-and-a-half years. My life is simple. I take the blows at work and recuperate in my room.

ALBERT: We used to fight over this red tin soldier. Remember? I wanted him on the watchtower. You wanted him at the gate.

OSCAR: What do you know about feelings?

ALBERT: Don't ask questions you wouldn't like the answer to.

OSCAR: I thought I was your most valuable friend, but only you were important to you.

ALBERT: We shared real truths between us.

OSCAR: And you ruined all that. *(Grabs his head as if in pain)*

ALBERT: What's wrong?

OSCAR: Nightmares. Arguments. When I ask Kate about our future, she says, "I've no plans to leave you."

ALBERT: Not because of me.

OSCAR: Liar. I've a penchant for summary. Get out.

ALBERT: I hoped you'd have cooled down—

OSCAR: If we don't talk long, I might. You took advantage of my illness, so you could have the excitement of my wife—Now, Kate's tormented because of…Alcee. (OSCAR gets manuscript and reads from it. KATE enters and over-hears.) "Amid the dusky and torturous outlines of flowers and foliage, there was her dear Alcee." (Pause) Alcee/ALBERT? Albert/Alcee?

KATE: I'm so grateful for the rain, which has freshened the room. (To ALBERT) Don't leave without a word of adieu.

ALBERT: Adieu.

OSCAR: (Reads to both) "Amid the dusky and torturous outlines of flowers and foliage, there was her dear Alcee."

(KATE takes manuscript from OSCAR and puts it on her desk.)

ALBERT: My coat is somewhere.

OSCAR: My wife's a cuddler. See, when I stroke her cheek, she leans into my hand, like for hours she's been waiting for my touch!

KATE: (She draws away.) Stop.

(Moving between them, ALBERT hands OSCAR an envelope.)

ALBERT: I wasn't sure I was going to give you this but—

OSCAR: What is it—? (HE opens the envelope and reads) Oh my God. It can't be. (To ALBERT) Your company paid my hospital—

KATE: Albert!

GHOSTS OF NEW ORLEANS

OSCAR: *(To KATE)* He financed my cure.

ALBERT: Kate didn't know.

OSCAR: You're ganging up on me. *(To KATE)* You'll have to pay Albert back.

ALBERT: *(To OSCAR)* Where did you think the money came from? The birds? The sky?

OSCAR: The carpetbaggers, the underground, I didn't want to know.

KATE: *(To ALBERT)* I'm moved, overwhelmed. Thanks.

ALBERT: I thought Oscar would be grateful, but he's not. *(To OSCAR)* Well, are you?

OSCAR: I want you bloody out my life.

ALBERT: I'm exacting payment in January. Eight hundred dollars a month. *(Looks at KATE)* I stepped out of bounds. Now I must step in.

OSCAR: *(Clutching his scalp, to KATE)* Get my quinine. You put Albert up to this…you parasite…*(KATE exits) (to ALBERT)*…leech.

(ALBERT moves towards OSCAR just as OSCAR starts to collapse. ALBERT helps him sit.)

OSCAR: I over-reacted? It's the malaria. I need more hot baths but - we can't afford…Afford. *(Laughs)* Funny. I thought Kate's mother financed my cure. Tight-assed widow! How much do I owe you?…In all.

ALBERT: Let's talk after Christmas.

OSCAR: The Note says eight thousand dollars, but I know…*(HE stops, looks around in fear and sees…)* My God. They're coming true…. The dead… everywhere. See them?

ALBERT: No.

OSCAR: I'm not dreaming…There he is! *(Points)*. The archbishop…

glowing like a golden triangle…floating towards me?

ALBERT: Where?

OSCAR: Shhh!. There!

ALBERT: Are there others?

OSCAR: *(Shakes head)* He's telling me… . He's slipping a gold sheath…on my little finger.

ALBERT: No…. It's just one of your nightmares.

OSCAR: Aaaah!!! They can't see well, but they can touch.

ALBERT: *(Reaches out to touch OSCAR)* Sit back; you're shaking.

OSCAR: *(Recoils from ALBERT)* First Kate. Now my wallet. *(Pause)* Albert, help me, please! I'm losing my mind. *(OSCAR thrusts the note into his mouth)*

ALBERT: *(Reaches for the note)* Don't eat that. *(OSCAR stops)*. I'm cutting what you owe me in half. Repayment for …

OSCAR: I'm losing my senses…*(To ALBERT, sobbing)* I won't accept it. *(To the archbishop)* I won't accept it!!

ALBERT: I'm not given to sham. I did, do find your wife attractive. Goodbye. You owe me nothing.

(ALBERT exits. OSCAR'S sobs turn to laughter as he does a macabre dance.)

OSCAR: *(Marches, dances, sings)* "When Oscar comes marching home again, hoorah, hoorah, When Oscar comes marching home again, hoorah, hoorah La-la-la-la-la, La-la-la-la-la, La-la-la-la-la, La-la-la-la-la, And we'll all be there when Oscar comes marching home." Kate! Come here, sweetheart.

(KATE enters with brandy and quinine.)

OSCAR: I should have gone on the stage. Enjoyed the fanfare, the curtain calls.

KATE: Should I call the doctor?

OSCAR: You kidding? I just earned eight thousand dollars.

KATE: Albert's gone?

OSCAR: He released the note. All his life men have circled Albert for money and I got it. *(Does a jig)* "When Oscar Comes Marching Home again, Hoorah, Hoorah, When Oscar Comes Marching Home Again, Hoorah, Hoorah. . ."

KATE: Why would he cancel—?

OSCAR: Maybe for you. Frenchmen are haunted by beautiful women. They eulogize them. Or maybe, he saw the ghost dance I've become. *(Laughs mockingly)* He has this immigrant innocence, which makes him believe in marriage and its possibilities.

KATE: Congratulations...

OSCAR: I regret any pain caused by my "perceived indifference."

KATE: Even harsh partnerships require consideration.

OSCAR: I love Kate because she is kind and—very strong. Because...

KATE: I'd like to hear why.

OSCAR: Because she likes chocolates, sitting by the lake—And displays the army fort I had as a boy. You know I love you. We were like cufflinks. First son would grab one and second son would grab the other.

(KATE and OSCAR are silhouetted behind the curtain as if in memory. We hear their young voices.)

YOUNG KATE: Guess want I'm wearing? You need to know what I'm wearing to speculate about what I'm thinking.

YOUNG OSCAR: No time. The greatest collection of intellects are at the table since—

YOUNG KATE: Thomas Jefferson ate here alone…I bought six purses.

YOUNG OSCAR: Six purses?

YOUNG KATE: One is for my mother. We're sharing it so technically it's for me. *(Ripple of laughter)*

YOUNG OSCAR: Buy a dozen more. I got money. Deep inside, it flames within me. Kisses?

YOUNG KATE: Careful, my dress is so tight that if I swallow a raisin I'll pop. *(Whispers)* I like it best when we're naked.

LIGHTS: Lights become realistic again. We are in the present.

OSCAR: I love you.

KATE: Men say that when they've stopped. You loved me once. You haven't loved anyone for a long time. You're out of practice.

(OSCAR kisses KATE and sees her fingers are bare.)

OSCAR: Shush. Where are your rings?

(KATE pulls out her rings tightly wrapped in a handkerchief. OSCAR takes them, puts them in his shirt pocket and adds his to the others)

OSCAR: Let's pawn them — at least. I'm going to make it easier. Lamy will drive you — to New Orleans— *(They say New Orleans together.)*

KATE: To New Orleans.

OSCAR: Every month—

KATE: Are you serious?

OSCAR: Provided you… do something—

KATE: Anything.

OSCAR: Writing is unhealthy for our children. Stop.

KATE: I can't believe you!

OSCAR: Play piano or beautify the house.

(KATE puts a cigar in her mouth. OSCAR grabs the manuscript)

OSCAR: *(Cont.) (OSCAR opens the manuscript. Reads.)* "She looked straight before her with a self-absorbed expression upon her face." *(Sniffs)* "She felt no interest in anything about her. The street, the children, her husband." Nice. "The flowers growing there under her eyes were all part and parcel of an alien world—which had suddenly become antagonistic." Thank God women don't get published.

KATE: I'll change my name. Would Amandine Aurore Lucille Barone have been published if she hadn't become George Sand? Moved to Paris and befriended—Balzac, Liszt, and—

OSCAR: Frederic Chopin. I know.

KATE: Would George Eliot have been heard as Mary Ann Evans?

OSCAR: You don't have her talent.

KATE: I've writing more lately, trying to make sense of the palpitations I feel. In my dreams, I'm running barefoot down familiar streets, trying to get home.

OSCAR: Put your shoes on.

KATE: I'm falling down a well. So many women have walked the earth, this very spot, and their stories have never been told. Why? Because we've been trained to contain ourselves. We're lovely but silenced creatures, tiny hummingbirds who settle for pink sugar water. I've been born in the wrong body or century. *(SHE undoes her clothes)* We should rip off these petticoats and heels that encourage us to be dependent.

OSCAR: Have you lost your mind?

KATE: When I talk politely, no one listens. I don't know how long I can stay, partnered with my pencil, talking to a bird. I didn't realize how profoundly smart women are hated. When I was a girl and later when pregnant—

OSCAR: Stop....

KATE: I was encouraged to write, read, reflect.

OSCAR: Stop... .If you know what's—

KATE: First to win honors for Mama— Then to rest for the baby. When I study for myself, I'm punished.

OSCAR: Because... you torture others. (*Quotes*) "She felt no interest in the street, the children, her husband." How can you write that?

KATE: You exhaust me so you can enjoy your paper and brandy. One more baby, one more caller.

OSCAR: I can't think of one good thing you've done.

KATE: You're a terrible father.

OSCAR: That's a boldfaced lie.

KATE: You squandered our money—Mama's money's been saving us.

OSCAR: I'm supposed to enjoy your—this Alceé? (*Seizes her manuscript*) I'll strike lines out.

KATE: I'm not going to discard my talents—

OSCAR: Talents? Lamy wants to have you committed!!

KATE: Lock my starving creative self in the basement, to languish without water or bread. I'll feed her like I did my children, watch her grow strong and proud.

OSCAR: I'm burning this!

KATE: Don't.

(*HE throws the manuscript in the fireplace. SHE dives for it.*)

OSCAR: Get back—

KATE: I'll die first.

(*HE shoves her aside, lights a match and burns the manuscript. KATE seizes a poker and swings at OSCAR.*)

KATE: Oh, Holy Mother.

(*A boy screams, "Mama, Mama." Another door slams and more boys cry offstage. KATE and OSCAR struggle. OSCAR staggers, seizing his chest in severe pain, and falls.*)

KATE: Oh, my God. What's wrong? Oscar? (*SHE listens for a heartbeat, shakes him*) Wake up. Talk to me. Mother of God! Oh, no. How quickly we leave the earth!

LIGHT: As the boys pound at the door, "Papa. Papa. What's wrong?" the lights fade.

SCENE EIGHT

(*A week later, December 19, 1884, late afternoon. It is raining. The room is draped in black: funeral wreaths, shrouded mirrors, pictures, and furniture. KATE sits alone.*)

INNER VOICES: "She was seeking herself and finding herself. She let her hand lie listlessly, as though her thoughts were elsewhere—somewhere in advance of her body, and she was striving to overtake them." (*SHE falls asleep*)

ALBERT: (*OFFSTAGE rings a bell*) Kate! Kate!

KATE: You can't come in. (*Hesitates*) Oscar's barely cold.

ALBERT: (*Enters*) I follow my feet, and they directed me here. You can't lock yourself up.

KATE: I can't find seventy-five dollars to pay for that coffin, so I'm in hiding—

ALERT: Done.

KATE: You shouldn't have—

ALBERT: You look rough.

KATE: I'm not in my right mind. I wake after three hours—

ALBERT: It'll take a few months—

KATE: The smallest thought throws me.

ALBERT: For the shock to settle in.

KATE: You saw the obituary. A description is given of Oscar so you can experience him slightly alive.

ALBERT: I'll remove these wreaths—black ribbon is an oxymoron. *(HE takes down a funeral wreath)*

KATE: Let them linger.

ALBERT: These flowers are wilting.

KATE: They're changing colors. If it's too warm, four o'clocks reflect sunlight; too cold, they absorb it. I'm moving into my aloneness.

ALBERT: They've taken the children?

KATE: Temporarily, maybe forever. Lamy claims I drove Oscar to suicide. The man's—

ALBERT: An ass.

KATE: My children hate me.

ALBERT: I'm sorry I can't comfort you properly.

KATE: Please go.

ALBERT: You need someone to…hold you.

KATE: Get out!

ALBERT: I'm not leaving when you're in pain.

KATE: Before you, everything was fine.

ALBERT: You didn't kill Oscar. Here's a copy of his will, and the extensive autopsy his relatives demanded. Oscar had forty grains of quinine in his bloodstream, four times the maximum dosage prescribed. He left his power of attorney to his brother, his body to science, and his debts to you.

KATE: *(Reads the will)* All his assets are mortgaged!! Twelve-thousand-dollar cash debt. Seven years taxes. Oh God.

ALBERT: Sit back. Breathe. Have you eaten anything?

KATE: No.

(ALBERT uncovers a basket.)

ALBERT: I decided to play the Southern gentleman. Here's some fresh bread—

KATE: Not hungry. *(She eats bread quickly while he gets soup.)*

ALBERT: Chicken soup heals all.

KATE: Being taken care of is a novel experience. *(ALBERT hands her bread with jam.)*

ALBERT: Your mother's coming?

KATE: No. Her health is weak. *(Pause)*

SOUND: *A dove coos.*

ALBERT: A mourning dove—You hear? I'm afraid to admit this—because I don't feel there is much future—I trust you completely—actually I have from the first. *(ALBERT reads slowly from The Awakening:)* "She sat once more upon the sofa beside Alcee. He had not stirred."

KATE: *(Reads)* "She put her arms about his neck. 'Good-bye, my sweet Alcee. Tell me good-bye.' He kissed her with a degree of passion which had not before entered into his caress and strained her to him."

ALBERT: Alcee is me, yes?

KATE: Yes. *(ALBERT kisses her slowly, then passionately.)*

LIGHTS: *Lights Down.*

SCENE NINE

(Five months later, May 19, 1884, noon. MARIA enters dressed like a fortune teller, carrying a picnic basket.)

MARIA: I'm not here.

ALBERT: Speak up.

MARIA: I have no voice. You were my voice. Oh, Albert, a rush of memory raised from my feet to my heart soon as you appeared. Remember that day we ended up throwing off our clothes and jumping in the surf. When you left, I cried for two years without stopping. You weren't my boyfriend; you were part of my soul—

ALBERT: Vampire. Don't mess with me.

MARIA: Fine. I'll depower myself. Take my teeth out. I have an unbelievable gift of being mute. I brought you daffodils. They're so yellow; when you hold them, you see spring. I understand your limitations. *(Squeezes his cheek)* I don't expect you to be thoughtful.

ALBERT: Let's get this straight. This is my body, not yours.

MARIA: I'm obnoxious, I know. Afterwards you'll love it. I went shopping. *(SHE hands him two bottles of wine.)*

ALBERT: I knew there was going to be a surprise.

MARIA: One for you, one for me. Adulterers have to drink more. We're always uncertain. We have to have a drink in our hand. I'm going to feed you a good cake at least once a year and tell your fortune. *(Takes his hand.)* I can read dreams. It's my genie ring. Rub it....Don't you dream?

ALBERT: I haven't had a nightmare since I moved out. Kate helped me beat back loneliness.

MARIA: You don't strike me as a person who'd let himself get too depressed.

ALBERT: I have my erratic moments.

MARIA: You're dragging Kate down. Louisiana law forbids marriage between adulterers.

ALBERT: She doesn't care about marriage.

MARIA: You should. There are two ways to do everything. Adultery is the wrong way. To marry Kate, you'll have to leave Cloutierville...forever.

ALBERT: I'll cut people out of my life before I cut Louisiana. I own half the state...How do you like being a widow?

MARIA: I'm alive, well, and meaner. I know how to manage money. We both need a change.

ALBERT: If I put my foot out the door, the wind may blow me away.

MARIA: I doubt it. You are a traveler. You know all the tricks to get out of town. Want to visit Colorado? *(Pause)* That's as close to a yes as I am going to get.

ALBERT: Are you free? *(Pause)* If not, how much do you cost?

LIGHTS: *Pause...Lights out.*

SCENE TEN

(Several weeks later, June 10, 1884, suppertime. KATE is glamorously dressed in lavender, writing. Wrapped gifts, candles in pairs; four o'clock flowers decorate the room. SHE daydreams.)

DREAM

OSCAR: *(Painting in a sand box. Sand falls in from the sky.)* It's wonderful up here, Kate. They keep pouring sand on top because there's a leak in the bottom. Even if the box is broken, it doesn't negate the spout.

KATE: Where are you?

OSCAR: Most things are unanswered so I'm back here with the bohemians. They rival each other in goodness. It's all blue here, like one endless sky. Been painting all day. I don't squeeze in. I take two spots. We are all so artistically motivated. I'll be the last person in the sand box, just like the captain doesn't' desert the ship. Today's my day. It's been a kind of secret day that only I can understand. The goodbyes from earth are coming at me hard and fast. You're the last. I'm setting you free, Kate— marry whomever you want. I want you to be happy. Never walk away from your cloud. Albert has an unbelievable gift of being reversible. But if you want him, let him appear. If you go looking for him, you'll never find him.

KATE: How can I reach you? *(Bells toll in the distance)*

OSCAR: Feed your soul. Nurture yourself.

SOUND: Chimes fade into dinner bells. OSCAR exits. KATE awakens.

BOYS OFFSTAGE: Take us riding, Uncle Albert. Please.

KATE: *(Calls offstage)* Get your baths, boys. Uncle Albert is tired.

ALBERT: *(Entering)* Now I'm a relative? *(Looks at the table)* What's all this?

KATE: Our six-month anniversary.

ALBERT: It's next week.

KATE: No, today.

ALBERT: You shouldn't have gone to so much… trouble. Listen, I've got good news. You've been officially named "tutrix" of your children.

KATE: Wonderful. Custody at last.

ALBERT: You can take them wherever you want. How about a celebratory drink?

KATE: Well, I suppose I should have something.

ALBERT: *(Notices some papers on the bar)* What's this?

KATE: I'm holding an auction, selling everything I can spare.

ALBERT: But you're running the plantation so skillfully.

KATE: I might be admired if I wasn't seeing someone else's husband.

ALBERT: Kate.

KATE: Yes, Albert.

ALBERT: This is Louisiana. Adulterers can't legally marry here.

KATE: Don't use that word.

ALBERT: I suppose we could pretend…

KATE: No one would believe we never had relations—

ALBERT: What if I swore we hadn't—?

KATE: Why would you lie?

ALBERT: It's the law.

KATE: Let's take a cottage on the Baltic Sea.

ALBERT: I can't leave Louisiana.

KATE: Elope to Paris. I wouldn't take advantage—

ALBERT: You'd be the first woman who hasn't.

KATE: Let's tell the world we're a pair.

ALBERT: I can't— When I think of a genuine relationship, with a woman who accepts me, I shudder. I've thought this through, many a black night. I've been alone while married for a long time. Uncertainty may be what attracts you–

KATE: I like who I am when I'm with you.

ALBERT: That scares me. I need to be honest—

KATE: Can't this wait till after supper? Open your gifts.

ALBERT: Some things you like about me have another side. But you may grow stronger from these "pain bursts," as I call them.

KATE: Let's hold each other, not talk.

ALBERT: I can't step up to the bar. I can't marry you.

KATE: I never asked you to.

ALBERT: But you will, you should… for your sons, at least. I stand before this huge cliff and I'm…going to Colorado.

KATE: Colorado?

ALBERT: I said I might need to see some land.

KATE: You can't leave now.

ALBERT: You're forbidding me?

KATE: How will I get through—?

ALBERT: I'll return in—.

KATE: If I thought this trip was a dream come true, I'd say hallelujah—

ALBERT: Back up. Say hallelujah. It's that important.

KATE: I thought your dream was with me.

ALBERT: It was… is.

KATE: Go on... leave! Monster.

ALBERT: Hit me. Hurt me, if you want. The truth hurts, but lies hurt worse. You acted with dignity. You deserve better.

KATE: I probably thought of you four times for every once you thought of me. People said you were a loner, fickle, violent. You don't get that reputation without some transgression

ALBERT: I gave you my heart–at least to a point–Then you found a wall, one I set up.

KATE: You want to get back on the carousel. Go. Find some younger, simpler woman. No intellect there.

ALBERT: Maria says you do fine alone.

KATE: She's a liar. *(Pause)* I made love with a man I hated so much; I had to take a four-hour bath. I told myself something good was coming. You were that brave thing.

ALBERT: Part of me loves you deeply, but a bigger part loves freedom more. You and I can continue to grow. You're walking your path. I'm walking mine. At some point maybe we'll come together—

KATE: I'll tell myself bad things about you. Your drinking—

ALBERT: My irresponsibility.

KATE: Fill my mind with your cruelties; forget the touch of your skin. List in detail–

ALBERT: My flaws.

KATE: Then, maybe my eyes won't hurt; I won't have to gulp back sadness—

ALBERT: I certainly care for you, a great deal, but not to spend the rest of my life with...

KATE: What? Who? Whom will I count on?

ALBERT: Aren't you mostly happy with your own creative world?

KATE: You disgrace me with your ambivalence. Perhaps I am too strong, too brave, too definite for your world… where spinelessness triumphs.

ALBERT: Maybe I should reconsider—

KATE: You can't pass a cat without stroking it. Find some nitwit like Maria.

ALBERT: It's not her —

KATE: You'll get sucked into her love jail. She likes you strong take-care-of-me men.

ALBERT: I do admire your loyalty.

KATE: No, you don't. You want me to be-. Go with Maria— she drips magnetism. She's got a lot of tiger in her, a lot of pit bull. She is suited to you. Go quick, leave. Get out. Before I stop you. Have pity and— Never come back. No matter how I cry. Or beg. Don't… call again. Have mercy on me.. Leave my sight.

ALBERT: And what will you do?

KATE: Take a ride with God. (*KATE turns away and ALBERT walks out, when she turns back…*) Lord, he's gone. He's really gone. I'll never see his face. No, not today or tomorrow. (*SHE goes to the window*) Wind's picking up, violating the leaves. Best to leave here. Get out of the circle of his influence. In a small town, there's no place he hasn't been. (*Calls out*) Boys! Boys! Mama wants you. Get packed. We're moving. To… ah, to Saint Louis. Where Daddy and Mama were married and once lived.

BOYS OFFSTAGE (*Ringing dinner bell*) Hooray!! After dinner we're leaving—

KATE: For Grandma's house. You're going to go to good schools and—

BOYS OFFSTAGE: Yepee!!

KATE: Travel. Visit the opera and symphony like Daddy and Mama did—

BOYS OFFSTAGE: Hooray!! Yeppee!

KATE: Yeah. And Mama's going to write. She'll write and write, and when she's tired, she'll write some more. *(KATE dances in a circle. We hear words from The Awakening that have a happy expectancy.)*

ALBERT: "Don't go; don't go! Oh! Stay with me," he pleaded. "Why should you go? Stay with me, stay with me."

VOICE OF KATE: "I shall come back as soon as I can; I shall find you here," She buried her face in his neck and said good-bye again. Her seductive voice, together with his great love for her had enthralled his senses, had deprived him of every impulse but the longing to hold her and keep her."

END OF PLAY

Uncle Victor

A PLAY IN TWO ACTS

*First performed in October 2000
at the Chamber Theatre,
Budapest, Hungary*

Photo: Matt Anderson
Pictured: Maria Mason, Barret O'Brien

Inspired by Chekhov's UNCLE VANYA

Dedicated to the North American Program at Bonn University, where the play was written, and Lothar Honnighausen and Claus Daufenbach, who provided the fellowship, giving me time to write.

CAST OF CHARACTERS

RANDOLPH TROWELL (DOLPH), a retired professor

ELLEN BARNES TROWELL, his wife, age twenty seven

SOPHIE MALLORY TROWELL, his daughter by his first wife

LOUISE MALLORY (MAMERE), mother of the professor's first wife

VICTOR, her son

DAVID AUGUST GREENAN, a doctor

MARIE GAUDET, an old nurse

ACT I
SCENE I

(The gallery of Waverly, the Trowell family sugar cane plantation in South Louisiana, 1899. AUGUST GREENAN, a handsome, awkward young doctor, 29, sits sleeping in a chair. The old NURSE hums a spiritual "Rock of Ages," stands, removes the bottle from in front of the doctor, then exits. MAMERE, an imperious but forgetful matron, enters with a candle.)

SOUND: *Wind*

MAMERE: Where's Rosalie, Bertha, Ella?

DOCTOR: Careful with the candle.

MAMERE: I got to come from way in back of my house. *(Calls out)* James! Andrew! Clifford!

DOCTOR: They're gone, Mrs. Mallory

MAMERE: Nobody gets the door at my house. *(Paces)*

DOCTOR: For God's sake, sit.

MAMERE: Bertha! Verma! Rosalie!

DOCTOR: I'm Dr. Greenan. Augie Greenan.

MAMERE: I can't remember.

DOCTOR: You sent me to medical school—

MAMERE: Nobody sweeps the gallery?

DOCTOR: From spare change in your kitchen tin—

MAMERE: Dust all over the woodwork. Grass overgrown—

DOCTOR: Let me help you.

MAMERE: Statues crushed. There's the head of one over there.

GHOSTS OF NEW ORLEANS

DOCTOR: Sit, Mrs. Mallory.

MAMERE: The gates are shattered. A sundial disappeared overnight.

DOCTOR: Shouldn't you be asleep?

MAMERE: I can't rest when Waverly is falling apart. Shutters flap. I don't want to tell Mama because I'm not sure if she's alive or dead. *(Calls)* Mama.

DOCTOR: She's dead.

MAMERE: I didn't know. How long?

DOCTOR: Few years after— *(DOCTOR starts to drink)*

MAMERE: The war. I remember! But where's my daughter?

DOCTOR: Miss Rachelle? She passed.

MAMERE: Her too? You're lying.

DOCTOR: Why would I do that? I'm a doctor. I'm too tired.

MAMERE: Because you think I can't take it, but I'm strong as a warrior, you see. I'm a Mallory, and I'll stand tall by Waverly like the front gate. I was the first child after six boys. That's why as a girl they called me Loui, and when I didn't inherit the family carriage, I took a sledgehammer and broke all the windows. I was tough as the boys. My father was so hard, he was a pilot fish. He fed off my mother, leaving her at the mercy of her mental phantoms, which became real with my brothers' deaths during the war. All five. *(DOCTOR says "five" with her. HE knows the story.)* Strength is an ordinary component of every woman. The sooner she breaks off the pattern of dependency on men, the better. But it's imbedded in our blood. We've been doing this since we were sitting round the fire, lounging in our big beds, excusing men who made us suffer and sewing our feelings into quilts.

(NURSE enters)

NURSE: I've such a backache. God. Five-thirty in the morning. *(Nods. To MAMERE)* What you doing up?

MAMERE: Watching. There're prowlers like termites waiting to eat us. *(Laughs)* Good you don't have a wooden leg.

NURSE: I ain't got time for jokes. I'm tired. You know I can't sleep when I hear you poking about. Come on back to bed.

MAMERE: I'm not sleepy.

NURSE: Not after you got me up. *(Takes her arm)* Look at you. Clothes a mess. Hair in your face. That ain't no way to come outside. My back's so stiff.

MAMERE: Quiet. Or I'll call Mama.

(NURSE and MAMERE exit. Alone, the DOCTOR drinks. NURSE reenters, tries to get the drink from the DOCTOR.)

NURSE: Why you got to come here at dawn? Wake the old folks. It's a crying shame. You can't start doctoring with a drink in your hand. How old are you? Twenty something. When you start drinking at twenty, at thirty, you're gone.

DOCTOR: Life stinks.

NURSE: I know you want me to go on to bed; that's what you want. But you ain't going to get that. I knew your Mama and Papa before they died and I sure ain't going to let you sleep with no bottle. *(Picks up her quilt and sews)*

DOCTOR: I don't need anyone.

NURSE: I know something's eating you from the way you grumbling, look-ing at me from the side. I done seen that look before.

DOCTOR: I'm fine. *(Wipes his eyes)*

NURSE: Why you drinking? You don't like doctoring?

DOCTOR: In Louisiana people are idiots.

NURSE: Now you started doctoring, you don't like us. It's too late for that.

GHOSTS OF NEW ORLEANS

They be people up and down the road is starving. Children who happy for a crust of bread. Old people so weak they can't get out the chair. You think 'cause you sad, and you drink, the world going to get better; well, you ain't the first one been hurting and you sure ain't going to be the last. You go to Church? You got that pagan smirk on your face. You done figured it all out.

DOCTOR: Look, I need some time—

NURSE: I ain't going to let you make love to no bottle when there's women all over South Louisiana wanting to be married to some fine young doctor. You lonely? What wrong with you, you don't see that? Me, I "jumped the broom" at fifteen. There are some things ain't right. Ain't right for you to be sitting here drinking. What kind of doctor you going to be with the shakes?

DOCTOR: I don't drink when I'm working.

NURSE: Not yet.

DOCTOR: I don't have the hardness for medicine. For this damn yellow fever. *(Speaks without emotion. HE is tired and burned out)*

NURSE: Sit still, can't you—

DOCTOR: I like twitching. If I'm still, I suffocate. Then there're always these unexpected shocks. Yesterday it was this boy, a field hand. *(Pause)* I've got all my patients' names and addresses in this little book but I don't know which ones are dead or alive. I'm always thinking, I'm going to be there when a patient dies, but most times I am not. *(Laughs bitterly)* I've been in mourning for three hours. But that's behind me. I apologize. Thing is…I don't know why he died. I could dress up some stupid explanations. I can't understand—

NURSE: Perhaps you ain't supposed to. There are some things we can't do nothing about. Rest. *(Takes bottle and exits.)*

DOCTOR: I don't know where to go from here. I'll let you know when I've an idea.

(VICTOR MALLORY, 42, awakens from under a blanket on the wicker love seat.)

VICTOR: *(To the DOCTOR)* What're you doing here?

DOCTOR: Thrashing about with good intent. You thought I was your brother-in-law.

VICTOR: Sixty-five years of self-indulgence. He's a catastrophe about to happen.

DOCTOR: How are you managing? You tell me the truth; I'll tell you the truth.

VICTOR: I'm sick because he's back. I not only direct the peripheral characters; I think I am one. Wait till you see the wife he's got, and the man can barely walk. When she walks in, everyone pivots in her direction.

DOCTOR: Marrying outside one's age range is the ultimate transgression

VICTOR: Why did the professor get everything from life, even a beautiful wife, even the second time?

DOCTOR: You don't know he's happy.

VICTOR: Please. She never tells him what to do. She just suggests a thing from which the result would be fabulous.

DOCTOR: Women don't interest me.

VICTOR: Lucky you.

DOCTOR: You idolized him before.

VICTOR: People who're figureheads represent a particular type of duplicity.

DOCTOR: Someone said he was the most famous professor at Tulane.

VICTOR: He's a cold, calculating fiend who's capable of kindness but it's a rarity.

(SOPHIE, 27, the professor's daughter by his first wife, enters.)

SOPHIE: Good morning, Doctor. I see you've already arrived.

DOCTOR: Good morning.

VICTOR: Sophie used to help me. Now, she follows her father around. We're in competition for worst place. We've to scramble for the crumbs.

SOPHIE: I'm helping Papa with an article for "Harper's."

VICTOR: Stuck on this father who drives her back and forth and screams for me.

DOCTOR: Famous men get lots of attention. *(To SOPHIE)* I'd like to stay the night, if you don't mind.

SOPHIE: Wonderful. It's always a splendid treat when you do.

VICTOR: *(Stamps ground)* The ground has a wetness to it. You feel it? You can't bribe the help to deepen the drainage outlets.

(RANDOLPH TROWELL, 65, in ill health, enters.)

RANDOLPH: Don't let me stop your stimulating conversation about carefully drained lawns.

(ELLEN, 28, gorgeous, enters in a décolleté black silk gown. SHE looks at the doctor, and he looks back. SHE pulls her robe around her.)

ELLEN: I didn't know anyone was here.

DOCTOR: Apologies.

RANDOLPH: This is Dr. Greenan. My in-laws financed him through school. Here's Ellen. The replacement wife. *(ELLEN exits.)*

VICTOR: We'll take that in the jocular vein which it invites.

DOCTOR: How are you feeling?

RANDOLPH: Great till I saw you.

VICTOR: *(To DOCTOR)* Part of his charm is his shamelessness. We'll ignore that.

RANDOLPH: Let's give thanks for something. It's not a bad day. It's a bad decade.

DOCTOR: Have you been feeling poorly?

RANDOLPH: *(Sits)* All I wanted was to sit a few days in a row, so God took standing from me. Do you know what that's like, always gauging whether you can make it someplace?

VICTOR: I never go anywhere.

RANDOLPH: Your personality reflects it. Victor's not too bright, but he can count from one to nine.

VICTOR: *(To DOCTOR)* He makes me feel like I'm about an inch lower than my left ear.

SOPHIE: Papa. Would you like some milk?

RANDOLPH: Coffee in my room. And cake. *(As SOPHIE helps him out.)* Preferably Bavarian Cream. I've an appointment with death, but first I've an appointment with life.

(RANDOLPH and SOPHIE exit.)

VICTOR: He swoops in like a mynah bird with mange. Lands and the room goes dark. Still he's got this wife. She was lovely yesterday, but she's even lovelier today. And the man's one of the great bores of the nineteenth century! *(Looks in ELLEN's direction)* What do you think about her? Nice to be young.

DOCTOR: I can't remember.

VICTOR: She's a romantic. To be that, she has to adopt a disguise. Needs twenty-four hours to wash her hair. She drifts about while I'm going into a serious decline.

DOCTOR: She's obviously not faithful.

VICTOR: Course she is. She's Catholic. And he had her first. There's no sin anymore, no salvation anymore, and I don't think there's going to be any

143

GHOSTS OF NEW ORLEANS

sex anymore. I'm a little strapped by life right now. His arrival was a great interruption. He doesn't belong here. The person who did died. He eats nonstop. Sleeps half the day.

DOCTOR: He's sensible.

VICTOR: Conniving. All the help know he came from nothing. He's screwed up the schedule, and this estate, which barely paid for itself, is in debt. The help used to come in at eight, now he eats at five in the morning, eleven at night. Servants lining up to watch. There's no cohesive force here. I move about like a guest whose host has left. He laughs when I say we are going bankrupt. My teeth chatter at night. I can't control them. Our expenses have tripled, and sugar prices have dropped.

DOCTOR: When's he going back to New Orleans?

VICTOR: Never. He's retired. He'll stay here forever, grumbling till he rots in place and I become chauffeur of the dead. I don't know why I didn't see through him. I guess I was too busy being young. Sister and I did every-thing we could to protect Waverly, but he finagled and got it for himself. *(Pause)* Mamere used to say, "Don't work for the second wife." How true! The first wife penny-pinches, only for the second wife to appear in furs and diamonds and loll about.

DOCTOR: You don't like your step sister-in-law?

VICTOR: She's the laziest, most exquisite thing I've ever seen. You think she'll leave Randolph?

(ELLEN walks in quickly. She gets some paper.)

ELLEN: Excuse me.

VICTOR: *(To ELLEN)* Ah, Sleeping Beauty. They say when Sleeping Beauty wakes up she's fifty years old.

ELLEN: Pardon me. I've the hardest time finding things. I'm between a this and a that.

VICTOR: Join us.

ELLEN: *(Glancing at the DOCTOR)* It's Sunday morning, and much too early to speak.

(ELLEN exits.)

VICTOR: Did you get a look? That dress could get me in a lot of trouble.

DOCTOR: She seems extraordinary to me.

VICTOR: Then she is, isn't she?

DOCTOR: But overdone.

VICTOR: I wouldn't mind a bit of overdone woman. I'm forty-two but I look fifty. What do you prescribe?

DOCTOR: Sit. Take a deep breath. And count to three.

VICTOR: What? One, two, three.

DOCTOR: Now, sit and read the Bible.

VICTOR: The Bible?

DOCTOR: "Thou shalt not covet thy neighbor's wife." I'm going for a walk.

(ELLEN enters.)

ELLEN: Victor, Randolph has instructions for you.

VICTOR: But is he nice? Used to be old people were the kind ones because they took time to think; now kindness isn't popular.

(VICTOR exits.)

DOCTOR: Sophie wrote your husband's not well.

ELLEN: Today he's improved.

DOCTOR: *(Awkward pause. Eyeing her dress)* Fetching dress.

ELLEN: My Natasha gown? I usually wear dark colors, so when I wear fuchsia I feel naughty. Why are you staring?

DOCTOR: I'm used to examining people.

(SOPHIE enters with coffee.)

SOPHIE: I'll set the table.

ELLEN: *(To SOPHIE)* Call the maid.

SOPHIE: We let so many servants go.

ELLEN: So ends another grand tradition of grace!

DOCTOR: I'll freshen up.

(DOCTOR and SOPHIE exit as VICTOR reenters.)

VICTOR: There's letters and packages for you and Randolph blocking my office. A trunk of—

ELLEN: My new hat.

VICTOR: From the most expensive modiste in New Orleans.

ELLEN: A little color in a gray life.

VICTOR: Is all this necessary?

ELLEN: Fabrics don't last long in this climate.

VICTOR: Style is costly. That's why I look like I do.

ELLEN: My husband'll reimburse you.

VICTOR: With what? *(Hands ELLEN some invoices)* This was bought on credit. You can't live in the grand manner if we don't produce sufficient cane.

ELLEN: Who's living in the grand manner?

VICTOR: This house is the size of three city mansions. When I suggest economizing, your husband looks off at the oak trees.

(MAMERE and NURSE enter.)

MAMERE: I got a letter from the Women's Guild.

NURSE: Your mother is her old self. It's a miracle how her fog has lifted.

MAMERE: They're creating an archive of the professor's unpublished articles.

NURSE: *(To VICTOR, whispers)* Maybe she should rise each morning at five.

MAMERE: We could use your help, Victor, with the cataloguing, especially the Tulane lectures.

NURSE: Your mother spoke French today. She was so sharp.

MAMERE: Nurse asked me all the phrases I knew. My family spoke French in the 1700's. *"On parle francais depuis des centaines d'annees."* I'd like to talk to my son in French, but for him, The Misanthrope isn't even a title. I suppose it's too late. Victor's forty-two but he looks almost as old as I do. When Victor was little, all he wanted to be was smart, you remember? Go like the professor on a ride of wealth and fame. I felt as confused then as I do now about where he's going. The boy doesn't think. If Victor wanted to fly, he'd paste feathers on his arms and jump off a bridge. Even as a child he was maudlin. Liked big black hats and capes. You couldn't call him inside; if he wasn't completely wrecked, scratched, blood somewhere, torn clothes, he didn't feel like he'd played long enough. I don't know what charm is, but I know Victor doesn't have it.

NURSE: Let's go read in the garden.

MAMERE: The professor's always buying, while Victor's always selling. Why can't Victor imitate him? *(MAMERE exits with the NURSE. The following lines overlap.)*

VICTOR: No one appreciates me or Waverly—

ELLEN: Who needs such a big house—

VICTOR: I'm orphaned in a way—

ELLEN: We spend our time on the gallery—

VICTOR: I've had to put up my life as collateral. Perhaps I should have left.

ELLEN: You could pack a suitcase and go now.

VICTOR: If only I had the energy.

ELLEN: Well, lie in the shade, wiggle your toes, and watch the sparrows till you get your personality back.

VICTOR: I don't want to be a drone.

ELLEN: Not too close.

VICTOR: I don't think one relationship should prevent another from flourishing. *(Walks over and puts his arm around her.)* You don't love Randolph. You don't hold hands in the dark anymore. That's the first step. Women who stay with men they don't love slowly deteriorate. One day you'll look in the mirror and think, whose worn face is that? You'll be old and you won't have tasted one of the great pleasures of life, sweetheart.

ELLEN: Don't touch me.

VICTOR: Three milligrams of Randolph will kill you. Walking him in, walking him out.

ELLEN: I'm no heroine. When I'm tired, I nap. *(Closes her eyes and tries to sleep.)*

VICTOR: Does he even talk to you?

ELLEN: I can live with him as long as—

VICTOR: You treat him like a spoiled boy, don't hold him accountable. Perhaps you won't outlive him. *(Grabs her face)* Look how your eyes have shrunk, your lips tightened, in the short time you've been here. He'll kill you just like he did my sister.

ELLEN: She died of a miscarriage.

VICTOR: Technically, but really from a broken heart. The professor ran to the city to forge a career.

ELLEN: I'm not like your sister. Let me rest. If by some merciful reason I fall asleep, I'll kill the man who wakes me up.

(DOCTOR reenters, followed by SOPHIE.)

DOCTOR: *(To ELLEN)* Look at that beautiful sky. Violet blue. Must be heaven, being embraced by that blue.

VICTOR: *(Looks at a letter. To the DOCTOR)* I forgot. A note for you. One of the field hands brought it. *(Sits with his ledger.)* The trouble with account books is they don't beckon. There's nothing interesting about finding some-one who will loan you money again and again and still talk to you.

SOPHIE: Eat with us?

DOCTOR: *(Looks off)* I can't stay.

(SOPHIE exits. ELLEN has closed her eyes and drifted off.)

DOCTOR: *(Crosses and watches her)* You asleep? Where do you go when you're not here?

ELLEN: Nowhere.

DOCTOR: There are so many ways stillness treats our needs. Look, the sun's rising through the trees. In a half hour it's changed dramatically. Nothing is more uplifting than light through oak leaves. *(SHE opens her eyes.)* See them, allowing the sun to come in, turning up to receive it. They've a heliotropic life *(Takes out his pocket watch.)* I wish we measured time by the sun and not by the clock, like we used to.

ELLEN: Me too.

DOCTOR: We know the sun's not going to be there forever. We appreciate the enchantment of the moment.

ELLEN: How far away do you live?

DOCTOR: Twenty miles up river.

ELLEN: Do you ride without a stop?

DOCTOR: If I'm tired, looking for emptiness, for some way to clear the
slate in my life, I stop my horse and watch the Mississippi. The movement
of the water, its changing currents give the soul its contemplation. *(Gazes at
ELLEN)* There's something mysterious and female about water, and that
river has a primal connection to it. Her power comes from the sky and goes
through the earth to the psyche of the underworld. She's deep, primordial
and lovely with an extraordinary sheen. If you meditate, put your soul into
her all the way, you can see her, feel her, lose yourself in her violence.
There are so many ways her fullness heals me. *(Pause)* Would you like a
drink? With more drinks, you see more.

ELLEN: Too early.

DOCTOR: Never too early. It's always too late. One refusal doesn't mean a
final refusal.

ELLEN: How do you have time to watch the water?

VICTOR: *(Watches the DOCTOR and ELLEN)* I could use a drink.

DOCTOR: I study whatever I can't get out of my mind. Most times it's the
Mississippi. Until I was fifteen, I went to sleep with the Great River in my
head, dreaming of lost treasure. Summers I used to work on the salvage
boats that raised ships from the bottom. That river contains water our
Indian ancestors rode on. It's in our bones. *(Looks up, breathes deep)*
Sometimes when I look at that river, she scares me. The Mississippi is violent, and high water magnifies her violence. She's complicated, folded
together, irrational, and she rises every night to meet these torrential rains.
(Chuckles) On the river, rain is never received with great joy; it's received
with mourning. A river should be predictable. The last thing you want is a
wild force. The Greeks imagined Neptune with a pitchfork and snakes for
hair. You can't control him easily. Once I saw a whole tree sucked under by

the current. Last week I watched a house sink in a storm. The land caved away, a hundred yards at a time. The tide washed against the front steps and boom. It was gone.

ELLEN: Why don't people do something?

DOCTOR: The Feds haven't fixed the levees since the war. Locals argue…refusing to build outlets while the water rises higher. How can a hill contain all that? When a levee five stories high cracks, the water will explode like a tidal wave.

Sound: Carriage

SOPHIE: Your carriage is here.

DOCTOR: Thanks.

VICTOR: A doctor who's concerned with nature. I suppose you devote Sunday to the orphans.

DOCTOR: Somebody should.

SOPHIE: *(To DOCTOR)* When are you coming back?

DOCTOR: Don't know. House calls are risky. You're not in control of time. Look at those white azaleas. My carriage seems as though it's surrounded by clouds.

ELLEN: See you soon.

DOCTOR: I hope. When I come here, I find such peace.

VICTOR: You have to come here to feel?

(DOCTOR and SOPHIE exit.)

ELLEN: *(To VICTOR)* Why needle the doctor? You dislike free spirits?

VICTOR: Doctors are always right, which is one of the annoying things about them.

ELLEN: How long have you known the doctor?

VICTOR: Since childhood. I never noticed. *(Pause)* I don't want to be one of those men who learn about love as he's relinquishing it. I watch you, and I'm...renewed; I ask myself...could you get a divorce...

ELLEN: And the professor?

VICTOR: You are not intimate with him?

ELLEN: *(Laughs)* In the South we go to great trouble not to get to the point. I admire my husband. He—

VICTOR: Bought you.

ELLEN: I adore gifted people. Could you take me to Paris?

VICTOR: Paris, Rome, London.

ELLEN: Who'd look after Waverly and hold up the family?

VICTOR: We family members steal from each other all the time. It's part of the tradition. *(HE kisses her violently.)*

ELLEN: The last thing I want is a raving lunatic.

SOUND: *Wind.*

LIGHTS: *Lights out.*

(ELLEN: costume change. VICTOR sits. When we hear crickets, bring up the lights.)

ACT I
SCENE 2

(The estate. Night. The professor sleeps, snoring. ELLEN sits watching him with uncovered disgust. He wakes up, and she is disciplined again.)

RANDOLPH: What's that?

ELLEN: It's me.

RANDOLPH: I'd an awful dream. I was in this swamp. The water was rising and I was sinking, waterlogged from the feet to the head, the skin floating off my body. I was moving toward my own death. Oh God. I don't know whether I drowned or not but I woke up with this headache.

ELLEN: You want…some Beaujolais?

RANDOLPH: Victor hardly knows a good wine. He's ignorant of civilized tastes.

ELLEN: Perhaps the doctor could prescribe—

RANDOLPH: I'd brilliant colleagues. Students waited in the hallway to hear me.

ELLEN: I remember.

RANDOLPH: Do you? There are a lot of dead people in my memory. I don't use it anymore. Where did all that genius go? *(Pause)* And why do you look at me with those dead eyes?

ELLEN: I'm not blaming you. It's not your fault—

RANDOLPH: There's death in life, too. Death to things that are young. Come here. It's only at the end of the day I start to feel my age. I feel fine till nine at night.

ELLEN: I'm getting older by the minute.

RANDOLPH: No, you're not.

ELLEN: I looked in the mirror and saw a wrinkle radiating from the corner of my eye.

RANDOLPH: Come, sugar. Don't upset yourself.

ELLEN: I don't want to get old, be ugly.

RANDOLPH: You won't. Time is on the side of things young. Let's get in bed, go to places where only you and I can fit.

ELLEN: You go on.

RANDOLPH: I can't sleep alone. I've to feel you by me to breathe. If only I didn't have this nagging pain...It's like being in jail . . .longing for what went before and fearing what will come.

ELLEN: I'm...sorry but I'm indisposed.

RANDOLPH: Don't cry wolf with me.

ELLEN: Maybe by the end of the week, I'll be up to—

RANDOLPH: You think I don't know I make you sick? Go sleep in the guest room. Let everyone know we aren't having relations. Parade through the house with your pillow. You've that shiny new ring, and you're an angry woman.

ELLEN: I...I...care for you.

RANDOLPH: You used me...you wanted money and prestige—

ELLEN: Who doesn't like comfort?

RANDOLPH: I don't mind if you want more rings, a new gown. I miss the lazy evening soirees, and even the drizzle that set them off. Embrace me.

ELLEN: Not in here.

RANDOLPH: Where then?

ELLEN: I'm not against affection—

RANDOLPH: Ah-ha. You want me to catch you. Play cat and mouse.

ELLEN: I'll join you.

RANDOLPH: I got you! Ah-ha. Put your hand here.

ELLEN: Oh, God, don't start!

RANDOLPH: Touch me.

ELLEN: Don't.

RANDOLPH: More.

ELLEN: Oh, God. Oh, my.

(HE forces her to kiss him in an attempt to make love.)

RANDOLPH: I'm taking what's mine.

ELLEN: Oh, no! Don't!

(MAMERE stands at the door with a gun.)

MAMERE: Stop! Or I'll kill you.

RANDOLPH: No! It's me...Randolph . . .

ELLEN: Put down the gun.

MAMERE: Who are you?

RANDOLPH: One of her foggy days.

ELLEN: His wife.

MAMERE: Impossible.

RANDOLPH: *(Screams)* Victor, come get your mother.

(RANDOLPH exits.)

ELLEN: What's wrong?

MAMERE: Everything's dusty in Rachelle's room. I don't know where she is.

RANDOLPH: Victor!

MAMERE: The goal of motherhood is the crafting of children. Rachelle was my crown jewel.

ELLEN: Sit. Tell me about her.

MAMERE: She was jovial—gathering people together artfully with some attention to detail. I can see her imagination breathing in things, even though she's disappeared.

ELLEN: That's nice.

MAMERE: You remind me of her, strangely. Beauty was what she was interested in, fixing herself up and making herself look pretty. *(VICTOR enters.)* She loved life. There was always a stimulating conversation going on between her and me.

RANDOLPH: *(O.S.)* Victor, where are you?

MAMERE: Victor? What do you want him for? Rachelle was happy at the core of her being, while Victor wears a permanent scowl. He's my nemesis. You can't separate him from his angry ghosts.

ELLEN: That's too bad.

MAMERE: It is, because when you're around him, you've heard every complaint possible. Five o'clock sherry with Victor is the closest thing to hell. I try to have a conversation but there's nothing there. If you connect the dots in the lines of his life, you'd draw an empty well. The only difference between Victor now and as a child is he wears suits, not knickers. Men grow up when they want to or they don't grow up at all. He's forty-two and still toddling about.

(VICTOR enters with RANDOLPH, walks over to MAMERE. She lifts the gun.)

VICTOR: It's Victor. Give me the gun.

MAMERE: Who?

VICTOR: Your son…the toddler, although most times I feel like the family slave. *(Takes the gun)* The gun, Mama.

(NURSE arrives. Hurries to MAMERE.)

NURSE: She stole the gun out the cabinet. I can't leave her for a minute. She likes to scare people, but she's harmless.

VICTOR: I'll put her to bed.

MAMERE: No, I'm waiting for Rachelle.

VICTOR: You know she's passed.

NURSE: *(To VICTOR)* Don't you be taking my job. *(To MAMERE)* Come on now.

VICTOR: *(To NURSE)* She's got to accept Rachelle's dead.

NURSE: Let her live with her own truth.

MAMERE: What'd Victor say?

NURSE: Nothing. Most men make you feel bad about things. I don't listen to them.

RANDOLPH: Will you all get out!

NURSE: *(To RANDOLPH)* Why don't you go to sleep with your wife?

RANDOLPH: I intend to.

VICTOR: I don't have a family about me. I've some estranged people who're driving me out of my mind—

NURSE: How can I bed her for the night if you don't keep quiet? Old people are like children. They want attention and closeness.

VICTOR: I'll walk her.

NURSE: No, you just play take-away. She so bored she don't know what to do with herself. You say I love you, but I can't pay for anything. She don't go nowhere. Buy nothing. Invite anybody to the house. I love you, you say, but you don't take no time for her. She want to go places, do things. You so busy running Waverly, you don't see. And you a Louisiana white man, so you don't have to.

(VICTOR, NURSE, MAMERE exit. Enter SOPHIE with a candle and soup.)

SOPHIE: Papa, you're feeling better? The doctor arrived.

RANDOLPH: Suppose he's here to steal our liquor. Go…comb your hair. I should work on you. A successful teacher doesn't change the mind, but the personality of the student.

SOPHIE: *(To ELLEN)* You look exhausted.

ELLEN: I am.

(ELLEN slips out)

SOPHIE: This chicken soup should restore your health. It's marvelous to think Cook makes great soup. It contains a strained broth and chicken.

RANDOLPH: Where did Ellen go?

SOPHIE: You're perspiring.

RANDOLPH: I want turtle soup…finished with sherry. Tell Cook to take one shelled, skinned, and cleaned turtle. About two pounds of flesh.

SOPHIE: Don't spill that.

RANDOLPH: It's tepid.

SOPHIE: If it's too hot, it'll burn your throat.

RANDOLPH: Reheat it.

SOPHIE: Heavens. Eat a few sips.

RANDOLPH: Too cold.

SOPHIE: Eat please. I can't keep running back and forth.

RANDOLPH: Well, don't.

SOPHIE: *(Swallows hard)* Papa, I need you to…improve…so you can help Uncle. Sugar is a difficult, year-round operation.

RANDOLPH: As your mother has passed, I take the liberty of telling you, you move like a field hand.

SOPHIE: I'll…work on it, Papa. You've never told us about your debts. *(SOPHIE takes out some papers.)* Money's due on these purchases.

RANDOLPH: Is it? Ha!

SOPHIE: Is Uncle authorized…to pay these bills? We've budgeted every penny. This month's income must go to insurance and taxes—so officials don't seize the house. So many repairs have to be done.

RANDOLPH: It's not expensive to make repairs. But you have to work along with people. And that Victor's not used to!

SOPHIE: If only it were that simple. Chairs need reupholstering. Doorknobs replating. The entire house needs painting . . .

RANDOLPH: Do it.

SOPHIE: How? A codicil…to the will gives Waverly to you till I marry and you're spending money on the wrong things. Soon all we'll have is soul and the clothes on our backs.

RANDOLPH: Are you trying to make me feel guilty I just gave the Church a statue…in honor of your mother, and the deceased members of the family?

SOPHIE: But how can you spend money, when…half of the help have asked for raises? The house is falling apart. Two bad crops or a serious flood and we'll lose Waverly. Now we've paid off the heavy mortgages, we need you to cut back…Uncle's working under wretched conditions.

RANDOLPH: Is that why he naps midday?

SOPHIE: We split the responsibilities. I care for the—

RANDOLPH: Here's how I see it. Victor's well has run dry, and his future's behind him. He's not broke, you see. He's having a hard time meeting the standards he's developed. I don't owe him a nickel. *(Dumps the soup.)* Get my wife.

SOPHIE: Get her yourself.

RANDOLPH: Get her myself?

SOPHIE: You want to squeeze this place dry, but there's no money left. I won't let you lay Uncle in a box like you did Mama.

RANDOLPH: I just bought a statue.

SOPHIE: Out of guilt! That's right! She wanted to keep you so bad she worried herself to an early grave. On your last visit, she made me do her up, powder, rouge, and all. She knew without beauty she wouldn't see you.

RANDOLPH: Liar. I came home the minute I heard—

SOPHIE: She was dying. Where did they find you? In some woman's apartment, Uncle said.

RANDOLPH: I see. Victor's turned you against me.

SOPHIE: Not true.

RANDOLPH: What did he or Rachelle ever do?

SOPHIE: Plenty.

RANDOLPH: Rachelle preferred Waverly to me, and Waverly fed her fears.

SOPHIE: Mama was valiant.

RANDOLPH: In death maybe but not in life. She was nervous near a horse. Scared of steamboats. Petrified of trains. I'd time to write because I married Madame Panic. I begged her to visit. She'd agree then change her mind or catch a cold. She was selfish. God rest her soul.

SOPHIE: How can you say that! About Mama!

RANDOLPH: She didn't care about me.

SOPHIE: She was so sweet.

RANDOLPH: To you maybe. She taught you to resent your father and she made sure I was a man you barely knew.

(Enter VICTOR)

VICTOR: I thought I'd barge in New Orleans style. Storm's building out front. *(To SOPHIE)* I'll sit with him.

SOPHIE: You've got to…get up early.

(SOPHIE leaves.)

RANDOLPH: You gave the order—

VICTOR: Yes. The cutting, loading and hauling start tomorrow. Cutting should be easier this year. I've restricted the acres devoted to cane.

(The following speeches overlap.)

RANDOLPH: Who authorized that?

VICTOR: Do I need authorization?

RANDOLPH: Decisions shouldn't be made precipitously—

VICTOR: I'm not your student—

RANDOLPH: All men must learn to think smart—

VICTOR: I don't have to listen to this.

RANDOLPH: You've made stupid, stupid decisions.

VICTOR: Men say, "I don't have to take this" when they should leave.

(NURSE enters.)

(VICTOR exits.)

RANDOLPH: Why am I so tired?

NURSE: You're sixty-five.

RANDOLPH: Do you know what it feels like to be surrounded by idiots, to be happily married, and not to be able to rest?

NURSE: You got problems.

RANDOLPH: I've a wonderful young wife who's driving me out of my mind. Waking up between hot sheets, a candle glaring in the window.

SOUND: Fade up slowly WIND.

NURSE: I couldn't sleep after the war. I'd walk around Waverly and think I saw soldiers. Three Yankee soldiers approached me but I scared them off with a gun. *(To RANDOLPH)* Storm's picking up. Let me take you to bed. I'll sing you a song my Mama sang to me. "Lord guide my feet on wandering paths."

(RANDOLPH and NURSE exit. VICTOR and ELLEN enter. SHE does not see RANDOLPH.)

ELLEN: Randolph? *(To VICTOR)* Good, he's gone. I'm worn out with him. The main cause for women's death is childbirth, cuts, then tedious husbands.

VICTOR: I love the way you talk, move. I don't care what you say.

ELLEN: *(Focuses on her drink)* Don't distract me.

VICTOR: *(Hurt)* I was trying to compliment you. *(Looks out)* Rains could flood the fields. Cane could all be drowned out. Does the professor worry?

ELLEN: Why do you do it?

VICTOR: Revenge is a good motive. It's acceptable in Southern circles. *(Takes a drink)*

162

ELLEN: Why don't you leave for the city, make something of yourself?

VICTOR: Whenever I get in the carriage to go there, my hands shake. I've to turn around and come back.

ELLEN: Once the professor improves, we'll go to Paris, I'll drink champagne in a café by Saint Paul's.

VICTOR: Notre Dame.

ELLEN: Watch boats glide down the Rhine?

VICTOR: Seine.

ELLEN: Drink Chateaubriand that tastes like rose petals and have Cotes du Rhone you can cut with a fork.

SOUND: *"Let Me Call You Sweetheart."*

ELLEN: The night Watchman. I'd better go.

VICTOR: *(Calls out)* Play.

(Night watchman plays "Let Me Call You Sweetheart." VICTOR hands her a box.)

A few elegant pleasures left. One is a wrapped gift.

ELLEN: Oh, my! Jeweled hairpins?

VICTOR: Great Aunt Jane's. Here, we do have heirlooms. Hold one to the moon.

ELLEN: It does glitter. But I don't go anywhere. I can't accept these...I'd best be leaving. Now in Paris, I'd take your jewelry. I'd camouflage these shiny pins among my satins, ribbons, and pearls. But where would I wear them here?

(ELLEN exits. Alone, VICTOR drinks excessively.)

SOUND: *Waltz.*

VICTOR: Ten years ago I saw her at a ball in New Orleans—glowing like a star in a velvet sky. Two lazy-eyed Louisiana boys stood by her, both thinking they were her escort. She was just there. Everyone else eclipsed. An invasion of beauty. If only I'd pursued her. She'd be lying next to me. *(Sound out.)* Thigh to thigh. Instead I financed his lectures, tours, articles so he could arrive with the masterpiece in hand. Why? Why?

SOUND: Scene change music.

ACT 2
SCENE 1

SOUND: "Oh Suzanna."

(Several hours later, VICTOR is passed out on the love seat. DOCTOR enters.)

DOCTOR: Play some more. *("Oh Suzanna" is heard on a harmonica.)* Your mantle clock reads, "Hours do not count unless they are happy." Well, I found the moon tonight. I celebrated my birthday watching the moon. Expressing my thanks to all those brave doctors from my past. I'm the first doctor in my family. And the last. *(Looks about)* Where's the corpse?

VICTOR: Don't mock Randolph...so loudly.

DOCTOR: You can talk frankly, but I can't. He wears a flowered waistcoat and pointed boots, while you won't buy yourself a watch. And your sister-in-law's so unlike the rest of you. Gorgeous but scattered.

VICTOR: Sometimes she reads Virgil to the professor.

DOCTOR: Ah, let's have a brandy—Dance and sing loud. *(Sings with watchman playing)* "Oh Suzanna, oh don't you cry for me. For I come from Alabama with my banjo on my knee. It rained all night, the day I left. The weather it was dry . . ."

VICTOR: You're going to wake the professor.

DOCTOR: Let's wake the whole house and bring her out.

ROSARY HARTEL O'NEILL

VICTOR: What a grand infantile comment.

DOCTOR: The things she can do with a ribbon or lace. She floats in with lavender preceding her. Brings in another century. I slept soundly till she crossed my path. Then, I lost the night. I would pay her to leave my thoughts. Now I'll go find her.

(DOCTOR exits and SOPHIE comes in. VICTOR drinks.)

VICTOR: "Oh Suzanna oh don't you cry for me, for I . . ."

SOPHIE: Give men two drinks and they all talk alike: loud, loud, loud.

SOUND: Out

VICTOR: The doctor needed company.

SOPHIE: Let him pamper himself. If the doctor wants to drink all night, fine. But you can't. Tomorrow you'll feed stalks to the grinders. You need to be alert. If you must indulge, have one of Papa's Cuban cigars.

VICTOR: A man of discrimination doesn't steal. *(Stumbles.)* I'm fine. *(VICTOR exits on his knees.)*

DOCTOR: Victor? Victor?

SOPHIE: He's gone to bed. Tomorrow he supervises men with knives.

DOCTOR: Cutting cane? I should respect that. *(Goes to get his coat, bumps into a table)* I feel so alert as the day commences. And foggy as it ends. I'm sorry. I better leave.

SOPHIE: You're tired. Sit a spell.

DOCTOR: I've so many patients. I can't just give them a remedy. I have to treat their gloom. Yellow fever everywhere, and no one knows the cause.

SOPHIE: Your voice is so soothing. You could improve anyone you talked to.

DOCTOR: You've hands like your mother. Long thin fingers. Oblong-shaped nails.

SOPHIE: You remember her?

DOCTOR: Vividly. Little boys love beauties. *(Pause)* You've grown into a woman and I hardly noticed. I'm sorry. I better leave.

SOPHIE: Won't you have a snack first? I enjoy eating at night. Should we have cheese or fruit?

DOCTOR: *(Continues drinking)* Both.

SOPHIE: Papa's a complete snob about what he keeps. The grapes are the size of plums. We've four or five proper wines.

DOCTOR: I think I can do two things at once: cure and live, and mostly I end up doing the curing thing. And doing it poorly. Have you been out there? The fields are under-staffed. Children and old people work till they drop. You can't be an effective doctor working in miserable conditions.. Where's the unlimited power of science? I believe in progress, but we've to face it. People destroy each other, and they don't build a better life. They're all alone.

SOPHIE: And your family?

DOCTOR: Mine? All dead. I barely remember my sister and parents and don't want to. No. I live for my patients. They become family. "Can you cure me?" they ask. My job's to say yes, but how. Most times, I sleep with the question. For yellow fever, all we know is the reality we've been brought up in. But that reality isn't big enough to save them. Some die horribly. They say human means "of the earth," out of which comes humiliation...The fortunate fade into a quiet frenzy.

SOPHIE: How do you deal with it?

DOCTOR: Death? Not well. I go off alone and sit by the river, immobilized.

SOPHIE: And what do you do there?

DOCTOR: I play this game I've concocted where I imagine all unborn infants as little drops. That some of us have to pass on for others to enter the cycle. Still, each time I shut a patient's eyes, a part of me closes. I'm an old man for a young doctor; maybe I'd die soon.

SOPHIE: You're not yet thirty.

DOCTOR: I've a rundown body, old like a used book. *(Guzzles liquor)*

SOPHIE: You're a spirit-filled person and you've—

DOCTOR: If only I could go back to being a boy and relive what excited me.

SOPHIE: If I had a friend who admired you, could you…have…any feelings for her?

DOCTOR: I doubt it. For a long time, I haven't loved anyone—

SOPHIE: You never want to…settle down?

DOCTOR: I couldn't be a husband or father. Women want successful husbands, but they don't want to pay the price. The price of success is time. What's that slogan? "Work, work, work, and when you're tired, work some more." Spouses will hate you for that. They'll turn green when you leave the house. *(Rises)* And I'm always leaving, aren't I?

(DOCTOR exits. Moments later, ELLEN enters.)

ELLEN: Storm's lessening. What delicious air. Smells like magnolias and brandy. Where's the doctor?

SOPHIE: Gone.

ELLEN: Already? Our destinies have been parted by a few indirect steps. *(SOPHIE starts to exit.)* Sophie, no, wait. I want to apologize for how cold I've been. Well. You've been so sweet, and I'm a witch. It's strange having a stepdaughter—

SOPHIE: Who's older than you? I know.

(THEY both smile.)

ELLEN: I want us to be close. I miss having girls my age I can talk to.

SOPHIE: Oh, it's so good to hear you say that!

ELLEN: Let's drink to friendship.

SOPHIE: I've this secret I'm dying to tell someone.

ELLEN: About the doctor?

SOPHIE: You guessed. I can't believe what I just did. I made a proposal.

ELLEN: Wha'd you say?

SOPHIE: I asked him if he wanted to settle down…But he didn't realize the someone was me. *(Passes the mirror)* How terrible I'm not beautiful. In church I heard someone say, "She's such a sweet girl. But no beauty like her mother. She ought to buy dresses that make her look younger. She seems so matronly." Matronly!

ELLEN: You've nice hair—

SOPHIE: People always say that—When there's nothing else. Mamere says, "Men can talk about the women who raise the best children, keep the best house, bake the best pies, but it's the beautiful women they come home to." *(Hands her a miniature)* Can you fix my hair like this miniature?

ELLEN: I don't want to look at pictures of other people's dead relatives.

SOPHIE: It went to a great exhibition. It was called "A Young Girl."

ELLEN: Who is she?

SOPHIE: Mama. Just lace my hair with silk ribbons.

ELLEN: Like in the picture. I can do that.

SOPHIE: Each night, I pray I'll wake up looking more like Mama, that one day I'll have tons of children and idle moments to play Mozart and remember her. *(NURSE has entered.)* Oh, Nurse. Tell Ellen how beautiful Mama was.

NURSE: Rachelle? She was one pretty woman. Even in her casket she looked about twenty-five. Long brown hair and big blue eyes. Rachelle was my little girl. Couldn't have none of my own. She liked big showy hats, purple ribbons, shoes, hats, and you. "Hand me my baby," she'd say. But mostly I remember she was beautiful. Beautiful the day she was born and beautiful the day she died. *(Pause)* Now you...you look like them Trowells, your papa's people, 'cept you 'bout your mama's height and you...you got her hands. That's right. *(Wipes her eyes)*

SOPHIE: Don't cry. I'm sure Mama's in heaven. Read our fortunes.

(NURSE reads Tarot cards.)

NURSE: What shall I look for?

SOPHIE: Oh, romance. For Ellen and me.

NURSE: Oh, my...The lover's card by the devil?

SOPHIE: Is that bad?

NURSE: Ain't always bad. Devil can mean...warm nights and—

ELLEN: What's that?

NURSE: Death card. Now...It don't always mean death.

SOPHIE: Could be the money problems Uncle's having?

NURSE: That ain't the feeling I'm getting here. To me...*(Looks at ELLEN)* Somebody want what ain't right.

(NURSE exits.)

ELLEN: I hope you all don't think I married the professor for money.

SOPHIE: Nobody said that.

ELLEN: I'd no dowry, true, but we'd wonderful times...I grew up in Ocean Springs, a town so small that people rushed to their windows when a stranger arrived. The Professor was an icon in New Orleans. He taught me to curtsy and to decorate a man's arm. *(The girls waltz.)*

SOPHIE: Is it hard being married to an older man?

ELLEN: Sometimes. Now we don't discuss anything because we don't—

SOPHIE: Get along?

ELLEN: But we go for drives together, sometimes. "I don't need much affection," he says.

SOPHIE: Even in bed?

ELLEN: Sophie! You want to embarrass me? Last Saturday, he fell asleep when I was kissing him, shut his eyes and began to snore. I shook him, but he wouldn't wake up. Next morning I thought he'd redeem himself, but he said nothing. *(THEY laugh.)*

SOPHIE: I too am baffled by love.

ELLEN: For the doctor? He's the "prince" of rural Louisiana.

SOPHIE: He discovered medicine on the plantation infirmary.

ELLEN: Worshiping a man is easier than living with one.

SOPHIE: I should stop myself, but it feels so good to think about him. *(Giggles)*

ELLEN: Let's…celebrate your discovery. Drink to friendship and the doctor. *(Footsteps. SHE calls out to the Watchman.)* Is that you, night watchman? Quiet when you pass my husband's window. But here, play something lively and loud.

SOPHIE: I'd better ask Papa. Too much noise upsets him.

(Exits. Harmonica plays, "In the Good Old Summertime.")

SOUND: "After The Ball."

ELLEN: It's so long since I've danced. Spun about a room. But tonight, I shall cry and dance and dance and cry. Then I'll nap in the guest bedroom: pull down the mosquito bars, wrap myself in sky-blue sheets, and gaze at the canopy of cupids, whirling through the stars. Drift to a nocturnal place partly in time, partly in eternity.

ROSARY HARTEL O'NEILL

(ELLEN dances to a frenzy. SOPHIE returns.)

SOPHIE: Papa says we can't dance.

(MAMERE enters, followed by the NURSE.)

MAMERE: Dance? Did I hear the word dance?

NURSE: She's up.

ELLEN: Let's kick up our heels.

MAMERE: And drink a mint julep.

NURSE: We'd some parties here.

SOPHIE: Shush.

MAMERE: Watching, smelling and—

ELLEN: Sampling bubbling sugar?

SOPHIE: Not so loud.

MAMERE: I stopped the hallway clock—

NURSE: When the guests arrived—

MAMERE: And kept it off—

NURSE: Until they left.

ELLEN: Were there roses?

MAMERE: Everywhere—

SOPHIE: On the mantles?

NURSE: Tables, and stairs—

MAMERE: Thirty bouquets—

SOPHIE: Of long-stemmed—

ELLEN: Red roses?

NURSE: And cake.

MAMERE: We danced out here—

NURSE: Caught a breeze.

SOPHIE: Sang and ate—

ELLEN: Duck?

NURSE: Snipe—

MAMERE: And quail.

SOPHIE: And drank—

ELLEN: Champagne?

NURSE: And dreamed of—

MAMERE: Marriages that'd take us—

ELLEN: To the ends—

SOPHIE: Of the world!

LIGHTS: *The women dance wildly as the lights fade.*

ACT 2
SCENE 2

(A week later. There is a table with account books and papers. A smaller table with the doctor's charts. Daytime. NURSE and the doctor are onstage. SHE is making a quilt and singing. HE drinks.)

DOCTOR: Who's the quilt for?

NURSE: Special girl. Which colors do you like?

DOCTOR: Yellow…and blue.

NURSE: Blue's the girl's favorite shade, but she likes fiery colors too. I'll put sunshine and sky in here. Which flowers you remember smelling as a child?

DOCTOR: I'm not much on quilts—gardenias.

NURSE: I'll look for that. I've a closet of scraps from my Mama and my Grandma. For years they sewed to keep their sanity, arranging scraps by color: coral, turquoise, plum, and toffee. Feel that beauty. *(HE touches the fabric.)* It helps cope with loss to have a real live patchwork quilt.

DOCTOR: I wouldn't know.

NURSE: Quilting is a hopeful way of dealing with life. I try to make sense of things by living each moment I sew. I play with patches and let my mind roam. Smell this? *(Holds up a scrap, which HE takes.)* Each color has a scent: intense red, rich amber, water blue, sweet vanilla. Wha'd you smell?

DOCTOR: Not sure.

NURSE: A drop of oak moss! I don't know about you. You come to dinner, but go home by yourself. You end up being connected to everybody and nobody.

DOCTOR: I can't afford a wife.

NURSE: Some women don't need money. They need a promise.

(SOPHIE enters with a vase, followed by VICTOR with some wildflowers, and ELLEN with writing paper. The following speeches overlap.)

SOPHIE: Papa wants us to meet here—

VICTOR: The minute the cutting begins, he starts. Cut down that cane and watch him pontificate—

SOPHIE: He wants to report about the progress he's made.

VICTOR: And what I've failed to do, while I exhaust myself with work crews. Sorry. I'm from a Jesuit education, so I always thought the heart of any great movement was terror. Yesterday, I lost my temper. I threw a book at him and told him to stop bullying me. I was amazed. He backed off.

ELLEN: He was in a foul mood last night.

VICTOR: I can't sleep, remembering his snipes. He feels great afterwards and I feel whipped.

SOPHIE: I'm sure he's doing what's best.

VICTOR: —For himself. He sits in his chair, sets up his suspicions, justifies being mean. I have to hold back or I'll spend the whole day hollering.

SOPHIE: He improved after my meeting with him. He said, "Did you notice I was pleasant?"

ELLEN: He's upset because he may have heart disease.

VICTOR: He's a—hypochondriac. This morning he left me a note that the right side of the house needed painting. As if I don't know. I purposefully avoid walking by that side, so I don't have to see it.

SOPHIE: It'll take months before he accepts he can't live like he used to. I'll check on him. *(Exits.)*

(VICTOR begins arranging flowers. ELLEN stretches out and polishes her ring against her skirt—looks outside.)

VICTOR: *(Watches her)* What are you doing?

ROSARY HARTEL O'NEILL

ELLEN: I'm counting the holes in the clouds. I suppose you think I'm incapable of meditation.

VICTOR: Just lazy. Follow your desires.

ELLEN: I wanted to spend the day writing letters, but I lack the courage.

VICTOR: You could straighten your quarters. Embroider? A woman who can't sew is as slow as a man who can't ride.

ELLEN: I'm going to lie in the shade. Watch the leaves. See how long I can do nothing.

(SOPHIE enters.)

SOPHIE: Papa's still eating.

VICTOR: That's it. I wait for no one over twenty minutes.

(Exits. SOPHIE toys with a flower.)

SOPHIE: I wish you could've seen them when Mama was alive. So full and thick. *(Pause)* Beauty is so seductive to men.

ELLEN: It's easy to seduce men.

SOPHIE: But not the doctor. He undertakes jaunts, jumping into his carriage with his charts, but he doesn't notice me.

ELLEN: I'm sure he likes you.

SOPHIE: I'm not sure. I keep looking back, reliving my memories. Wondering if he has this same excited discontent. I'm afraid to be around him for fear he'll see how lightheaded I am with him. Everyone knows I'm in love with him. The servants, Nurse, Uncle. I can't bear the embarrassment. What should I do? I weigh his pauses for meaning.

ELLEN: I'll question him.

SOPHIE: Oh, would you? It's hard to say, "Won't you marry me?"

ELLEN: I'll get the doctor to the side. I'll tell him not to return if he doesn't love you.

SOPHIE: And if he does—

ELLEN: I'll say when it comes to rings, size doesn't matter.

SOPHIE: Oh, Lord, I'm so delighted—

(Exits)

ELLEN: *(Alone)* What good's this mausoleum to a girl whose blood's raging. Has she ever been courted? He doesn't love her. And I'm wild for him. Suspended in animation, actively captured. She doesn't see our chemistry because she's too compliant. Maybe…I should help her. *(The DOCTOR enters, carrying charts and maps.)* Shouldn't you be going?

DOCTOR: The only reason I go home's to see my dog. I've a giant Schnauzer whose parents are champions. He was sired in Russia. *(Takes out a chart)*

ELLEN: How do you have time for these charts of the river with so many patients?

DOCTOR: Some nights I'm bone idle, and the Mississippi fills up the evening for me. I update these charts. *(Unrolls a map)* Years ago when the Choctaws roamed, the river front was dense green, thousands of trees…You're not interested.

ELLEN: I am. What are those marks?

DOCTOR: Holes where trees were.

ELLEN: And the x's?

DOCTOR: Houses destroyed but not replaced. Homeless are everywhere. People lock their gates against men who don't have the energy to come up the drive for a crust of bread. I ease the moans of the dying.

ELLEN: How do you face the family?

DOCTOR: When I look into their cold eyes and whitened cheeks, and say, "I'm sorry," they know.

ELLEN: Just out of curiosity, is it over with you and Sophie?

DOCTOR: You don't need circuitous tactics—

ELLEN: So, the answer's "no"?

DOCTOR: You know why I'm here. I don't come for food. Victor's food would worm a dog. Let's go somewhere.

ELLEN: Where will we go?

DOCTOR: Walk on the levee, dine over a crack before it's sacked and closed. Contemplate the beautiful bruised colors of the Mississippi.

ELLEN: Like an aphrodisiac.

DOCTOR: Yes. Feel the wind, smell the fecundity in the air.
Erase ourselves in the screaming blackness. *(Pause)* Come here. It's more interesting to embrace when there's a sense of penalty.

ELLEN: Please leave.

DOCTOR: You feel nothing for me? I caught those glances. That scared sadness.

ELLEN: I'm getting my husband.

DOCTOR: While you're talking, he leaves the room—Interrupts when you get enthusiastic. *(Pause)* First time I saw you in that black silk gown, your hair flowing by your face, I thought you might be a siren.

ELLEN: No closer!

DOCTOR: *(HE takes her in his arms.)* I want to smell your hair.

ELLEN: Move—

DOCTOR: Like sweet olive trees.

ELLEN:…no.

DOCTOR: Or a trail of honeysuckle—

ELLEN: Don't . . .

DOCTOR: Falling, half-lost toward—

ELLEN: Stop.

DOCTOR: Lush camellias and beds of wood violets. *(SHE breaks away. A hard silence.)* I've gone into a terrible decline waiting for you. Replaying your words. Reliving scenes because they haunt me when I'm calming myself before going into surgery.

ELLEN: You…shouldn't—

DOCTOR: Soothed by your particular strange voice . . .

ELLEN: Do that.

DOCTOR: Thinking what it'd be like—

ELLEN: Oh, God…no.

DOCTOR: To have what I want.

(Grabs her and kisses her as VICTOR enters with a bouquet of roses. The following lines overlap.)

VICTOR: You should ring a bell when it's safe to enter.

ELLEN: We're just good friends—

VICTOR: —Good friends . . .

ELLEN: —It was nothing.

VICTOR: Two and two are four; not three or five.

ELLEN: I'll fix those roses.

ROSARY HARTEL O'NEILL

VICTOR: Don't touch them with your…white hands of deception. They belong in a…glorious church with frescoes…You're becoming a witch…and that's a…uh, death sentence—The number of witches burned over the centuries is nine million. Shriveled women with pendulous breasts—*(VICTOR faces the doctor.)* And you…you! You don't like women. You do everything but the carnal act. My best friend stabs me in the back.

DOCTOR: I thought you knew—

VICTOR: Sorry. I wasn't paying attention to the obvious.

(As the DOCTOR exits, SOPHIE enters and whispers to ELLEN.)

SOPHIE: Did you talk to the doctor? What did he say? Tell me quick. *(ELLEN sighs.)* Your eyes say it all.

(SOPHIE covers her mouth. The PROFESSOR enters with a bowl, sees VICTOR with the roses standing by ELLEN, and speaks sharply.)

RANDOLPH: I just tried the bread pudding. I've got to consume the whole thing. *(Sits and eats. The others watch and wait.)*

SOPHIE: Did you have a good nap?

RANDOLPH: So-so.

VICTOR: Only so-so?

RANDOLPH: *(Jovial)* So-so is good for me. You all may hate me, but I…I won't go on a glider and do nothing but idle.

VICTOR: No one wishes you to.

RANDOLPH: Sit in a rocker with parasites for friends, then take my place among the tombs bordered by ironwork. Sophie, get the books. I want to thank Victor for handling my property. The man's worked nineteen years and we agreed he'd make all the little decisions, and I'd make the big ones. And so far I've never had any decisions. All kidding aside, I've serious matters to discuss. As you know, I appreciate how generous you've all been. Victor does the best he can, but Waverly has been a burden. Poor fellow wasn't raised to do much. And when was the last time Mamere had a new gown? When I tell you all the good news, I don't want you to thank me all at once. I've gone to considerable lengths to assess the value of our assets and I've discovered we're millionaires. Millionaires on paper, that is. I, of course, was born a poor boy, so money doesn't mean that much to me. Money can't buy happiness. Yes, I had to work for an education, wear used clothes, save string. I'm a well-known professor but I've had to rely on Victor, Sophie and Mamere for advice on practical family matters. I'm old, sick. I never thought I'd see my sixtieth year.How many good days do I have left? Still, I can't think of myself. I've a young wife and an unmarried daughter to consider. *(Pause)* We can't go on living here. We're not country people. What's the point of having a beautiful wife if you can't be seen with her and take her out? We can't afford to live in New Orleans on the income we get from Waverly. Were we to sell the woods, swamps, or mineral rights, those are one-time transactions and couldn't be repeated. We need a way to guarantee ourselves a fixed income. Now, I've devised a plan that'll please everyone, including Victor, and I'd like to outline it to you.

VICTOR: How long will this take?

RANDOLPH: A few minutes. I need everyone's opinion. The average return on the sugar plantation is about three percent a year. I propose we sell the place, invest the proceeds in managed funds at six percent and set aside a few thousand for a small house in New Orleans.

VICTOR: Wait. I think I'm going deaf. Repeat what you just said.

RANDOLPH: That we invest the proceeds in managed funds and buy a small house—

VICTOR: No. No. You said something before—

RANDOLPH: I propose we sell the place.

VICTOR: That's it. Sell "the place." THE PLACE. Great idea. Fantastic! And where do you propose I live? And Mama? And Sophie?

RANDOLPH: Let's not jump ahead. We don't have to decide all the details—

VICTOR: Wait, I...I'm losing whatever sense I had. I seem to recall, tell me if I'm wrong, that "this place" belongs to Sophie. My sister and I put it in trust as a dowry for her. Sophie is to take charge of the property when she marries or when you die.

RANDOLPH: Sophie's whom I'm thinking about.

SOPHIE: Don't bring me into this. I want what is good for you all.

RANDOLPH: Of course this place is for Sophie. Who said anything to the contrary? I wouldn't sell without her permission. What I'm proposing is for her benefit.

VICTOR: Preposterous. I don't believe what I'm hearing. I must be asleep or in some nightmare.

MAMERE: Victor, don't raise your voice at Randolph. He knows best.

VICTOR: I need a drink. Some bourbon. God. Give me some sherry, straight alcohol. Anything. Go on, say whatever you want. Say it. Say it. Go.

RANDOLPH: I don't understand what gets into you. Why are you so upset? I know my proposal's not ideal, but it is a way out. If you all think I'm being extreme, okay, I won't insist.

VICTOR: I maintain what I can, but the lack of money makes my job impossible.

RANDOLPH: I'm not blaming you, but vegetation's gone wild, brickwork's in a shambles—

VICTOR: You think I don't see? Still, I made sure you didn't go a day without a drive in your red fringed carriage.

RANDOLPH: True…but—*(Looks at ELLEN)* What's a young woman to do here, walk slowly, parasol in hand, feeding the ducks? Avoid the sun. Try not to use light too much inside as it intensifies heat. Let her life simmer for a long time so it won't spoil. *(Looks at SOPHIE)* And poor Sophie, she's orphaned in a way. What husband will she find? A farm hand? Males under thirty-five are the real ghosts on Louisiana's plantations. I see now. We must adjust to the new situation and perhaps sell Waverly.

MAMERE: I don't understand.

RANDOLPH: If Victor's at the auction, he can bid and keep it in the family.

SOPHIE: He's still paying off your excesses: thirteen check shirts, twenty-seven silk handkerchiefs, thirty-nine broadcloth vests—don't tease him now.

RANDOLPH: I'm not. I feel bad. Waverly's got a manager who's desperate and worries all the time. In the city, from sale revenue, he could enjoy peace of mind. We'll tell the Sheriff we want the best price—

MAMERE: You don't mean to . . .

RANDOLPH: From the best buyer—

NURSE: To sell this estate . . .

RANDOLPH: And we're shopping around. It shouldn't be difficult—

SOPHIE: After Uncle sacrificed his life, his…youth.

RANDOLPH: I don't think he works hard. He says he inspects the fields. Most times he's off exploring the countryside, reading journals, and gossiping with the help. I don't mind. He should enjoy himself. Meanwhile, the invoices rise. *(Opens book)* We can't pay for these repairs. The roof leaks; the ceilings are cracked; and all the floors giving in places. *(Pause)* Look at the debit columns. How can we sustain a sugar business that at best breaks even? A business that depends on good weather in a state where weather's precarious.

SOPHIE: Our ancestors did it.

RANDOLPH: On the backs of slaves. *(Pause)* We can't even meet the taxes and insurance. *(To SOPHIE)* I'm looking out for your concerns. Let's leave before we have to be carried out.

VICTOR: Enough! What do you know about hard work? Lying about like a lizard in the sun.

RANDOLPH: Don't take out your—

VICTOR: All lizards used to be reptiles—

RANDOLPH: Don't punish my wife. Nothing's decided yet . . .

VICTOR: I've worn myself out. Up at dawn noting every task is done—
Under rigid control with stringent economy.

RANDOLPH: It's good you did.

VICTOR: We've the mortgage paid off—

RANDOLPH: We appreciate it—

VICTOR: Sophie has a dowry.

RANDOLPH: I know, but you're half a saint. You've the promise to get
there, but you're still carrying the cross.

VICTOR: I don't believe what I'm hearing. I denounce all rights to my
inheritance, except for the rear cottage—I don't know why I did this, but
Sister said, "I'd like Sophie to have Waverly. Normally an estate passes to a
son, but Sophie's your heir, and she's—"

SOPHIE: Plain. Yes.

VICTOR: Sister didn't say plain. She said you were—

SOPHIE: Ugly.

VICTOR: Quiet. I slave to bring Waverly into solvency.

SOPHIE: Even sold bricks from Mama's gardens.

VICTOR: The place finally brings in revenue. Granted, it's a pittance, but
you can't sell Waverly—

SOPHIE: Without consulting Uncle.

RANDOLPH: I can. I hear him and I don't agree with him.

SOPHIE: Mamere, we can't let Waverly go.

NURSE: When you think of what this house has witnessed.

RANDOLPH: It's not my fault we don't have enough money.

VICTOR: I won't let you do this.

RANDOLPH: I'd like to save this plantation. But I'm your brother-in-law I'm not God. Waverly's sinking, moron. "They ain't going to be nothing for nobody," we don't bail out.

VICTOR: You're so brutal.

RANDOLPH: Why can't you get it...get it through your thick skull. Waverly's going down the drain. Grab your life vest. In one swoop we're going under.

(RANDOLPH tries to stand. VICTOR pushes him down. They fight.)

VICTOR: No, we're not.

RANDOLPH: It's hard to believe you're a grown man in your forties. Since I arrived, you've tortured me. You're envious. I was a successful professor for thirty years, but that's over. I apologize. After twenty-nine days at Waverly, I've had enough. I won't turn into a blind man. Live here in a big bed and draw the shutters. I'm going to sell Waverly, and you can either go screaming and crying, or you can walk out with dignity like sensible adults.

VICTOR: *(To RANDOLPH)* You won't get away with this.

SOPHIE: We're losing Waverly!

MAMERE: Not Waverly. Mama hid her silver in a compartment on the wall. And my brothers carved initials in the floor.

VICTOR: Sister wouldn't have stood for this. Who would have thought Randolph would have finagled her will.

MAMERE: Everyone said he was so brilliant, he threw off a light.

VICTOR: And now...After climbing the university ladder, he's created a trumped-up trusteeship to justify theft.

MAMERE: Poor Victor can't get to the first rung of the ladder.

VICTOR: Oh God…What should I do, Mama?

MAMERE: I don't think you'll learn until right before you die.

VICTOR: We can't let him sell Waverly.

MAMERE: No, it's a millennium house with open doors, high ceilings and cross-ventilation. It'll take one thousand years to forget all that.

RANDOLPH: Mrs. Mallory.

VICTOR: Don't go near her.

RANDOLPH: You look so young.

VICTOR: Talk to her! Touch her!

MAMERE: *(Pats RANDOLPH's hand)* I suppose you can't stay at Waverly and amount to anything?

RANDOLPH: No. We'll ease into the new glitz with gleaming luggage and for you a Canadian fox fur coat.

MAMERE: Well…if the professor says go, let's go. I just realized how capable he is. I'm so used to Victor—

VICTOR: How can you say that, Mama?

MAMERE: I was being facetious.

VICTOR: Go ahead. Turn my life into a joke! *(To RANDOLPH)* You're a snake. Satan!

(Exits)

RANDOLPH: I don't need your permission to sell what's mine.

SOPHIE: Uncle's irreplaceable.

RANDOLPH: The cemeteries are full of irreplaceable people.

ELLEN: Don't leave him so upset.

SOPHIE: Make up, Papa!

RANDOLPH: To keep Waverly, you need a wizard with a pot of gold….You can't reason with a jackass. *(A shot is heard behind the scenes. A shriek from ELLEN. NURSE runs out, followed by SOPHIE.)* Somebody go get…get him. He's lost his mind.

(VICTOR staggers in. ELLEN and VICTOR struggle in the doorway.)

ELLEN: Give me the pistol…

MAMERE: Lord!

VICTOR: Where is he?

SOPHIE: Stop!

ELLEN: Give…

NURSE: It's loaded.

VICTOR:…Thank…God.

ELLEN: I'm taking it.

VICTOR: Move.

MAMERE: Wait…I…

NURSE: Careful!

SOPHIE: Watch out!

VICTOR: Where…is he?

MAMERE: Don't shoot.

VICTOR: I'm going to...kill him. Ahhh! *(They struggle. VICTOR frees him-self from ELLEN. Runs about looking for RANDOLPH.)* I'll find the...the...coward!

ELLEN: Oh God, no...

VICTOR: And kill him.

SOPHIE AND MAMERE: Don't! No!

ELLEN: Duck!

VICTOR: Lucifer!

(VICTOR fires at RANDOLPH. Bang. A pause.)

RANDOLPH: Vicious bastard. You think you can come in here—

VICTOR: I missed him.

RANDOLPH: And take my life.

VICTOR: *(Furious, VICTOR fires again and misses.)* Damn. Hell. Can't...even shoot...A lousy gun.

(RANDOLPH is overwhelmed. ELLEN leans against a wall and almost faints.)

ELLEN: Get me out of here.

RANDOLPH: What've I done?

VICTOR: After how I treated him...*(VICTOR puts gun to his own head.)*

(SOPHIE screams)

SOUND: "Dixie Land."

VICTOR: No more bullets.

(ELLEN laughs)

ACT 2
SCENE 3

(Later. NURSE sings. DOCTOR drinks. Then HE searches his medical bag for something. NURSE rises.)

DOCTOR: Don't leave.

NURSE: I got to help them pack. It's a sad day. That's all I got to say. Can't you do nothing to set things right? Give the poor girl some hope.

DOCTOR: Who? What?

NURSE: Sophie needs to get married. I send her in here, and you do it.

(Exits quickly. Footsteps. VICTOR enters and tosses the gun to the DOCTOR.)

DOCTOR: Where've you been?

VICTOR: I'm not sure. I don't know whether I was drunk or not but I woke up with this headache, looked up at the ceiling, and thought, "Am I in hell?"

DOCTOR: Give me what you stole from me.

VICTOR: *(Ignores him)* You think I'm mad? A person torments you hourly, you take one shot at him, and they say you're crazy. And you...

DOCTOR: When you let men bully you—They'll persist.

VICTOR: I wore patched sleeves—

DOCTOR: Darned socks.

VICTOR: Oh, give me something. I'm disgusted.

DOCTOR: Half of humanity is disgusted, but you're acting like an idiot. Maybe three hundred years from now, people will know how to be happy. They'll look back at us and laugh: working unsuccessfully—trying to speak right, to find answers, to cure things. They'll be smarter and wiser and they'll resurrect hope. *(Pause)* Don't kill yourself with that morphia you stole from me.

ROSARY HARTEL O'NEILL

VICTOR: You can do my post mortem.

DOCTOR: That's nice. I get to identify the fact my morphia killed you? If you need drugs, let me introduce you to my best friend Johnny Walker— Because you can stop drinking—

VICTOR: I can't face Randolph.

DOCTOR: You'll have to.

VICTOR: Why can't I sleep and never wake up! I cheapened myself for lust. (To DOCTOR) You—BETRAYED ME—my best friend. You knew I loved Ellen. A FRIENDSHIP DIED HERE. You were more intelligent, more sensitive than the rest. BETRAYING ME FOR THAT... THAT... nothing's left. (Pause) I'm forty-two. I'll live another twenty or thirty years. How? If only I'd wake up in a different place, in a younger, more virile-looking body. I'm wearing out. You don't see it. It's the old enthusiasm that's gone. Tell me how can I start a new life. They must teach you what to tell patients. That's what I need to know.

DOCTOR: (Extends gun) Here, kill yourself. Shoot. Be done with it.

(SOPHIE enters.)

SOPHIE: Oh no. I'll put that pistol somewhere safe.

DOCTOR: First help me get the morphia your uncle stole from me.

SOPHIE: (To VICTOR) You stole morphia?

VICTOR: I can't take living.

SOPHIE: How come women can take it? Men can't...I am just as unhappy as you are.

VICTOR: Oh, here. (Shoves her the bottle) But you better pull things together—

SOPHIE: What should I do? What?

VICTOR: Figure it out. You're so capable.

SOPHIE: All right…I will. *(Hands DOCTOR the bottle)*

(ELLEN enters, looks at the DOCTOR, SOPHIE, VICTOR.)

ELLEN: We're leaving.

DOCTOR: I can go now.

ELLEN: How are you feeling?

VICTOR: Don't patronize me.

ELLEN: The professor wants to speak to you.

DOCTOR: That's good.

VICTOR: I can't handle more degradation.

ELLEN: Forgive him for his flaws.

DOCTOR: You could do that…don't you think?

ELLEN: And the good things he taught—

SOPHIE: Will live in you.

VICTOR:…I'm sorry…demanding people offend me—All right. One final sermon.

(SOPHIE and VICTOR exit. The DOCTOR looks at ELLEN.)

DOCTOR: Can't you sit?

ELLEN: It'd be foolish.

DOCTOR: Foolish me. Shut your eyes.

ELLEN: I'm so tired…The professor wants everything—

DOCTOR: Rest. Try feeling once and for all satiated—

ELLEN: *(The DOCTOR takes her hand.)* What are you doing? Oh no…

DOCTOR: Checking your pulse. That's all.

ELLEN:…well, be quick.

DOCTOR: Your breathing's rushed. Excuse the cold hands—

ELLEN: Don't. —Will you try to believe that I am a good person?

DOCTOR: You don't love anyone. You are a hedonist. Why not follow your feelings?

ELLEN: Stop!

DOCTOR: I'm amenable to just looking.

ELLEN: No. I…I can't meet your needs…

DOCTOR: Good.

ELLEN: I'm sorry if I've given you the—

DOCTOR: Let's celebrate uncertainty.

ELLEN: Impression that I wanted an—

DOCTOR: Let's run off somewhere! Oh, Ellen. I'm giving you a chance for a face near you, by you, a face that loves you. *(DOCTOR takes her in his arms.)*

ELLEN:…I think…I can't deal with . . .

DOCTOR: My feelings for you! And what we could do about them! Can't you see something's missing from your life? You're bound to give in to a brush with passion. Do it where there's nature to hide you. A man that loves you. Even this far. I feel you. I sense the blood in your veins. I see your body living in me, shining through me. Run away with me—

ELLEN: I won't. I . . .

DOCTOR: And you'll no longer weep for your life. *(DOCTOR grabs ELLEN.)*

ELLEN: I...I can't go. Not now. I come from a different world.

DOCTOR: You could change.

ELLEN: I feel too old...If a woman is going to stray, it'll be in her early twenties. By her late twenties, she's resigned to how miserable life is.

DOCTOR: Yes, you should go away. There is something strange about you. You and your husband just showed up here one day. We were all busy working, doing things. You infected us like yellow fever!...I haven't done a thing for over a month, and there are a lot of sick people out there. So what do I do now? Abandon my practice? I see you every day and suddenly I won't see you again. I'll breathe, eat, drink and sleep but there will be no life!

ELLEN:...Forgive me. *(SHE rushes to him and kisses him passionately)*

(Sound of footsteps. They break apart. Enter RANDOLPH, VICTOR followed by MAMERE, NURSE, and SOPHIE.)

RANDOLPH: I just want to tell you, Victor, you're an incredibly good man. Forget the past.

VICTOR: . . . How can I?

RANDOLPH: Don't talk about it. Forgiveness is a superior act to vengeance.

VICTOR: You're right but I'm not open to change; change unnerves me.

RANDOLPH: Imitate me. I like to learn and to teach, and I flatter myself that I'm good at both.

VICTOR: Still, you're owed an apology. For what I did out here—

RANDOLPH: Not another word. *(Looks up)* What a clear sky.

VICTOR: I didn't notice. I've been through so much, I anticipate disappointment...even bad weather. I carry an umbrella even though it hasn't

ROSARY HARTEL O'NEILL

rained for days.

RANDOLPH: I hate to leave…but I've to get Ellen in the carriage before dark. *(SHE nods.)* I want to drive by the chapel where we married and check on the family tomb. That sepulcher was inspired by Michelangelo's Pièta. And the tombs of the Medici princes. *(To ELLEN)* Give me your hand, sweetheart.

SOPHIE: Say a prayer for me by Mama's grave—

RANDOLPH: I'll describe the flora and fauna that inspired Audubon—

MAMERE: Isn't the professor a genius? He's the ambassador of this family. If only Victor could have learned something from him.

RANDOLPH: Ah, it's Victor we should thank, Mamere. Soon as I get to the city, I'm going to send you the right fluff. A little fur for your coat.

MAMERE: Such extravagance!

SOUND: *Carriage bells ring.*

(Carriage arrives for PROFESSOR.)

RANDOLPH: You must excuse me.

SOPHIE: Oh, Papa. I don't want you to leave.

MAMERE: You sure I can't go with you? *(HE nods no.)* Well, mail me the first draft of your next article so I can study it.

NURSE: She'll look every day. Don't forget to write.

RANDOLPH: I'll get Ellen to send a long letter. *(Chuckles)* She's nothing better to do. I'm being facetious. *(HE and VICTOR embrace.)* Life's short, and there's no time to thank people enough.

VICTOR: I'll pay you the same as before.

RANDOLPH: Don't trouble too much. You've worked for twenty years—

VICTOR: Everything shall be as it was. Maybe I can do better.

RANDOLPH: For now…Ellen and I'll live like little love mice. One room's enough for us honeymooners. (*Looks at the DOCTOR.*) I'd a catharsis last night. Talked to the wee hours with my wife. We'll be cozy in closer quarters. (*HE puts an arm around her and SHE breaks free to hug SOPHIE.*)

ELLEN: I'll miss you.

SOPHIE: Write to us. When you settle down.

RANDOLPH: Goodbye, everybody.

VICTOR: (*Kisses ELLEN*) We'll probably never meet again.

RANDOLPH: I'll remember you all . . .

ELLEN: Maybe not.

VICTOR: Pardon me for anything I've done.

ELLEN: Of course.

RANDOLPH: We're off. I'll remember you all. So much emotion and appreciation. I'm surprised. Delighted. I'm taking a lifetime sabbatical with my bride. Ellen, put your arm through mine. Smile and wave goodbye.

(*RANDOLPH and ELLEN exit, followed by NURSE, and MAMERE. DOCTOR speaks to SOPHIE.*)

DOCTOR: So long. Please bring my carriage around?

(*SOPHIE goes out. The DOCTOR and VICTOR remain. The DOCTOR drinks with no food. He is becoming an alcoholic. VICTOR loses himself in his ledgers. Each man murmurs to himself but the words overlap.*)

DOCTOR: We should wave them off.

VICTOR: I was never one for long goodbyes.

DOCTOR: They're getting in the carriage.

SOUND: *Sound of carriage bells.*

VICTOR: Sophie hasn't balanced the books.

DOCTOR: Ellen takes with her some kind of unspeakable music.

VICTOR: When you stop subtracting figures, you think you've more money than you've got.

DOCTOR: She didn't proceed with explanations. She appreciated mystery.

VICTOR: Invoices are lined up against me.

DOCTOR: Her life and mine were intertwined. We should've been friends forever.

VICTOR: I've got to hurry to see which bills can wait.

SOUND: *Carriage.*

DOCTOR: She came when the leaves were full on the trees and went when they were gone. How quiet it is. There's no rain or wind. Just the sound of a lone squirrel. Terribly silent and safe here. The dim light full of meditative sadness. I've this sense that life is leaving me. Mmm. They're gone.

(Enter SOPHIE.)

SOPHIE: They're gone. Strange chill in the air rolling in from some polar region. Glad I packed blankets. I waved them down the drive like Mama used to do. Stood and waved till there was no more sound, but the flapping of a heron in an oak tree.

SOUND: *Carriage arrives.*

(Holds up a spray of lavender)

SOPHIE: The last of the lavender. It doesn't like our climate. It stayed with us longer than we thought it would—

VICTOR: *(Mumbles to himself)* Delivered to...Mr. Carrerre.

SOUND: Sound of bells and carriage wheels.

DOCTOR: My carriage is here. Nothing to do but say goodbye. *(Picks up his bag.)*

SOPHIE: Must you leave?

VICTOR: Sophie!

DOCTOR: Moving's something everybody does.

VICTOR: *(Stamps a letter)* Account delivered. Two dollars and twenty three cents.

DOCTOR: I've this mare with a bad leg. I need to get her home.

SOPHIE: When will you be back?

VICTOR: Sophie, he doesn't know.

DOCTOR: Write if you need me. I'll come, of course.

SOPHIE: Can't you leave tomorrow?

(DOCTOR starts to leave. SOPHIE gets some crackers.)

DOCTOR: I want to use up all my energy. I don't want any of it to go untried.

SOPHIE: Have some nourishment at least.

DOCTOR: No, thanks.

SOPHIE: A drink?

DOCTOR: *(The DOCTOR drinks bourbon. Blots his mouth with a handkerchief, puts it down.)* No need to walk me out.

SOPHIE: I want to.

SOUND: Carriage leaving.

DOCTOR: No.

(MAMERE and NURSE enter, MAMERE with an article and NURSE with a quilt.)

MAMERE: Someone's leaving? Oh, the doctor. I thought he was courting Sophie.

NURSE: Shush now.

MAMERE: I told you it was too soon to work on that trousseau.

NURSE: Mind your own business.

MAMERE: Everybody knows the ring should come before the quilt!

VICTOR: *(Nods and continues writing.)* March the third. Twenty dollars. Friday the fifteenth, twenty dollars again.

(Pause. The sound of bells. SOPHIE enters, puts a candle on the table. Picks up his handkerchief.)

SOPHIE: The doctor is gone. He left his handkerchief. I've a collection of handkerchiefs. I'll keep this for him.

MAMERE: Did you get a promise? *(SOPHIE nods her head, no.)* Tell him you don't need a big ring.

NURSE: Quiet.

(SOPHIE lights a candle)

VICTOR: The house seems empty, as if the walls were laughing.

(SOPHIE sits at the table with VICTOR and writes. VICTOR counts. MAMERE reads to herself. NURSE hums "Amazing Grace.")

SOPHIE: It's been so long since I sat at this table.

VICTOR: It'll take a week to get it all straight.

MAMERE: I helped Rachelle pick out her linens when she married.

VICTOR: Thirty, thirty-five.

MAMERE: The professor liked my silver pattern.

(The night watchman begins playing "Let Me Call You Sweetheart." VICTOR looks up.)

SOPHIE: Your books look neat.

VICTOR: It's hard to believe I won't run out of money.

SOPHIE: We must be stronghearted.

VICTOR: *Richard Coeur de Lion.*

SOPHIE: Pray.

VICTOR: For good luck in bad times. Sounds contradictory.

SOPHIE: All prayer is heard. It might not come when we want it, but it's coming.

VICTOR: For most people Waverly is just a name.

SOPHIE: How can you despair when we're surrounded by beauty? Every oak tree is overloaded with an abundance of leaves, so many that they fall.

(NURSE hums.)

VICTOR: Twenty three dollars and forty cents. Five dollars…Everything is gone, *mon amie.*

SOPHIE: No, it's not. We can't control whether or not we're successful, but we can control how hard we work. If we keep working, we'll be rewarded. One day we'll wake into the land of angels and dreams and see God in all his brightness. Do you hear? It has just started to rain. The sky is also crying for us.

SOUND: Ending Music

THE END

Photo: Matt Anderson
Pictured: Barret O'Brien, Deborah Lee Smith

John Singer Sargent and Madame X

A PLAY IN
TWO ACTS

CAST OF CHARACTERS

JOHN SINGER SARGENT—28, handsome, a good athlete, formally dressed American. A bit naïve, he is courageous and daring and will defy everyone to protect his painting. No experience in love.

JUDITH GAUTHIER— late thirties, French art critic, beautiful. She champions artists and underdogs and admires Sargent.

CLAUDE MONET—middle aged established landscape artist. A powerful art critic and teacher, he is working to improve his sensitivity to his students' struggles.

AMELIE GAUTREAU—24, "Madame X." Exquisite. The most beautiful woman in Paris, she is from New Orleans and yearns for love.

DR. SAMUEL-JEAN POZZI *(nicknamed Dr Dieu (God) because of his promiscuity and the fame of his gynecology)*—Early thirties, with dashing good looks. He collects artists and destroys their souls and is enamored of Amelie Gautreau.

SARAH BERNHARDT—mid-thirties, the most famous actress in France, with a mother complex and a sexual history with Dr. Pozzi.

EMILY SARGENT—24, a delicate girl with a childhood deformity. She is John Sargent's sister who follows him about and lives off his fame.

HENRY JAMES—middle-aged, austere English novelist and critic, who champions Sargent for his talent and is one of his greatest admirers.

OSCAR WILDE—29, dapper London poet, dressed in dashing urban attire. He believes in Sargent and the beautiful of Paris and is always available for a clever remark.

Claude Monet and Henry James.
Oscar Wilde and Sam Pozzi
Judith Gauthier and Sarah Bernhardt

VICTOR HUGO and RICHARD WAGNER are walk-ons with
no lines.

SETTING

Multiple interior and exterior set. Belle Époque Paris and
London, 1882.

PROLOGUE:
THE LADY IN BLACK

(AMELIE GAUTREAU appears in portrait pose & dress of MADAME X)

AMELIE: Welcome. I'm not a character. I'm an exhibit. I'm the only living
descendent of Madame X. I'm here to tell you beauty is more powerful than
money, because I have it and I have had both. I had beauty long before I
had money. My husband's money can't get me in anywhere I can't get
myself in with beauty. I'm saying educated beauty, not like a sexy beauty. I
fought real hard to maintain my position, to have beauty and class, as you
will see.

Lights fade. Lights go up on Stage Scene and Act One

ACT ONE
SCENE ONE

(Dr. Pozzi's salon, 10 Vendome Place, Paris. A rainy May afternoon. Offstage, Victor Hugo reads from his novel and Richard Wagner plays the piano. Onstage, in a silk kimono, Judith Gauthier arranges Japanese flowers. She is beautiful, 37, full figure, large, expressive eyes. John Sargent rushes in under a dripping umbrella. Twenty-eight, he is handsome, robust, a good athlete, formally dressed.)

JOHN: Amazing house.

JUDITH: It's the doctor's Palace of Creativity. Any artist who is anybody eventually comes here. *(Shakes his hand.)* Judith Gauthier.

JOHN: Daughter of the—

JOHN AND JUDITH: Famed novelist.

JUDITH: And nun of art.*(Laughs, holding his hand.)* None in the morning, none in the evening.

JOHN: John Sargent. Student painter.

JUDITH: Rapidly ascending.

JOHN: I'm here for a nomination—to the Salon.

JUDITH: Good.

JOHN: You're the critic who wrote that attack on me and—

JUDITH: Madame Gautreau from New Orleans—

JOHN: "Ambitious Americans seize our medals and glory."

(JOHN checks his pocket watch, peers out the rainy window. Two old men walk across the stage. One studies sheet music, the other a book.)

JOHN: That's not…Victor Hugo and Richard Wagner.

JUDITH: I furthered their careers.

SOUND: Doorbell rings.

(Claude Monet hurries in, drenched. Portly, he hides an artist's portfolio by the door.)

CLAUDE: Wicked out, rainy and cold.

JUDITH: Claude Monet. Let me introduce—

JOHN: We know each other.

JUDITH: *(To CLAUDE.)* Your coat.

CLAUDE: *(Hesitates, coughs. Gives JUDITH his wet coat.)* It's too hot with it on, and too cold with it off. *(Pause)* Don't you go to class?

JOHN: I try to go. I went to the door. Did you bring the letter?

(CLAUDE coughs. Pounds his chest. Music from "The Ring Cycle" echoes off-stage.)

JUDITH: Wagner. Playing catastrophically—

JOHN: *(To CLAUDE)* You come in panting.

(Hugo crosses, reading.)

CLAUDE: Victor Hugo! You know John Sargent.

(HUGO shakes CLAUDE'S hand…profusely, never looking at Sargent, exits.)

JUDITH: Brandy?

CLAUDE: God, yes.

JOHN: Coffee. I don't want to be loose. I want to be tense.

(CLAUDE coughs and pounds his chest.)

CLAUDE: The Professor's dog died. He's not coming.

JOHN: Does he do this a lot?

CLAUDE: Some Frenchmen have never been nominated for the Salon.

JUDITH: John's from Philadelphia—

(JUDITH exits.)

CLAUDE: The Professor says, "Haven't we done enough for John already?"

JOHN: I didn't know I was out of favor.

CLAUDE: No one is in favor now.

JOHN: Artists, we're no better than squirrels. Spend all day looking for food.

CLAUDE: Hold off a year.

JOHN: Unlike you, I've no government stipend—

CLAUDE: The professor suggests you do Louise's portrait. She's social.

JUDITH: *(Pokes her head in)* The school will get a commission.

CLAUDE: Here's that letter.

JOHN: It's in the handwriting of you-know-who. I don't want to touch it.

JUDITH: John shouldn't have to consider financing the Professor.

CLAUDE: *(Reads a paper)* He says: "If nominated, Sargent will have to organize the hanging, pay all assistants and costs. If Louise's portrait sells, the studio will retain eighty percent."

JOHN: This is blackmail.

CLAUDE: Leverage. The Professor has got to—

JUDITH: Put his empire in place.

JOHN: The man wears the persona of genius without having done the work—

CLAUDE: My coat?

JOHN: Two hours of painting, thirty hours of eating and talking.

CLAUDE: *(Gives JOHN back his portfolio.)* Your submissions.

JOHN: Most students collect around him wanting a trade.

CLAUDE: Sorry.

JOHN: But I was more than his student—

CLAUDE: In art, rejection is the norm.

JOHN: I painted his first official portrait...

(JUDITH gives CLAUDE his coat. He turns to JOHN.)

CLAUDE: You don't realize how important the Salon is to the future careers of the stars of France. You're a newcomer. A neophyte. This competition was made to further emerging French painters from the Ecole des Beaux Arts. The fact that you, an American, are considered at all is unusual. Be satisfied. Many Parisians went out of their way to admit you into France's leading art school. We teach you and close our eyes. But now you want all the prizes. You aren't wise. Shouldn't it be enough that we include you with the French. You're not even European. Your family has no connections. They totter back and forth between countries, only arriving when the wealthy have left. Many artists are calling in favors to keep you at this state school. Now you want to be nominated to the premier competition with the top French youth. If you win, which you invariably might, how do we explain the school's use of state monies for your education. Why don't you exhibit in New York? Come to Giverny. Do landscapes.

JOHN: Portraits are what I do.

(CLAUDE exits.)

JUDITH: Why insist on entering the Salon?

JOHN: Employment depends on repeated proof of ability. Good art sells, but marketed well, it sells better. The public must be reminded; one striking performance isn't luck.

JUDITH: You were wonderfully overqualified—

JOHN: I survived there, because I was cloaked. When you put your talons on, you're dusted. I don't want to walk the fine line between chaos and control. Never complaining! Keep the gothic alive for some horrible mother's dwarf-like… I can't believe I'm so committed to a teacher I hate.

JUDITH: Your Professor is a dud, but don't let that fool you. He is a power in Paris.

JOHN: What should I do?

JUDITH: Paint a star.

SOUND: *Sounds of crashing, crowds scream, soft crying.*

JOHN: Amelie Gautreau!

JUDITH: Getting out of her carriage before the doctor's office.

JOHN: What a luscious beauty. She looks fourteen—

JUDITH: She enters the best rooms of Paris.

JOHN: She's this weird binary opposition between promiscuity and classiness.

JUDITH: King Ludwig attended the Opera to see her climb the stair. Elizabeth of Austria posed her as a garden statue—

JOHN: How does such an American get touted the beauty of Paris? Don't tell me! She's a Civil War orphan from New Orleans—and the French have adopted her—I know I'm mesmerized too. Lovliness launched her into the world of power. Perhaps she could protect me. An American painting an American; that the French might accept. Her beauty would entice Parisians to the portrait. So instead of being lost on the ceiling, it might be hung eye to eye. Amelie Gautreau; there's a face could start a career.

SCENE TWO

(An anteroom to Dr. Pozzi's house. AMELIE GAUTREAU, 24, enters. Exquisite, she suggests a Greek goddess, with an ample, upturned bosom, narrow waist, long elegant neck, sculpted shoulders. DR. SAMUEL-JEAN POZZI greets her. Well-built, early thirties, with dashing good looks, he wears a close-fitting business suit.)

AMELIE: Doctor!

DOCTOR: It couldn't wait.

AMELIE: I forget I'm not your only flirtation.

DOCTOR: You're the one that matters…Amelie!

AMELIE: I'm two months pregnant.

DOCTOR: Holy Mother! Thank God you have a husband.

AMELIE: But, I've a marriage blanc—a sexless marriage. He's too old to---

DOCTOR: Slip once, then have the baby. "Come early."

AMELIE: After my husband touches me, I vomit for twenty-four hours.

DOCTOR: I'll give you a pill.

AMELIE: Couldn't you and I marry?

DOCTOR: I am married. You're married.

AMELIE: It's your baby! What should we do?

DOCTOR: Say you're carrying your own vestigial twin. And—

AMELIE: Have an abortion? You said I wouldn't conceive—

DOCTOR: I said bi-manual manipulation—made termination painless. You've had good relations for the first time.

AMELIE: But I want the baby.

DOCTOR: The most beautiful woman in Paris can't be pregnant.

AMELIE: Talking to you is like speaking to a wall. I walk up and bang, hit my head.

DOCTOR: Come here.

AMELIE: Don't touch me.

DOCTOR: We can still have intercourse.

AMELIE: Good Lord! You're not even worried.

DOCTOR: You won't show for months.

AMELIE: No, I wouldn't expect you to feel for someone.

DOCTOR: My mother died at thirty-six, always pregnant.

AMELIE: Why should that concern me?

DOCTOR: I have nightmares about your confinement. I'm the son of a Protestant minister. I know the power of scandal. Some innocent must be blamed. A student like...

AMELIE: I won't do this.

DOCTOR: We'll say while painting he fell for his model—

AMELIE: What about compassionate solutions—

DOCTOR: Beautiful women are aphrodisiacs.

AMELIE: Surely there is another—

DOCTOR: How about John Sargent, who's sitting next door?

AMELIE: I won't do th—

DOCTOR: He's sexually naïve, American.

AMELIE: Don't even think—

DOCTOR: He needs a star for his portrait and you're a candidate.

AMELIE: It's too convoluted.

DOCTOR: Nothing's too deep for snakes not to move gracefully.

LIGHT: Lights fade.

SCENE THREE

(Dr. Pozzi's salon moments later.)

LIGHTS: Lights up on the doctor entering.

DOCTOR: Sam Pozzi. They call me Doctor Dieu (God).

(A corporeal glance passes between them.)

JOHN: John Sargent.

(DOCTOR holds his hand a bit too long. JOHN withdraws it awkwardly).

JOHN: John Singer Sargent.

DOCTOR: You're all dressed up—formal collar and cuffs. You couldn't paint like that—

JOHN: It's important to give canvas the respect it deserves.

DOCTOR: You're civilized to the fingertips.

JOHN: Thanks, but I must go—

DOCTOR: You don't socialize?

JOHN: I guard against time stealers.

DOCTOR: Won't you look at my art? Indulge me. I'm a hoarder. If I buy

ROSARY HARTEL O'NEILL

too much, I'll add on a wing to the house. *(Looks down.)* Here's a tortoise inlaid with gold and pearls. Marble from India, floors from Honduras, garnet-crusted frames. There's Degas, Monet, and your portrait of the Professor from last year's Salon.

JOHN: My! I never knew.

DOCTOR: You're a national treasure waiting to be recognized.

JOHN: Don't exaggerate.

DOCTOR: Or so Amelie Gautreau thinks. I quote, "What to John is ordinary is to most painters—"

AMELIE AND DOCTOR: *(Amelie enters.)* Extraordinary.

AMELIE: John Sargent. I've heard of you by rumor. You have that man thing about you. Women want to say hello.

JOHN: *(Paralyzed seeing Amelie.)* Madame Amelie.

AMELIE: Married to Pedro—whatever his name is. I'm the other half. *(She puts out her hand. He pecks her.)* You've kissed your dog softer than you've kissed me.

DOCTOR: Amelie may need a portrait.

(Exits.)

AMELIE: My husband is a millionaire in bat guano from Chile.

JOHN: So something ostentatious and grand? And the purpose of the portrait?

AMELIE: To replace children. Every chance he gets, Pedro jabs me about not wanting them.

JOHN: You could care less about that?

AMELIE: When I die, I die. In his case, we live again through portraits.

JOHN: You don't believe that.

AMELIE: What does a good portrait involve?

JOHN: About two hundred hours of sitting.

AMELIE: I'd have to give up sixty parties. It's too time-consuming.

JOHN: You're forced to live that way to survive.

AMELIE: *(Cries.)* I'm trying to do the sensitive thing that makes Pedro feel good—

JOHN: So you want a full-length?

AMELIE: Can you paint my pure white skin? More marble than human.

JOHN: The musculature has vibrancy.

AMELIE: Capture how rice powder "spiritualizes" my flesh and carmine reddens my lips.

JOHN: Like in the paintings of Franz Hals.

AMELIE: Glorify my flawless skin.

JOHN: The Dutch artist.

AMELIE: It's all about spoiling myself for now. To combat wrinkles I stay a day a week in bed and apply creams all over my body. I bathe, bathe, and bathe again. I use pearl powder, violet powder, rouge, bisque for the eyelids, belladonna for the eyes, yellow shine and mineral potions for the hair. I varnish my face, fix on Russian ringlets, wear pre-Raphaelite dress. To make sure my gown won't clash with an interior, I make a trial visit to any house I'm invited to for a party…And your weakness as a painter?

JOHN: No personal life. Most parties bore me in ten minutes.

AMELIE: You protect your energy.

JOHN: Painting won't let me rest. My hands are always itchy.

AMELIE: I could feed your passion.

JOHN: How?

AMELIE: My greatest preoccupation is romance. Thank goodness for loose gowns in which a married woman can relax at five o'clock. Daytime fabric is heavy, like removing upholstery. The teagown is as undressed as one can be in public and still be clothed. *(As if preparing to undo it.)* Below my robe I am seductively naked.

JOHN: I'm going to practice saying no. "No, no, no."

AMELIE: The most wonderful things are waiting on the other side.

SCENE FOUR

(The Salon continued. Crash offstage. Doctor rushes in.)

JOHN: An accident?

DOCTOR: They wait to crash till they're near a doctor.

(HUGO and WAGNER enter carrying John's sister, EMILY SARGENT, a pretty girl of 24, with a hunch back.)

JOHN: My sister.

SISTER: *(Reaching for JOHN.)* You forgot your sketchbook.

JUDITH: She ran before the carriage.

SISTER: John! You're supposed to check with me.

DOCTOR: Is she bleeding?

SISTER: I can't keep up with him.

JOHN: Are you in pain?

SISTER: I fell.

DOCTOR: What part hurts?

SISTER: My...arm.

JUDITH: Can you move it?

SISTER: I'm fine. Did John get the nomination?

(All but JOHN and JUDITH exit, carrying Sister. JOHN knocks on the closed door.)

JOHN: Will Sis be all right?

JUDITH: I suspect. Coffee? *(JOHN shakes his head.)* How long has she been—

JOHN: Following me? A few years. It's very sad. I tell her to make friends, but she hasn't found "her tribe." She's fragile, and accident-prone. She was dropped as a child. I was born first. Later children died. At birth, she could fit in a shoebox. *(Paces.)* Sis said a novena for me to win that nomination. But the path of glory is strewn with corpses. Mom has used up our savings. Papa's health is weak. What future awaits Sis if I fail? Marry a poor man with one foot. Let her husband's mistress move in. Her only distinction is her hair, so long she can sit on it. Hasn't cut it since she was born. She calls it her "too long to let hang hair."

JUDITH: I've seen girls like your sister in the wards of Charity Hospital.

JOHN: What's keeping the doctor?

JUDITH: She needs a goal because she'll never have a normal life.

JOHN: *(Paces, looking toward the doctor's office.)* I'm her purpose.

JUDITH: Good. We can both watch you paint, while she recuperates in my room.

JOHN: We couldn't inconvenience you.

JUDITH: There's a wing for visiting artists.

(DOCTOR enters with SISTER, who is wearing a sling.)

DOCTOR: Your sister's got a sprained arm. I waived my expenses.

SISTER: He gave me a ring with a single human teardrop.

JUDITH: *(To SISTER.)* I'll braid your hair, put you in a kimono—

DOCTOR: I need to watch her.

JUDITH: You and your brother can live here!

JOHN: I don't think so.

JUDITH: Don't you know about the balance teeter-totter?

SISTER: Let's stay. Please.

JUDITH: Maybe you've had so much badness; it's time for good...

(Exiting with SISTER.)

SCENE FIVE

(Next week at the doctor's. AMELIE touches JOHN as they go through trunks of costumes. SHE holds up a gown.)

AMELIE: I love clothes but I loathe portraits.

JOHN: I won't impose my views.

AMELIE: Women put up with idiosyncrasies in wealthy artists, 'cause they get a lot—

JOHN: I'll make you even more beautiful.

AMELIE: But to be painted ten hours a day by a student.

(She turns away.)

JOHN: I'll immortalize you as the prettiest woman alive. Talk to me.

GHOSTS OF NEW ORLEANS

AMELIE: I can't.

JOHN: I need to see what you see. Be in your mind—your body. *(Pause)* Feel what troubles you?

AMELIE: Dark thoughts come into my head all the time, so the rain won't let up.

JOHN: Was there a time when you didn't have these holes?

AMELIE: New Orleans was the cure. No one gets to be a big fish in Paris. It's too unforgiving. When I came here, it was not a welcoming place. This city doesn't have the flamboyance, the Caribbean feel New Orleans has. After the war, I brought my body to Paris, but I left my soul in New Orleans. There was a thinness in my world there that allowed me to see possibilities. So many happy hours, days, months with my family beside the Mississippi River. I always felt I could go back and be the little girl and be protected. I guess no place that took you away from there is going to look good. But I've got to try not to care so much.

JOHN: You've always been displaced but now you're feeling it.

AMELIE: I've tapped into a rich gold vein here.

JOHN: But you've shot your heart out.

AMELIE: I have to close my eyes; it's unreal.

JOHN: Your world is strife with black sins.

AMELIE: *(Pours a drink.)* Let's get drowsy on champagne.

JOHN: Whatever, if you'll let me do the portrait.

AMELIE: What if I dislike something, like my left eye?

JOHN: Everyone has a skeleton in the closet, some …

AMELIE: What if I hate the portrait?

JOHN: What if you love it?

AMELIE: I've never seen someone anticipate winning so quickly.

JOHN: We live not seeing our faces, so the other becomes a mirror.

AMELIE: But I don't want a—

JOHN: I'll give you one hundred percent attention.

AMELIE: Most men try to fashion you into something that works for them.

JOHN: You can do things while I paint.

AMELIE: Good. I'll daydream intensely, allow my body to open up, my imagination to soar. Fantasy makes you feel so nice. The visual interconnect with the skin, the sensory organs. Time stops. I like to dream. Doesn't matter if it's good or bad. I like to not think. *(Drinks.)* Counting time by heartbeats. You have to slow things down, focus on the body. Most people can't do that in their waking hours. They have to go to sleep—Me, I can do that standing in place. *(Drinks.)* Dreams are wishes. What would you do with a wishing well? You're so strong and sweet. Have you never loved a woman?

JOHN: I have a close family.

AMELIE: You choose to be isolated.

JOHN: I view others as interference.

AMELIE: It's easy to be alone, painting. But the inner voice never dies. You should stray. All affairs end. Some end in a day, a year. The next day, sometimes I feel real bad. I feel dirty because there has to be some bond. That's not true for most men…There's no permanent thing. There's different degrees of temporary.

JOHN: Let me paint you.

AMELIE: Fine. But this weight of platonic love has to be surgically removed from your brush.

(She caresses his cheek.)

SCENE SIX

(Later. JUDITH, SISTER in a kimono enter with Sarah Bernhardt, mid-thirties, with wild golden hair.)

JUDITH: The great Sarah Bernhardt.

SISTER: My. I used to follow you. Today it's called stalking.

SARAH: Gushing is always distasteful.

JOHN: Hello, Miss Bernhardt.

SARAH: I'm Sarah to the world, why shouldn't I be to you?

JOHN: Sarah.

SARAH: Singer Sargent. That's not French. I'm not going to beat about the bush.

AMELIE: 'Cause you don't have much bush to beat. Ha.

SARAH: Please! I'm Amelie's godmother and counselor. There are those who are family by birth and those who are family by acclamation. I've devoted myself to this girl's image. She wants to assimilate herself as quickly as possible to the appearance of a woman of a certain class. It's not easy. Soon as she got breasts, men descended like bees to butter.

AMELIE: John is doing my portrait.

SARAH: You're going to put your face in the hands of an amateur. What do you say for yourself, Mr. John Singer? *(To JOHN.)* Your father is a failed physician. Your mother a dilettante. Your sister a cripple.

JOHN: God! I need a pet that bites to show you how mean you are.

SARAH: We have a name for painters like you—invasive painters.

JOHN: Right. I don't do vanity portraits—nice portraits of very shallow people.

(Exits with his SISTER and JUDITH.)

(Alone, SARAH confronts Amelie.)

SARAH: You're headed for the guillotine. It's just a matter of when the cart gets there.

AMELIE: The doctor said John's portraits are good and original.

SARAH: Yes, but what's good is not original, and what's original is not good.

AMELIE: I like him.

SARAH: You've bonded as expatriates do.

AMELIE: He shines gentleness.

SARAH: Watch out. We don't need him all over you like applesauce. I don't trust men who are anarchists.

AMELIE: It's healthy to fight people who are not important.

SARAH: He was rejected from the Salon. Expunged!

AMELIE: You can't treat a—

SARAH: A portrait artist should be regenerative, enhance the face.

AMELIE: With John that's—

SARAH: Impossible. It is his own insistence on himself. He was home-schooled and brought up with some woundedness around money. The only thing he'll reach for is your wallet. You can't be eccentric without being rich. Now, I've been painted thrice and each artist was wealthier than the last.

AMEILE: John's not dangerous.

SARAH: When you bring his name up, it polarizes the room. *(Pause)* When he's tested, he'll turn up violent; it's part of his life. He's always going to break out of the corral and head for the woods. He's like a wild horse. You can ride him for a while but then he'll have to buck you. Strengthen your bone character. Fire him. Let him beat the male drums. There is certain stability even in cruelty.

AMELIE: I'm so glad he's available.

SARAH: You can't stop birds of prey from flying overhead but you can stop them from nesting in your hair.

(SARA exits.)

(JUDITH and SISTER enter with HENRY JAMES, OSCAR WILDE dressed in dashing urban attire.)

JUDITH: I'd like to present our writers from Britain, Henry James and Oscar Wilde, who come with—

OSCAR: With letters, occasional bunches of outrageous flowers—

HENRY: I didn't know a painter…could make me levitate.

(A bodily look goes from the men to JOHN, who turns away clumsily.)

JOHN: I need to work.

OSCAR: I didn't know you had to struggle. I thought you just appeared.

HENRY: Your portraits are delicious!

OSCAR: I could eat them. And you're gorgeous! If you go into a city and they don't adore that outfit, get the hell out. During my last term at Oxford, I declared, "Reformation of dress is of far greater importance than reformation of religion." Tight lacing is bad both from the health and aesthetic points of view. A small waist gives no air of grace but exaggerates the width of the shoulders and hips. My motto is it's stupid to suffer for beauty. Why not suspend dresses from the shoulders and obviate the need for a corset? We all have these tummies. I look in the mirror and made my peace with it. Now I don't see it anymore.

JOHN: Why are you here?

OSCAR: We like beautiful things, being beautiful things ourselves.

JOHN: Seriously.

OSCAR: I don't like these gawking groups that watch plays and hang out at dinner.

HENRY: But anyone who is anybody passes through Dr. Pozzi's Palace of Creativity.

OSCAR: I'm sure your cardiologist would never approve of what we do. *(Rolls his eyes.)* We gain some on the merry-go-round and lose some on the swings.

JOHN: I need to get back to work.

OSCAR: *(To HENRY.)* I like him so much—

JOHN: Are you finished? To me, when a person takes my time, they steal my soul. Since I'm not famous, you don't value that. It's only by the sheer excellence of what I do, I can say I'm a painter. I'm damned pleased when my work gets hung. But then I've got to worry if anyone will buy it and like it. So to expand my appeal, I saturate myself with interesting people and double the amount of sittings.

OSCAR: Is he or isn't he?

HENRY: *(To OSCAR.)* I don't know why anyone would want to be androgynous.

OSCAR: Declare one side or the other. And—Hire a bodyguard at once.

HENRY: Paris is not a welcoming place. If you're from Philadelphia.

OSCAR: You'll get slapped with one hand and crowned with the other.

HENRY: Come to London.

JOHN: I know no one there.

OSCAR: Strangers are friends you haven't met.

HENRY: Rich Brits love money but they do squander it from time to time

SISTER: Wait! Could I have your autographs?

OSCAR: No. You've already got too much paper in your house. I'm afraid you'll die tragically. And John, if you end up having a tawdry affair with Amelie, would you call me at once. *(Kisses AMELIE'S hand.)* You can always tell a bracelet by its garnets and a house by its finials. *(Shakes JOHN's hand.)* I'll never touch your finial because it's next to your switch.

(HENRY and OSCAR exit. SISTER and JUDITH follow them out.)

SCENE SEVEN

(Later. JOHN and Amelie look through a clothes trunk.)

JOHN: Where shall we begin?

AMELIE: With the buttons. As a child, I wore gold buttons. See, here's my little white dresses from our plantation.

JOHN: Some things shouldn't be saved. You have to say it's finished.

AMELIE: Right. If you're living far from New Orleans, you can't miss it. When I broke through some of the really hard memories, I sobbed for days. All these thoughts hurried inside me. I know how silly it sounds, especially when one lives in Paris, but I still see the images of New Orleans and can't focus on what has happened there. I grew up on a plantation outside New Orleans. It was just a part of my life and then out of nowhere, it was gone. The Civil War took it all, the mansions, the money, the men. I haven't been back to the city since the war. I cannot look. I fear I shall never return. I know New Orleans can be rebuilt and remade into a thriving city. But it probably will not happen in my lifetime, and I wonder if the new world that replaces the old will be worthy of its ancestor. *(Takes liquor.)*

JOHN: Why are you drinking?

AMELIE: Because there's nothing wrong with it.

JOHN: You've got to snip negative thoughts.

AMELIE: I can't enjoy where I'm living because I'm too busy taking care of where I was.

JOHN: You have to develop something in you which allows you to grieve—

AMELIE: I can always go back to New Orleans.

JOHN: But not now.

AMELIE: Mama and I have lawyers after us. Greedy brothers and—

JOHN: Try on the white dress.

AMELIE: All desperate after the Civil War. I knew at eight years old I'd never have the answers to their questions. I remember looking in the mirror saying that.

JOHN: You have to garner your strength and face your –

AMELIE: After the acclaim of the portrait I'll do that.

JOHN: When you return "the most beautiful woman in Paris," you'll take New Orleans back.

AMELIE: Now it's filled with ghosts that could penetrate me.

JOHN: Right now they could. Mmmmm…I don't like the dress.

AMELIE: When I think about never going back to New Orleans, I could bawl. That city that I loved so well is not in my world anymore. I could walk backwards there with my eyes closed. It's a big little town. I never thought I'd rupture with New Orleans in such a violent way. I've no friends left there. They all picked up and left. Some did not have much change to where they lived, their mansions defied their poverty, but they could not bear being there any longer. There were too many threats to their lives. Whatever one may have thought about New Orleans, it was truly unique. It was one of those places where if you had been transported by fairies and you woke up, within ten minutes, without asking a soul, you'd know where you were. Sometimes out of the blue, I'm overcome with homesickness. I don't know where it comes from—Doc says maybe I act sad to control others.

JOHN: You like to see yourself surrounded by love.

AMELIE: Maybe. You prefer the blue shawl?

JOHN: You should feel good about yourself without anyone else.

AMELIE: That's a weakness to need people…

JOHN: Try the pink cape. I'd think you'd take joy from your looks.

(SHE changes before him.)

AMELIE: Beauty rarely gives me enough. Men take me from the box, unwrap the tissue, let me out, wrap me up, put me back in the box.

JOHN: Try another dress.

AMELIE: How will you choose?

JOHN: The composition must be right for your soul. *(Pause)* I'm happier when I come here than I was at the studio where I studied. Whenever I went there, someone threw a lance at my stomach. Then I sensed arrows coming before I walked in. I can't return there honorably, because it's steered by cowards. I survived, because I don't need praise. We're too American to be totally admired.

AMELIE: The portrait will change that.

JOHN: Most people have chiseled success from a bedrock of pain.

AMELIE: If you were to claim your laurels—

JOHN: I'd go find passionate work elsewhere.

AMELIE: But they're hanging you at the Salon.

JOHN: Your beauty, not my name.

AMELIE: For now. When you started sketching me, the voice said— "Things will change." I've progressed more in four days than I have in twenty years. I can make my own decisions. I'm not always asking others to tell the good little girl what to do.

JOHN: You did that?

AMELIE: Relationships were too confusing

JOHN: Men love you because you shine gentleness and they want to experience that.

AMELIE: I like it when we're alone.

JOHN: Do you?

AMELIE: This is my prayer, so you can take as long as you want to answer. Come to my chateau in Brittany. It's the first place I went to by myself. There's a spacious walled park filled with oak trees. In the country, the mind has more juice. You can listen to the crickets, watch the flowers grow, and allow yourself the pleasure of overwork.

JOHN: Fine. I did so much not painting this week, I'm exhausted.

(THEY kiss.)

Scene Eight

(2 months later: Amelie's chateau, Les Chenes Paramé, Brittany. Someone plays on a distant piano. Lights up on JOHN and AMELIE kissing; after lovemaking, he puts his hand on her round stomach –"Our baby is so happy." He wraps her in a sheet to paint her. DOCTOR POZZI arrives.)

JOHN: Doc, what a...surprise!

DOCTOR: Lovely house. Old Paris green. Walls of light and windows.

AMELIE: It's a big house to have nobody in.

JOHN: Turn to me.

AMELIE: We sit in a different chair to eat each night. These chairs belong to me, and I want to enjoy each one.

DOCTOR: Have you finished the painting?

AMELIE: John went too far one way, and he's working his way back.

DOCTOR: Where is—your husband?

AMELIE: Mexico. We like seeing him once a month.

DOCTOR: Enjoy your independence.

AMELIE: I'll be in a cage soon enough.

DOCTOR: *(Trying to kiss her.)* Don't I rate a kiss?

AMELIE: John dislikes when I leave my pose.

DOCTOR: How precious; the model is so devoted.

JOHN: You're being funny?

DOCTOR: No, I'm being mean.

DOCTOR: Excuse us—

JOHN: *(Bitterly.)* I'd prefer not to.

(JOHN leaves. SHE collapses on a bed.)

AMELIE: Well, what do you think?

DOCTOR: I've multiple personalities, and none of them like him.

AMELIE: You're jealous.

DOCTOR: John is macho and prissy, traits that make a man obnoxious.

AMELIE: He's acrid, true—

DOCTOR: Bourgeois at best. The middle class is on top of all this molten lava of hatred.

ROSARY HARTEL O'NEILL

AMELIE: I let him go by me like bad weather. As soon as we met, it was not a question of if, it was a question of where... These Capricorn men can be so difficult. And there is definitely a lot of lesson stuff in Capricorn Alpha males for me! All three of the really important men in my life...Capricorn! And I'm an Aquarius Rising, which is almost the same as being a Capricorn myself. Inevitable minor clashes. So...we'll see if John is mellow enough, or if he chooses to pout...I hope not. I go crazy without him...and truth to tell, he without me, 'cause when he is pouting I get all his erotic energy in the brief before bed/getting up personal time he allows himself—yes, it comes down to how he deals with painting...and that's fine...then his family...and that's a habit, and... By the end of the day, his 6:30 a.m. to 11:30 p.m. days!...he can hardly relax...so it takes a bit of doing to chisel that open. I'm utterly clear he loves me...and trusts me...but his pace when painting is different than mine, and it frustrates him.

DOCTOR: You can't quit your obligations.

AMELIE: I tried to tell him but—You have no idea the sacrifices he makes—

DOCTOR: I've tickets to the ballet...

AMELIE: Isolation is required—

DOCTOR: People will forget you!

AMELIE: When John paints best, he feels purged—

DOCTOR: Painters act superior because they spent the day in contemplation.

AMELIE: They are superior.

DOCTOR: The man's a parasite.

AMELIE: A recluse, painting eighteen hours a day.

DOCTOR: I've bought portraits from his type and once they had me, they bloody screwed me.

AMELIE: You don't enjoy much of what artists offer, because—I'm not criticizing—you dislike contemplation.

DOCTOR: I've the biggest art collection in Paris.

AMELIE: With John, I feel totally alive. It's exciting to be in a place where things are birthing.

DOCTOR: Have you told him about the pregnancy?

AMELIE: *(Dreamily.)* This portrait is my way to become the person I'm meant to be.

DOCTOR: If something happens with this—

AMELIE: *(Drinks from a small vial.)* John's like the astrologer exploring my world with a telescope. He wishes to know who I am fully. He sees deep inside my beauty and says I'm an enchantress. *(Drinks more.)* Somehow, through the portrait we both live more profoundly.

DOCTOR: *(Takes the vial.)* How much arsenic have you been taking?

AMELIE: Enough to turn lavender without killing myself.

DOCTOR: Ye gods!

AMELIE: Peacocks eat poison to make their tails bright.

DOCTOR: You need to be conservative within the confines of your eccentricities.

AMELIE: A little arsenic is like having foreplay without the act.

DOCTOR: When will you tell John about the baby?

AMELIE: He knows. John is very attached, and that's not a bad thing.

DOCTOR: *(Puts a hand on her stomach.)* You're starting to deform.

AMELIE: Tighten my corset.

(HE dresses her and tightens the corset.)

DOCTOR: The most beautiful woman can't be fat.

AMELIE: Ooh, I'll squeeze in. I won't add an inch.

DOCTOR: That's my girl. Does this hurt?

AMELIE: No, pull more. *(SHE grits her teeth in pain.)* I don't know how to function as a mother. I've gotten rid of so many people, I feel like a dead person. A child can be quiet and dumb and still get her way. But can a mother?

DOCTOR: Kiss me.

AMELIE: Not now.

DOCTOR: Oh no, am I the ex-boyfriend?

AMELILE: I have no strength—

DOCTOR: Who knows if the painting will be worth hanging?

AMELIE: I'm going to purchase it for thousands of dollars.

DOCTOR: No. You've fallen into the vortex of flattery. I'm lucky I've never been that tempted. Has John decided on the pose? No? That's dire. You've boxed yourself into such a black corner. All you can do is cut your way out the backside. You'll have to take whatever he gives you now.

AMELIE: I can't waste time with you.

DOCTOR: You said beneath my coat I had wings—

AMELIE: If I need you for something, I'll tell you. If I don't...tell you. I don't need you...for whatever you were...hoping I would...

DOCTOR: How much have you been drinking?

AMELIE: I don't mind...getting drunk on good champagne but I don't want to— *(DOCTOR yanks her corset.)* My God. You're hurting me. Stop! (Amelie has violent cramps.) Mercy. Oh no. Help.

(JOHN walks in, pulls the DOCTOR and AMELIE apart.)

JOHN: Are you hurt?

AMELIE: Oh! I'm –

DOCTOR: Bleeding.

JOHN: Oh, no!

AMELIE: It's awful. The pain. Oh Lord!

JOHN: You're turning blue.

DOCTOR: She's hemorrhaging, fool.

AMELIE: I'm giving birth to a pure viper.

DOCTOR: Quiet.

AMELIE: *(Screams at the doctor.)* Like you.

JOHN: What's wrong?

DOCTOR: Help! Lift her to the bed.

JOHN: She's having a…

DOCTOR: My baby!

CURTAIN

ACT TWO
SCENE ONE

(The chateau, Brittany. Two days later.)

(JOHN paces. Wailing offstage. JUDITH and SISTER enter.)

SISTER: I brought you paints.

JUDITH: Doc's giving Amelie a— He's cutting off his appendage, as he calls it. She acts sad but inside she is saying, "Yes."

SISTER: They pretended the baby was yours.

(SISTER runs out.)

JOHN: *(Looks about.)* Where's my suitcase?

JUDITH: They're killing it, but it wasn't yours.

JOHN: I get a few arrows in me and I fly. Otherwise they'll keep shooting at me.

SOUND: More offstage wailing.

JUDITH: You can't leave!

JOHN: I've had the dogs of prey the last two days.

JUDITH: The Salon's coming up.

JOHN: I was naïve and I had my soul crushed and –

JUDITH: You didn't see Amelie the way she was, but the way you were.

JOHN: I walked into wolves naked and let them chew –

JUDITH: The woman was duplicitous.

JOHN: *(HE keeps packing.)* I never had a girl because deep inside I knew the pain involved. I had so much in my life, passion for my work, my friends, family.

JUDITH: If I thought I was losing you, I would fight for you. I would walk through fire for you.

JOHN: Amelie was –.

JUDITH: The reason we get distraught when our lover goes, we think God has left; but God hasn't left, a human being has. Paint.

JOHN: I can't bludgeon myself to do it.

JUDITH: Feeling will come out your brush and flood onto the canvas.

JOHN: I can't find a satisfactory pose. I sketched her seated with her head raised, then lowered, playing the piano. I did a watercolor of her with a book and a brisk oil of her holding champagne. I drew her kneeling on a sofa looking out the window. Nothing worked. The only way to redeem her portrait is dynamite…

JUDITH: Even if Amelie loved you, she could die—

JOHN: When the doctor took her off, I knew it'd never be the same. Suddenly she's with this –

SOUND: *More screaming. SISTER runs in.*

SISTER: She's been trying to kill the baby.

JOHN: God.

SISTER: Three of Mother's babies died, but she wanted them to live.

SOUND: Wailing offstage.

JUDITH: Paint Amelie at my chateau next door.

JOHN: Other women I can draw as a clinician, but Amelie I could only do as a dreamer.

JUDITH: Don't quit.

JOHN: Her portrait is about something that didn't happen.

JUDITH: Well, draw something that did.

JOHN: Most of us can only let so much go at a time. It's a terrifying process to let the old life go and experience something you've no idea where it is going to take you.

JUDITH: Most women are existing, not living. Reflect how you feel now.

SCENE TWO

(The chateau, moments later.)

(JOHN walks to a window. AMELIE enters.)

JOHN: Amelie!

AMELIE: How did you know?

JOHN: I was used by girls when I was younger and discarded.

JUDITH: *(To AMELIE.)* Lie down.

SISTER: *(To AMELIE.)* Don't walk.

(JUDITH and SISTER exit.)

AMELIE: Forgive me, John. The sun is coming up over the horizon, a red orb.

JOHN: You get this love experience from nature.

AMELIE: From you.

JOHN: Interesting artists are distractions.

AMELIE: You glided into my life like some god man.

JOHN: They come, they go.

AMELIE: And when I thought you loved me—I merged with you and I was—happy.

GHOSTS OF NEW ORLEANS

JOHN: That wasn't the real you. That was a performance: it was my suit, the haircut, the lighting. I talked, and reality and fantasy merged—

AMELIE: You loved it here. Being in the beauty.

JOHN: Because you are in my world everywhere. When you suffer, I can't sleep. I go to the shore and listen to the waves crashing, until the screeching seagulls wake me up. When you are blue, I ruminate…three-hundred-sixty thought-degree circles. I shouldn't paint this, do that. Now I want to be sad. I want to walk with a chip on my shoulder. Because no one cares about me.

AMELIE: You worry all the time?

JOHN: Now I use evidence. It's called implication, evidence and extrapolation.

AMELIE: Once in a while, you have done something wrong. So when you feel depressed—

JOHN: I'll dispute it and choose to get out of it.

AMELIE: Maybe I haven't gone completely—my body still works. Thank God.

JOHN: How could you kill the –

AMELIE: It was damaged. Not a person. My body rejected it.

JOHN: A baby can't defend itself because it's dead—

AMELIE: My chemistry wasn't there to handle it.

JOHN: It can't come back, say you did it wrong.

AMELIE: Doctor says our genes are programmed for grim consequences.

JOHN: Do I have a gene for insanity?

AMELIE: Don't feel bad. I wasn't a mother. I was someone who was transformed into—I'd long since departed to some far-away place. There was no growing in me, just beautiful emptiness…I'm not supposed to think of the baby, and you shouldn't either.

JOHN: Why is it the male should not be soft and the female can be ruthless, cold-hearted, downright mean?

AMELIE: Because the female controls that power.

JOHN: You are shrewd, although you like to present yourself as fluff and mirrors.

AMELIE: I can barely speak when I look at you. Even now, miserable and bleeding, all I want to do is hold you naked… *(She drinks.)* I love watching the champagne bubble. It's like spirits dancing across water; now it's sparkling.

JOHN: Is that why you indulge yourself, to wipe that sorry feeling out?

AMELIE: Once you've had morphine, alcohol is just a garnish. *(Quietly to JOHN.)* You want some?

JOHN: I suppose the baby died a horrible neglected death.

AMELIE: My body self-destructed. Our bodies tell us what to do, if our minds won't. *(Long pause. SHE drinks.)* Till today, the doctor hadn't offered to sponsor my portrait. Every so often he sent out a feeler, tested the waters. Paris is not just a mecca for beauties and painters, but also for arts patrons eager for fame. It's hard for him to give you glory like that. Now he feels sorry for me and he'll help. Not think of—Oh, John. Won't you finish the portrait —

JOHN: Lots of portraits were painted that shouldn't have been. Lots of canvas bleached in vain.

AMELIE:—now we know it will be well placed? Paint me—in this. I feel the need for the quiet of black.

JOHN: It's a treacherous gown.

AMELIE: Waiting for an enchantress. Half ghost, half cat! I used you. Sorry. I know what you feel even if I can't change it. Forget about me; think about the portrait. It could launch your career. I'll get it featured in the best room in that Salon. People will worship your talent. Oh, let me. I know how to do this. When you hear the rush of that opening crowd, you'll forgive me.

JOHN: I need to do something dreadful to that dress. Rip off a strap. Now twist in profile, hold that. I think I've got something. Now talk ...about ...romance.

(HE starts to draw her.)

AMELIE: For good intimate relations you have to have champagne or rudimentary love. A fleeting feeling—crystallized through the fire of experience. I like the release flashes that go off in my brain; I also like to hear a man scream. It makes me feel I've a purpose, to help him become free.

JOHN: I never felt free.

AMELIE: You should let yourself go. Tie in with nature from millions of years ago. If you give up all the barriers and feel your primeval rushes, you are going to release good and hard.

JOHN: Stand by that table. *(Stammers.)* I will draw you with my brush...beginning with the shadows...and gradually evolving...your profile from the background by means...of large, loose volumes of shade, half-tones...of light, refinements of form, finally...bringing the masses of light...and shade closer together, and assembling your true figure.

AMELIE: Say you love me, John; say it now. You love me! Love me.

SCENE THREE

(Dr. Pozzi's Salon; CLAUDE and the DOCTOR. enter)

DOCTOR: How could he paint her like that? Unattainable beauty reduced to narcissism.

CLAUDE: Even so, I admire it.

DOCTOR: Part of him hated her.

CLAUDE: The portrait is a retreat from previous submissions.

DOCTOR: His colors are somber, his brushwork too finished, and his conception simplistic and unflattering.

CLAUDE: You're sleeping with her again. Ah! The highest trades are in bed.

DOCTOR: After he came back to Paris, he went back into—

CLAUDE: Sargent is going to follow his instincts and damn the world.

DOCTOR: I tried to reason with him over dinner. Impossible.

CLAUDE: He refuses to rein in his style.

DOCTOR: The man steals all his images.

CLAUDE: Yes, but he steals with genius. Sargent's rise has been a magnificent steady –

DOCTOR: This is where your little locomotive runs off the track— Manet's "Olympe" was knifed because he painted a real woman nude. Sargent is headed for disaster—If he doesn't tone down the painting.

CLAUDE: Should we warn him?

DOCTOR: Go to maids' quarters in an eighth-floor walk-up?

CLAUDE: I'll go alone.

DOCTOR: Actually, bad reviews could help you. Surely it troubles you his name is mentioned twice as much as yours. John could win your government stipend. Why not mentor him in landscapes?

CLAUDE: He doesn't want to change.

DOCTOR: Aren't you on the steering committee?

CLAUDE: I can't let personal feelings interfere with—

DOCTOR: I'm not asking you to vote against the portrait. I'm saying you could talk to a few people. Tell them about—well, colleagues find him vitriolic. Once, resenting a silence, he slashed a canvas with a sword and roared out of the studio.

CLAUDE: Still, he has the appeal of a romantic mystery. From his arrival, he provided a spectacle of energy unleashed.

DOCTOR: Oh no, here he comes.

(JOHN enters.)

JOHN: Have you seen my portrait?

CLAUDE: I've studied it.

JOHN: Good. I don't feel a painting lives till my friends view it.

CLAUDE: It's clear you admire Tintoretto.

JOHN: I was dissatisfied and dashed some pink over the—

DOCTOR: Gloomy background.

JOHN: Vast improvement, don't you agree?

CLAUDE: Yes—I mean, perhaps.

JOHN: I played down the urge to localize my sitter.

DOCTOR: But why give the starring role to clothes?

JOHN: What do you mean?

DOCTOR: And such colors?

CLAUDE: Raisin and claret-soaked plum.

DOCTOR: Were you thinking of a fruit compote?

JOHN: Why the slap?

DOCTOR: Let's hope the portrait expands your clientele beyond expatriate Americans.

JOHN: Amelie's gotten me the biggest room in the Salon. The painting will be hung at eye level. People will see how focused we Americans can be. If the portrait is successful critics won't control which paintings get seen and which get skied.

DOCTOR: No one will like her this way.

JOHN: Fine. It's the way she was, wanting to be loved, trail-blazing toward it. The black goddess is what she became.

Scene Four

(The Awards Ceremony, Dr. Pozzi's Salon, later. CLAUDE, backed by the DOCTOR, stands at a podium. AMELIE, JOHN, SARAH, SISTER, JUDITH, OSCAR, HENRY and stand-ins WAGNER and HUGO fill the audience. JUDITH and SISTER run to the podium.)

JUDITH: You people are a testament to the importance of John's talent.

JOHN: *(To SISTER.)* I've got the flies.

SISTER: We're moving into the A crowd.

AMELIE: I can't get enough exposure.

DOCTOR: You lap it up like chocolate. *(Squeezes AMELIE's arm.)* Right?

CLAUDE: Come here, John. Tell us about your work. Ladies and gents. John Singer Sargent.

JOHN: I start every morning, painting hours at a time. My plan is to make a complete sketch, which dries so rapidly that the next morning I might paint another study over it. I want to paint what my eye sees, not what my mind instructs me to see.

CLAUDE: You may recall Sargent's portrait of Professor Duran provoked much interest. Today's work was judged by forty critics—including the amazingly decadent, desperate but still whimsical Oscar Wilde and Henry James.

OSCAR: We're here. We're wanting—

HENRY: And we're ready to be amazed.

CLAUDE: Our master of ceremonies is Dr. Sam Pozzi. To continue, Sargent strides deep into that territory called influence. He has set out on the trail of light, of strong contrast. *(Pause)* Envelopes require someone to open them, and Miss Bernhardt's hands are it.

SARAH: Sarah!

(CLAUDE passes her an envelope, which she reads.)

SARAH: *(Cont.)* Oh my! "The painting looks monstrous and decomposed? Indecent!"

DOCTOR: *(Taking over.)* "He has placed the subject in a sorry dark pool."

JOHN: It's just one notice—

DOCTOR: "People find the portrait atrocious."

OSCAR: *(Calls out.)* For me it is a perfect painting.

DOCTOR: "Sargent has made Mme. Gautreau horrible in daylight." *(Reads more.)* "He paints her ears rose, her hair mahogany; her eyebrows in dark thick lines, her white shoulders disgust us." *(Reads.)* "The fallen strap reeks of decadence."

(Sounds of heckling. Doctor defers notices to CLAUDE.)

CLAUDE: *(Reads.)* "The profile is pointed, the eye microscopic!"

AMELIE: I'll die of shame.

CLAUDE: "The right arm lacks articulation, the hand is deboned."

AMELIE: Let's go, John—

JOHN: I want to hear it.

CLAUDE: *(Reads.)* "Detestable! Boring! Monstrous! 'Madame X' lacks technique."*(Sounds of people rushing.)* Order! *(Louder noises.)* Ladies and gentlemen.

(JOHN goes to leave. AMELIE, SARAH, and the DOCTOR stop him.)

DOCTOR: Are you sick?

JOHN: You don't have to be sick to die.

CLAUDE: You owe Amelie a public apology.

JOHN: *(Removes sword.)* Artists have to be vigilant and have weapons. You critics live in the dirt, the muck, and we have to let you know we're going to stand up to you and kill you. But artists shouldn't have to battle. We shouldn't have to be brutes to survive. Oh yeah, it's OK, mock my painting. I'm fine.

DOCTOR: Take down your portrait.

JOHN: No.

DOCTOR: You'll have to fight me.

JOHN: So!

JUDITH: *(To JOHN.)* You'll hurt your hands!

JOHN: Fine. My portrait stays in Room 31, at the Salon Competition!

DOCTOR: I say it comes down.

JOHN: You'd like to squash me along with the hundreds of artists you've erased—creeping up to their attics, embracing failure in a bottle. I want to tell the painters s in Paris, the Americans, the Mongoloids, the Turks, that for every 3000 artists you critics level, they'll be one John Singer Sargent who raises his painting on the pedestal and says "It's not garbage; it's great.

(JOHN and DOCTOR fight. DOCTOR pulls out a knife. JOHN shoves him backs, leaves.)

JOHN: Move, or I'll bludgeon you to death!

LIGHT: *Blackout.*

SCENE FIVE

(JUDITH, SISTER, OSCAR, HENRY at a graveyard in London.)

HENRY: I know what the controversy was in Paris. It's all about the ripped strap on her dress, the violated attire. We have to do something.

OSCAR: Why is that so shocking?

HENRY: John broke a primal rule in portraits – never defile a client.

JUDITH: We can't let him give up hope and…

OSCAR: …go sit in some godforsaken London graveyard.

JUDITH: I thought he was staying with you.

SISTER: He's humiliated, can't face anybody.

HENRY: It's discouraging to see promising artists do themselves in.

SISTER: I know. I know! Some see their faculties going and blow their heads off. Others tie stones to themselves and drown. Some drink themselves to death. Some famous ones whose lives are unspeakable choke to death on drugs, and sleep in their own feces.

HENRY: Surely there are critics like me who appreciate the painting.

OSCAR: The swanlike, pre-Raphaelite dress.

JUDITH: Bad reviews can't last more than three weeks in the public mind.

SISTER: The portrait is still up.

JUDITH: More critics can review it.

HENRY: The curiosity factor is on our side.

JUDITH: We must contact other critics.

HENRY: How about the London Gazette?

JUDITH: Good. They only allow professionals to critique.

OSCAR: Because they don't feel students should be led by the blind.

SISTER: I know an art reviewer in Normandy.

OSCAR: I've an old lover in Brittany.

JUDITH: I once reviewed in Dublin.

HENRY: And I in London.

OSCAR: I've a close cousin in Scotland.

HENRY: If we create enough controversy, everyone will want to judge for themselves.

SISTER: Certainly some people do not like the doctor.

OSCAR: I'll contact his enemies.

HENRY: We will change the opinion of "Madame X."

JUDITH: One critic at a time.

Scene Six

(A graveyard, London. JOHN sits on a tomb, sketching. The DOCTOR enters in a heavy coat.)

DOCTOR: Why are you hiding out in London? You'll catch your death.

JOHN: The only thing I can control is myself and I've a tenuous hold on that.

DOCTOR: You're living on a grave?

JOHN: I sit on a different tomb to draw each day. Those tombs are unmarked and I want to enjoy each one.

DOCTOR: You are a road warrior. That's fascinating.

JOHN: I'm an alien. The Salon took away my claws. I've got to get my power back.

DOCTOR: John, I hope you don't mind if I polish my stick while we have a final talk.

JOHN: I do.

DOCTOR: *(Polishes pistol.)* Your eccentricity is causing questions in the legal department of the Salon. People are not sure who you are. When I agreed to sponsor your portrait, I thought it was just for you to hang it and avail yourself of some services, but you've gone too far. Hold back—maybe participate in one of the lectures. People know your work, they've seen your painting; don't be so eager to push it at others. Several people have come to me and asked me who you are, to be going to England like this. I certainly like your charm and enthusiasm for your work and I don't want you to lose that, but you should withdraw the portrait.

JOHN: You are a devious rat. Soon as you got with the Salon's Board of Directors, you voted down my painting. There are twice as many negative adjectives in the dictionary as positive ones. I cringe when I hear how you people talk. You are abusive; irrational –

DOCTOR: If you are going to attack, give me a day so I can get a crowd.

JOHN: Critics. Rather than develop your abilities, you are going to find ways to abort artists. We don't always know when it'll happen. You take away the artists who are outside your vision and promote losers. It's pre-Civil War management. "Bury the slaves in insults until they scream."

DOCTOR: Do you know whom you're fighting? Bernhardt, Wagner, Monet, Hugo—

JOHN: The weak never attack unless they have overwhelming numbers. It's a turf war. You all got together over coffee in an unspoken conspiracy against me. The way I dress, the way I act. You figured I was moving in. You smelled me a mile. You're a snake. Snakes merge with the leaves. Look like they are leaves until they move.

DOCTOR: (*Calls out.*) Sarah! Talk some sense into this moron.

(*SARAH enters. DOCTOR exits. JOHN hides behind a tomb.*)

SARAH: I don't know where you are. It's exciting that you're not to be found.

JOHN: The torture continues.

SARAH: Things here are quiet. People do not seem to be around you the way I expected.

JOHN: One tomb to the other. That's about it.

SARAH: The press flatly denounced Amelie's appearance! Nothing could be said worse than has been said in "Le Monde."

SARAH: So the best of the young professionals leaves France.

JOHN: They don't notice their shelves are bare because they have eaten everything and are fat.

SARAH: I don't like you, but you're the only one who can paint. You can't imprint these fools with standards if you don't come back. You were one of the lynch pins that kept the Salon exciting. So you're staying in England.

JOHN: Sometimes I go across into Ireland.

SARAH: Relocation takes a big emotional bite.

JOHN: I like it here—with my friends who don't know me. My parents never settled down. We lived in rented accommodations off season. "At home" meant unbracing climates; dull European towns, total isolation. We had no idea whom we might see from year to year. So I am undaunted by a new country.

SARAH: But to be alone for days, it stratifies, ossifies, hardens you. I still remember your pride as you accompanied...

JOHN: Amelie through the little Salon gate.

SARAH: Return to Paris—withdraw the portrait. The portrait means more to her than you. There you put all your talent, but she put all her fame. *(Pause)* The portrait had a line before it all week. I dodged behind doors to avoid friends who looked grave. I took Amelie to see it by the corridors. People jeered. All day it was one series of fierce discussions. In the afternoon the remarks became "Strangely shocking." Well, you're nothing till you're crucified. There's one thing about bad press: it drives roots into the ground and like a tooth, you have to yank them out. Amelie's prepared to discuss her purchase offer if you withdraw from the competition. Remove her portrait from the Salon. Amelie's not a nymph you can paint nude. Don't disgrace her with this character assassination. Let the Salon take the painting down.

(AMELIE enters. SARAH, exiting, calls to AMELIE.)

SARAH: *(Cont.)* Tell him how appalled you are!

AMELIE: You're isolating yourself. How poetic!

JOHN: You could do the same.

AMELIE: Can't you at least paint the strap back in? I'm so mortified—

JOHN: The portrait is realer than you. I painted with so much emotion, I could barely see.

AMELIE: I remember...

JOHN: I thought you liked it.

AMELIE: I did, do, but Pedro hates it. I can't give you any money for it. What will you do?

JOHN: I won't dope myself...

AMELIE: The main thing I did today was choose not to take a pill.

JOHN: Good.

AMELIE: Don't.

JOHN: I care.

AMELIE: I'm starting to sniffle. Sometimes we need to hear validation—My eye makeup is dripping— Because we die inside. I had to be able to cry again, and you got me to cry and I've cried continuously for days. I cried for all the years I've lost because I did not have the courage to be anything but be beautiful. You need to remind me that being true is what I like—

JOHN: You need to spend more time with good people.

AMELIE: But—

JOHN: When you do so, the world will open up.

AMELIE: How can I when I feel so shamed?

JOHN: Humiliation is—where most of us live.

AMELIE: I can't go though more pain…

JOHN: You've got to stop —

AMELIE: I want you to talk to me more, smile more; I don't want you running from me. When I'm alone, this kernel deep inside says something is missing. That's a new suffering. Being with you in the country released something. Your voice was like a little diary when I got up. It confirmed to me I was alive. I want to wake up every morning beside you—watching the breeze across the pond and the deer across the field. (Pause.) There is a place we could meet. I don't want to lose you.

JOHN: You saw I could stop it.

AMELIE: I go crazy without you and, truth to tell, I want you to take all my clothes off. Lie on top of me.

(SARAH enters with the mail and the doctor.)

DOCTOR: So much negative mail.

SARAH: One mistake in Paris, you're that mistake for life.

DOCTOR: To remove the portrait, the Salon needs this form notarized.

SARAH: Sign it. And rectify the situation..

JOHN: *(To AMELIE.)* The art world doesn't care about you or me.

SARAH: We're at the point all subtlety is gone. Short of clubbing John over the head, there's no shortcut.

DOCTOR: *(To JOHN.)* If you keep that portrait up, I will sue you. I'm your sponsor and—

JOHN: Viper! Somebody ought to defang you. *(Scoops up stones and throws them.)* Get out. All of you.

(The DOCTOR, SARAH, and AMELIE exit. OSCAR and HENRY enter.)

HENRY: Why are you throwing rocks?

JOHN: The activity calms me.

OSCAR: Come to the house. Judith's arrived.

HENRY: Some people are loyal. Oscar and I have attended all your shows gleeful a foreigner was outwitting Paris. I'm American, and Oscar's Irish, and we've succeeded as imports in London.

OSCAR: If you have charm, nothing else matters. If you don't have charm, nothing else matters.

(A sensual glimpse passes from OSCAR to JOHN, who turns awkwardly away.)

JOHN: Leave me be.

(Exits.)

HENRY: Shouldn't we talk to John? Try to convince him to—

OSCAR: Rule. With men who have a history of bachelorhood, you can't push them. You want them to take the time to value themselves.

HENRY: John has a lot going, so we need—

OSCAR: Sooner or later he'll figure out what he needs to give up to live here permanently with us. We spoiled him. Give him a chance to feel that was the honeymoon and now he can have a life in London. *(Using a feminine voice.)* "Yes, dear. Yes, dear." Say I love you with relative frequency. "Good night, dream of us." *(Pause)* The rest is the cold ruthless warning: stay true to your talent, stay clear-eyed about it.

HENRY: But shouldn't we ask him if he wants to settle permanently in London?

OSCAR: Never ask a man a question that requires him to give up himself to make you feel better.

HENRY: What do you mean?

OSCAR: Don't ask him a question you don't know what he will answer. Right. Remember, most men are hunters.

HENRY: It's so damn old-fashioned.

OSCAR: Evolutionary. John is out there and he has to win. If you push him into a corner, he is going to fight. It's not a thought pattern, it's an intuitive thing, and what comes out his mouth may be hurtful. If he says he is tired—

HENRY: Let him be?

OSCAR: Because that's his way. He hasn't worked it out yet, or he can't verbalize it yet. *(In a feminine voice.)* Just say, "You'll feel better. Paint tomorrow. We love you, good night."

HENRY: But I need to talk to him at length. John lives in loneliness. He doesn't see we're wayfarers too and wouldn't be jealous.

OSCAR: You are a writer. You like to spell things out. You are always analyzing emotions and context. Painters are, whatever their level of intelligence, very focused on their work, and only when they have done painting can they talk to us. At least the ones who are heterosexual. Most of them aren't verbal enough. Even the "sensitive" ones. I think it's a sexual thing but I don't want to be quoted on it. We have too many friends of different persuasions.

HENRY: But I want to tell him of our counter-attack.

OSCAR: Just swallow it. Recognize that the graveyard is a place that has meaning to him, and for the foreseeable future he needs to live here. We are still new in his life.

HENRY: Not that new—

OSCAR: Not as new to us. We make a commitment and we go full out. We are writers. We are trained to do that. Painters, basically, they want arm candy. That's nice. They want a model, not a problem. Partnerships are hard for painters of most generations, especially bachelors. They have great intimate relations. Let it ride. Don't press. Just keep your eyes open and be watchful. Don't press.

Scene Seven

(The graveyard. Later. JUDITH is onstage. OSCAR, JAMES, SARGENT enter.)

JOHN: The doctor and Amelie are suing me.

JUDITH: I feel your pain.

JOHN: They're afraid.

JUDITH: It's as if they stabbed me.

JOHN: Should I withdraw the painting?

JUDITH: You are a creative genius, and people are envious.

JOHN: I walked too far out.

JUDITH: You're aggressive and it grates on people. So what? They are evil people and you walked into their sandboxes. We artists have to carry a knife and be prepared to fight.

JOHN: I can't deal with the pomposity of the academy.

JUDITH: You have to watch for the feet that come out to trip you. When they see you climbing, they feel guilty so they knock your ladder over. You are living a courageous peril-filled life. When you are living like that, sweetie, you're up every morning and you are on it.

JOHN: I was thinking about painting in the missing strap.

JUDITH: Oh, my God. No!

JOHN: All the Salon would have to do is acknowledge some part of my work. I was a thoroughly committed student. A full day at Teach's atelier, four hours of life classes. There's a real need for someone good at the Salon and I'm not going to be there—

JUDITH: A lot of us are recovering young artists.

JOHN: I miss the known, the familiar, and friends. I've embraced these people for nine years.

JUDITH: They're in collusion against you.

JOHN: I want my old life back. Most of the time it was a safe routine.

JUDITH: Somebody is going to be sacrificed. They're going to throw a body in the fire—the one who's weakest. Stay away.

JOHN: And Amelie.

JUDITH: If it was just she and you, it could be different. But there's the doctor.

JOHN: He is a weak chunk.

JUDITH: Who got ahead because of his wife's railroad empire.

JUDITH: Get angry. Stay angry. Pray to your ancestors who had the courage to leave.

JOHN: But I have no money.

JUDITH: You know who you are—John Singer Sargent, and what you are capable of. *(Pause)* You are following the voice inside that remains unquenched despite repeated attempts to kill it. *(Pause)* You march relentlessly towards human potential, forgetting laziness permeates our condition. *(Pause)* Because of your strength - you become a target.

JOHN: What should I do?

JUDITH: Continue to make brave choices. Understand sadness will walk beside you. Move where inspiration takes you and release lassitude. *(Pause)* For you drive hominid evolution. Your force will echo through generations. Whether you are recognized is immaterial. *(Pause)* You live for others who want to be brave, but cannot, for the future of our race. *(Pause)* You must interact side by side with the devil—and not be baked in his power—rather outshine him by your actions. He will make you clearer—this is the true reason for evil in our world. *(Pause)* You will not fail...We won't let you. There is one intelligent soul who understands your purpose and if there is one, there are more.

JOHN: To know you're not defenseless, that your ship has guns.

JUDITH: You are descended from greatness—you must be great also.

Scene Eight

(Later. The graveyard—CLAUDE and JOHN enter.)

JOHN: Why a lawyer's office? Someone paying you off?

CLAUDE: Actually other members of the Salon felt badly about—

JOHN: Get to the point.

CLAUDE: Come back to the bohemians.

SOUND: A carriage passes, and bells ring.

JOHN: I don't like bells. You have that sound over there and you can't stop it. *(More bells.)* I knew when the portrait went up in Studio 31, the Salon and I were getting a divorce.

CLAUDE: You projected love on the portrait, so you think you're not loved. I can't support this portrait, but I support you.

JOHN: You're not reliable. There is no indication you're capable of loyalty.

CLAUDE: Can't you find peace in accepting our differences?

JOHN: No.

CLAUDE: You shouldn't have to function in exile.

JOHN: My whole life I lived in the wrong climate. Traveling with my family to off-season hotels—trying not to look indigent. It was a Diaspora. I was unmoored. I had no relationship with place. There was a harshness and necessarily so. I felt like a marionette.

CLAUDE: Still—if you love what you do, you have a companion inside your heart. We all miss you.

JOHN: In Paris there was a lot of pleasure in seeing the same faces. The class meant nothing. It was the everyday routine. 'Course schools are always asymmetrical. One likes one student more than the others, and it goes back and forth—keeping the balance. Still, as difficult as the studio was, I would rather have it in my life than gone.

CLAUDE: Come back before—

JOHN: I felt lucky to have you with me. You were stable and had threads to other people. You raised the talent level by entering the room. *(Pause)* And the Salon was like a modern-day palace. People don't live like that anymore. It was a gentle pathway to the kingdom of dreams.

CLAUDE: It certainly is.

JOHN: But it doesn't take long to kill something. Ambitions die young in the souls of people. People wonder why I stayed with that entry-level art school. And after a while I wonder too.

CLAUDE: Quite a few people believed in you. They still do. *(Pause)* The artists want you to stop this dreadful episode and accept a check from Amelie for five thousand dollars for the purchase and storage of the painting. All we want is to take it down.

JOHN: And if I don't comply?

CLAUDE: Let's not —

JOHN: Tell Amelie I own the portrait and will hang it as long as I please.

CLAUDE: Tell her yourself.

(JOHN starts to leave when AMELIE walks in shrouded in black. SHE is tense, fighting some inner demon. SHE carries a flask.)

JOHN: How are you?

AMELIE: Barely alive. Only the day has changed.

JOHN: That's it.

AMELIE: Today is Friday and no invitations. It's been Friday all day.

JOHN: Yes.

AMELIE: That's what happens when you get panned, the bad part, the only bad part. *(Offers him a drink from the flask.)*

JOHN: No, thanks.

AMELIE: There's so much backstabbing going on in Paris, you have to watch where you sit.

JOHN: And your doctor?

AMELIE: He runs the Salon without opposition, and when he gets some he kills it. You look tired.

JOHN: You know what's keeping me up at night. But during the day, I'm coming into my own. I've got everybody on the run, a lot of red faces. I'm going to lie low and let the other people shoot. Save my gunpowder till the end.

AMELIE: Oh, John. I came prepared to keep a tiny profile but I've changed my mind. I feel like I have a big black W on my chest that says, "Witch, witch." So I started hiding in the house. I cried enough tears to fill up a river and I stayed a coward and protected my feelings. Just stay a coward, I told myself, "If he cares for you, he will do something. He will send you a—" *(Offers him another drink.)*

JOHN: No, thanks.

AMELIE: *(Cont.)* Last night I dreamed we were married, and our ship was sailing to New Orleans. Like a tortoise, it was slipping into the sea, going into the deepest part. The fog spangled before us like a wonderful breath in midday. New Orleans is where I got my feelings from. The city has a human frame because I've loved it so long. We were different people there. I was strong and sweet. You were brilliant and so amazing and humble. Warmth had come through. Red had come through your hair. I saw it in the light. Everyone applauded as we walked down the street. I knew the roads. I just didn't know the names. Nothing was finished. I knew I needed to marry rich. I needed to marry possibility. You had made yourself special by not being able to be pinned down. We lived in the French Quarter, across from a Voodoo priestess' house, you see. It had no number, so I didn't know. And we talked quietly to each other late at night. Your words jeweled in my head. You said:

JOHN: Love strips us, makes us more whole.

AMELIE: I'll never go back in the doll box. I'll throw everything away outside.

JOHN: There's something about you. You are happiest when you're undressed.

AMELIE: So I've decided to empty my clothes allowance. Name your price and I'll buy the painting. This tormented image must be…temporarily removed.

LIGHTS: Lights fade.

(JOHN exits, paces before the graveyard.)

SCENE TEN

(The graveyard, London. JOHN and JUDITH enter the stage. SISTER enters, followed by HUGO and WAGNER with fanfare.)

SISTER: We came for the party.

JUDITH: It's not a party; it's a decadence festival.

JOHN: I can be as decadent as anyone.

OSCAR: I try to come late, so you'll know no matter what happens, I'll always be there.

SISTER: They're rescinding the lawsuit. The Parisians are retreating. Crowds have been demanding to see the portrait. Some bridge oceans, for two minutes before it. Your public wants the painting rejudged and put on permanent display.

JOHN: What?

JUDITH: You've conquered the British press.

JOHN: Holy—fantastic!

OSCAR: Those who don't have strong opinions, who are not locked up, may touch John's sweater.

HENRY: *(Enters, reading a paper.)* The London Gazette printed Oscar's review.

OSCAR: "Sargent is a master. Gautreau, a visionary beauty."

SISTER: Harper's says, "Sargent's portrait triumphs—"

JUDITH: You gave, gave, gave, and now you are going to get, get, get.

JOHN: Still more reviews?

HENRY: "Sargent's picture has a knock-down truth—"

OSCAR: That's what I wrote!

JOHN: *(Reads.)* "A wonderful rendering of life—"

OSCAR: "Beside him, his competitors stammer…"

JUDITH: I said that.

SISTER: This is just the beginning.

OSCAR: I don't want to talk about a revolution, but it's coming.

HENRY: Sargent is in training. His idea of painting is going to rebuild the world.

OSCAR: *(Reading.)* In eight hours, he was praised by thirty-nine critics. That's four-and-a-half an hour.

JUDITH: The Salon is getting you rejudged.

SISTER: After talking to the committee, I walked out with a spring in my step.

JOHN: You did what?

SISTER: Someone had to represent you to the jury. The public is causing a riot. Pounding the doors to Studio 31. They line up at dawn, sleep out front—Claiming the portrait has Italianate influence and sourcing it to the "Florence of your birth…" They say nature, living and breathing, is reflected in your portrait.

JOHN: It makes me feel good to hear the destruction going on.

JUDITH: They are calling you the greatest portrait painter of the Third Republic.

JOHN: I can't believe it.

SISTER: Commissions are pouring in from—

JUDITH: Museums all over the world.

OSCAR: The portrait's got a cult following

HENRY: Some are calling it "Madame X."

JOHN: I removed Amelie's name.

SISTER: You can lease the portrait.

JUDITH: And live off the proceeds—

SISTER: The rest of your life. What do you say?

HENRY AND OSCAR: Melancholy Dane.

JOHN: I guess it's the best painting I've ever done.

ALL: Scandal has brought you fame. *(All dance.)*

(AMELIE enters in the portrait pose and dress of MADAME X.)

AMELIE: My portrait didn't ruin John's career but it ruined mine. I had more paintings done by famous artists who tried to please, putting me in white, in cream. No portrait could rival John's. I tried to buy it back for phenomenal fees, using that as an excuse to see him again, but he never complied. From then on he was thrust in the vortex of his dazzling career. And I, the most beautiful girl in Paris, became the unknown MADAME X.

END OF PLAY

Beckett at
Greystones Bay

A PLAY IN ONE ACT

CHARACTERS

SAMUEL BECKETT— A writer, 27, smashing looking—
tall and athletic, broad shoulders, angular features.
Dishelveled clothes, grubby trousers, dirty raincoat several
sizes too large on a thin frame, which has a text in one
pocket and a bottle of stout in the other.

A CACOPHANY OF VOICES FROM HIS PAST
Loud, soft, haunting, brash:
Brother's voice
Father's voice
Mother's voice
Edna's voice
Cousin Margaret's voice

SETTING

Greystones Bay, Ireland, winter 1933. Dusk. The coastline
of Greystones is made of a large beach, rocky formations
and a bay which hosts a small harbor. SAM'S father is
buried in a nearby cemetery.

ROSARY HARTEL O'NEILL

SCENE ONE

(The action takes place in the mind of SAMUEL BECKETT with offstage voices from his past. These may be portrayed electronically or by actors. We're on a bleak stony beach. Winter. 1933. Dusk. Twilight shadows soak up the tattered sand. SAM limps in, carrying a pail with stones. His index finger is bandaged in gauze. HE conveys an impression of elegance, though threadbare. His short reddish-brown hair is brushed to the right, revealing an aquiline nose, and haunting eyes. HE has set up camp by a weather-worn chest. It contains bandage supplies, books, cigarettes, matches, and food. HE faces the audience, responding to images of people he envisions in the sea. When HE does so, faces appear on the rear scrim and/or actors representing these characters stand up in the audience. HE yells out.)

SAM: Go. I need to finish my book.

(Takes out a pencil and pad, writes. A whisper like a hoarse breeze. Lights dim. His father's image startles him.)

Oh! Is that…you?

SOUND: Sound of breathing.

It can't be, but it is. Sit. Goodness. Well.

SOUND: Sound of breeze.

I'm glad to see you. You look good. Your hands aren't swollen any more. Did you come because they want to psychoanalyze me?

SOUND: An eerie rustling sound.

What's that? When I came back from your death bed, I felt completely lost. I crawled onto this beach and lay here for hours, like a husk. I don't know who I am or what I'm doing. I'm living a dying thing. You have already cut me loose, but I refuse to let you go. Bad move. Mother's lonely. Brother's getting married. Your dog, Wolf, died. Mother cried for two days….

(FATHER'S voice: "You must go.")

You hated psychiatrists. If I can be out here in this place that you loved, I know my mind will clear up. I'll finish the book. Say something? Anything.

GHOSTS OF NEW ORLEANS

(A low, barely perceptible heartbeat and shallow breathing. FATHER'S voice: "Go.")

No.

SOUND: A clanging noise like a metal door closing. Ghost disappears.

Don't leave. Father.

(Fading wind. HE reaches toward the sky.)

To quote Keats: "I have clung
To nothing, loved a nothing, nothing seen
Or felt but a great dream. O I have been
Presumptuous against love—"

(Sees image of his BROTHER. Screech of seagulls.)

(BROTHER'S voice: "See the psychiatrist.")

Oh, Brother. I can't. When you write on the beach, its majesty gives you hope. It hits the eye with possibilities. You'll find more crazy people inland where they are not challenged. *(Breathes heavily.)* I don't speak much, but I can to prove my sanity.

(We hear FATHER'S voice, "Fight, fight, fight, and when you're tired fight some more.")

That's what Father said. He was strapped to the bed because even after that massive coronary, he tried to pull himself out. Father said I was a star and—

(Murmur of word "star" echoes on the breeze.)

"Everyone wants to shoot a star." Sam's voice, "Pow. Pow. Pow." But Father said—

(HE mumbles along with his FATHER'S voice: "What you don't have, you don't need.")

(Sound of "need" on the wind. SAM rummages for a match. To BROTHER.)

Smoking stiffens my courage. Other times I whistle. *(Takes out a tin whistle.*

Demonstrates.) I'm a writer, for God's sake. I can't let them burn that out of me. One day my name may mean something. Now it doesn't mean I need a big-city psychiatrist. Those people are outlawed in this country. That's right. They're forbidden to practice here. *(Angrily.)* You try to change someone; it's a big blow to his soul. I'm not sick. Artists work in solitary confinement because we fear people are completely mad. Course we could be crazy. *(Laughs.)* Time for a joke. A writer lived with his publicist until she quit doing publicity. Said she was tired of being number two. "No," he said. "My writing is number one, I'm number two, and you're number three."

(BROTHER'S voice: "Come inside.")

As you distance yourself, you see family as intrusions. Great artists have all proven to have deformities of their psychological profiles. Writers are powerful people, not group-oriented husks. A book may be beautiful but it's also gratification for control. I'm the heir to Dante, Proust, Shakespeare.

(Doubles over with a stomach cramp. BROTHER'S voice: "You're sick.")

True, I sleep with you to stop my panic, but it stops. *(Breathes quickly as if suffocating.)* Arrogance—keeps me writing through a chain of failures.

(BROTHER'S voice: "It's a shallow existence.")

No, it's defiant. The world is watching writers. The world needs hope. The homeless need us. The hungry need us. Those in prison need us. Our calling is high and holy. *(Pause.)* What is the universe asking you to give up to follow your path? *(Pause.)* Nothing? No one's called to the easy life. Nevertheless—

"There never lived a mortal man, who bent
His appetite beyond his natural sphere
But starved and died."

John Keats, my mentor, died in glory at 26.

(BROTHER'S voice: "Stop those thoughts.")

The mind's natural prey is itself. *(Takes books out of the chest.)* I take satisfaction from organizing my books. These baby steps give me pinpricks of joy. I always carry a book. It's my cross against life's vampires. *(Lifts book against the sky, paces.)* I can hold up the book and say stay away because this is the power I have. Every artwork is a prayer. The authentic poem, picture, song, they're prayers releasing hope in the onlooker like the response to a psalm. Priest: The word of the Lord. Respondent: Thanks be to God. Language lifts my soul. Words and I saved each other.

"When by my solitary heart I sit,
And hateful thoughts enwrap my soul in gloom:
Sweet Hope, ethereal balm upon me shed—"

(Rattle of breeze—To BROTHER.)

Mother doesn't like Keats—well, no matter. It takes a lot to kill my enthusiasm.

(SAM grinds cigarette, chews it, rummages for a match.)
(MOTHER'S voice: "Your suffering is mental, son.")

Night sweats, shudders, breathlessness…*(Gasps for air.)* even total paralysis, it's make-believe.

(MOTHER'S voice: "You should teach.")

Colleagues wheeze by to have a look, offer me a yawner course. I don't want to talk to stupid people. You have to work too hard. I resigned because, because…not because I was ill. *(Catching his breath.)* I need to be around brave people. *(Gasps.)* These students, they're tombstones. Nondescript. *(Feeling an abdominal pain.)* What could be more violent than killing a part of myself for money? I have to numb myself to that ambition that propelled me through all those years of intensity. If I'm going to do that I'll put a gun to my head and shoot it. *(Grabs his chest as if having palpitations.)*

Yes, Mother. I apologize. I don't want life to be about minor disputes. I took the job, didn't I? Once they had me, they bloody screwed me. There was such hatred of high standards; I walked through the campus like a target.

SOUND: Voices: indecipherable murmurings.

These men talk more than they think. Tiny thoughts after each huge diatribe.

SOUND: Voices: a crescendo of mumbling.

ROSARY HARTEL O'NEILL

I'm too overqualified. I don't mean that egotistically. I mean that factually. *(Pause.)* I'm a book on the shelf, insurance for the rare student.

(MOTHER'S voice: "Don't flatter yourself.")

(To MOTHER.)

If I give teaching time to writing—I could create something superior. "Every deep thinking mind tries to clarify thought. This is only perfectly attained in writing." (Says Schopenhauer)

(A clawing wind. HE tightens the jacket about him. BROTHER'S image reappears. To BROTHER.)

I don't blame Mother. To always think alone, it hardens you. *(HE gives up on the cigarette and tosses it.)* I'm not compulsive. For months, the only joy I had was my writing and part of me craves that. *(Pause.)* At some point, an artist is no longer a part of the university team, a member of the family, a half of a couple. You are ostracized or you self-ostracize. *(Pause.)* Writing became my safe harbor. Paper would receive my tears. Paper would hold all for me till I could figure it out. *(Pause.)* But I gave my soul to a cause that evaporated. All my writer friends stripped off their veneer and put on a suit and tie. *(Tightens fist.)* God, my finger hurts. *(Punches the air.)*

(BROTHER'S voice: "You were the heavyweight champion of school.")

Some things can't be fixed. If you're a psycho, they can't fix you. *(Pause.)* Time for a laugh. A minister told his congregation, "Next week I plan to preach about the sin of lying. To help you understand my sermon, I want you all to read Mark 17." The following Sunday as he prepared to deliver his sermon, the minister asked for a show of hands. He wanted to know how many had read Mark 17. Every hand went up. The minister smiled and said, "Mark has only 16 chapters. I will now proceed with my sermon on the sin of lying."

(SAM unwraps gauze and tends to a festering boil.)

The suffering of the skin is the caustic encrustation of feelings defied. I have to inspect my body every day for ticks, for toxicity.

(BROTHER'S voice: "Get straightened out and you'll write again.")

I haven't stopped writing. I've got a lot of attention out of being ill, so I'm always going to be doing that. *(A cold breeze. HE blows on his numb fingertips. Removes a shrimp shell.)* I studied whether a crustacean can suffer in my last story. I gave Mother three copies. *(Pause. Laughs.)* Not shells, books. No, I don't want my writing to offend. I'm not mocking anyone.

(HE unwinds long strips of gauze which drift in the breeze.)

(BROTHER'S voice: "See the psychiatrist.")

Back, Brother! You're in my light. My neck's oozing, my foot's purple, I think I'm bloody dead. I even have a—bump on my bottom. I can't sit long. But I can write standing up. *(HE exposes finger, neck, and foot wounds.)* Disappointing? I know.

(BROTHER'S voice: "All through life you kept in shape.")

Golf is still what I'm best at. Golf is not a team sport, like publishing. There's one person standing at that tee, one person lifting that club. When I swing, I imagine I'm powerful like Schopenhauer, the great pessimist. *(SAM puts a shell over his nose, changes his voice.)* He said, "Art is not like science, merely concerned with reasoning, but with one's soul. Each must count for what he is in reality." Schopenhauer—who received a reply that most of his first publication had been disposed of as waste paper. Later when I lance all my boils, I'll pretend I'm Keats, moving toward beauty.

"Beauty is truth, truth beauty—"

Surely you know that. I don't just collect quotes. I memorize books. Keats goes deep into depression, and that makes me feel better.

"I have been in love with easeful Death,
Called him soft names in many a mused rhyme,
To take into the air my quiet breath—"

There's been a rupture of everyone I was close to. Not you, no.

(HE blots a boil. Takes out a razor and fresh gauze.)

(BROTHER'S voice: "Mother's worried.")

Yes, I've read Mother's daily notes, her copies of the "Times," with her exhortations that I might earn money by writing for the obituary section. I'm not running from responsibility. I washed and shaved Father after his coronaries, even though he found it intolerable and started to cry. I changed the bedpans, and drove Mother to the hospital. *(HE blots another boil.)* In our family, she gets to hold the leash. She's the rigid one. I'm not. Oh no. This weepiness is humiliating. This panic-stricken stasis of Keats, crouched in a mossy thicket annulled, like a bee in sweetness, drowned with the fumes of poppies. *(Begins to lance finger.)* It's okay to cry as a purging tool like a spring rain. Ooh.

(BROTHER'S voice: "You want a pill?")

No! How much rest do we need to make up for a loss?

(BROTHER'S voice: "A blanket?")

I'm not cold. Smile, Brother. Only friends I want are…those who are profoundly happy.

(BROTHER'S voice: "Fresh bandages?")

Not so close. I realize there are absences I've had for years and I'd made no progress in reducing them even though I'd read and thought a great deal.

(SAM lifts a stone to the light.)

Look at that? Here, I'm back. Part of me that was empty is full again. I want to wake up every morning watching the breeze shimmering over stones. My eyes drift deep into the gray greens. I distract myself by counting the colors: the amber tans, pearl blues, gray browns. I'm falling in love with stones.

(SAM wanders off alone, stares out to sea. Tide laps in and out.)

I take stones home; lay them into the branches of trees. It's a pre-birth nostalgia to return to the mineral state…to an untouched spring that hasn't been contaminated. When I walk through a stony landscape I study the grays, the different contours. You can be in hell among the stones and still be happy. *(Picks up stones.)*

(BROTHER's voice: "Come back.")

GHOSTS OF NEW ORLEANS

I don't want to go inside, feel a loss of beauty. Be exposed to the illogical cowardly things that go on in there. The house never was mine. It will go like the tide sliding over stones. When I look at their silver sheen, I feel peace. I'm in touch with God when I'm here.

SOUND: *Wave sounds rip the water. Distant hum of a motor boat.*

Father loved little boats. Once we were out on rough waves and I panicked and he crawled over and slapped me. And I calmed down because Father never hit us.

(Sam collects stones. Distant song from the church. "I will raise him up. I will raise him up. I will raise him up on the last day.")

Another dirge from Saint Mary's. The man died of a heart attack. There's one more Mater Dolorosa.

(BROTHER's voice: "Ma wants you to be a pallbearer.")

I don't like being around concentrations of people. I have to be so vigilant; I consider it a waste of time. "The dark impression of that Nothing, which we fear like children, the darkness." Schopenhauer. How can I lift the casket, walk in the church, the man I knew so well, gone with no way of changing that? I'm not going to make choices, which are not in my interest. I choose to live in a gray world of low extremities.

(BROTHER's voice: "Be a pallbearer.")

Hang around the casket. Watch the lid close. Click. I can't walk behind the hearse.

SOUND: *Sound of tolling church bells. Recites.*

"Where are the songs of spring? Aw where are they?
Think not of them, thou hast thy music too,—
While barred clouds, bloom the soft-dying day."

SOUND: *Gulls caw. Speaks to BROTHER.*

When the house sells, I want only the piano and the green settee.

(Looks up, sees his father. To FATHER.)

Father, you needn't come home? In full regalia, hat, coat, polished shoes, I don't have high fever. You don't have to keep me in place, sit by, and tell a story.

(GHOST vanishes.)

Now that's the task of the radio, the record player. The role of the story-teller has evaporated.

(Tide laps out. BROTHER'S voice: "Treatment is the only hope.")

I can't submit. It'll kill my inspiration.

(BROTHER'S voice: "It'll unleash your artistic force.")
Sometimes I taste the excitement of being free. Other times...

(MOTHER speaks: "You're selfish, a hypochondriac.")

(To BROTHER.)

In my family my illness is a fantasy. *(Pause.)* I'm not angry, Brother. But I keep having to forgive the same people and that's hard, because every time I forgive them, they do another nasty thing to me. *(Rewraps finger.)* Not you, Brother. Mother. The town. It's never been a city that—. My stories always get axed. I'm too much a part of here to be considered anything special. People who don't write don't know the challenge to remain stable in a world that rejects what you do. When I see a publisher, I put on a face. *(Pause.)* I like reading in waiting rooms. I've got 15 different books I study about art, philosophy, psychology. I survive because I'm tenacious. *(Chuckles.)* No, that's not part of my control thing. If publishers think you're marshmallow, they'll shoot their whole quiver into you.

(BROTHER'S voice: "Relax.")

How can your work be valuable when everyone wants to rewrite it? You have to be vigilant. Let these cowards know that if they muck up your book, they're going to die. And let the cowards move on. Sometimes I don't want to do that...*(Looks up, points.)* like that bird that chased the others off. He held his ground. But human beings shouldn't have to act like buzzards. Oh yeah, it's OK, scrap me again. I'm fine. *(Winces.)* Ooh. I've got to lance this finger.

(BROTHER'S voice: "Rest.")

Sometimes I think of how it might be if I could sit back and smile at my life instead of having to rewrap a boil. *(Laughs.)*

SOUND: *Tolling church bells.*

(To BROTHER.)

Do I like sex? I am what you'd call a randy individual. R-A-N-D-Y. I don't like sex, I love it. Brothels, dirty books...everything. Ecstasy organs do give joy, but...chasing physical traits can lead you on the road to ruin. The crossroads for me was when I had perverts wanting to have sex with me. *(Laughs.)* After a while, lust goes away. Our main job is to reproduce, which I failed at.

"But put therein some drug designed
To banish woman from my mind." (Keats)

(BROTHER'S voice: "Why not quote yourself?")

Because Keats found an audience. *(Pause. Laughs.)* It's not inadequacy. I don't have to look up; I can look even with Keats. He was luckier, more focused. *(Pause.)* And yes, I would like a woman in my life.

SOUND: *"Ave Maria" peals from the church.*

(SAM collects stones.)

Any intellectual realizes another deeply-connected human being cushions you against adversity. It's like yeah, I could march into this battle alone, but if you stood with me, it'd be easier. As an artist, you look obsessively for a mate because you're so unmatched in every other area. I'd like someone who likes silence, nature, touch—but I can get by with a more peripheral relationship. I don't need constant interaction. Just...the promise. I was hoping I didn't have to work...that my dream woman would come to me.

(BROTHER'S voice: "You pick girls you can't have.")

You're either going to get stung by women or your conscience will sting you cause you're alone.

(BROTHER: "You held out till college.")

True. Before, I always looked away. My excuse was, "They aren't good enough for me." But I wasn't ready to bare my soul. "Dark violet eyes; Soft dimpled hands, white neck, and creamy breast—"

(BROTHER'S voice: "Edna.")

I held back love for so long, when Edna came before me, I couldn't stop my dazzled senses.

(BROTHER'S voice: "What a beauty.")

We met twice that first day, exchanging general, then more intimate views, and I considered this significant. I got hooked on the fantasy—for weeks the most important thing was the words we shared.

(To EDNA.)

You like novels, Edna? We could read Proust together.

(EDNA'S voice: "Marvelous.")

(Overlap of EDNA'S voice reading with SAM'S.)

"For a long time, I used to go to bed early. Sometimes when I had put out my candle, my eyes would close so quickly that—"

(To EDNA.)

You want to meet each day to read? Yes, oh yes.

(EDNA'S voice reading with him.)

"When a man is asleep, he has in a circle round him the chain of the hours, the sequence of the years, the order of the heavenly host."

(BROTHER'S voice: "Don't go back there.")

(The cackling of sea gulls. SAM scoops up pebbles. Hurls a stone. To BROTHER.)

Edna was living a life completely unknown to me, but I basked in the drivel of time I was given. Edna was not talkative, so I envisioned her profound; she was depressed, so I imagined her deep; sarcastic, so I found her witty. I didn't realize cruelty had seeped into her behavior. When we finally kissed, I became subsumed in her.

(BROTHER'S voice: "Don't torture yourself.")

She disappeared with my best friend to the country. Did they have sex? She and he knew each other before. *(Pause.)* For years, he and I were close, but soon as he got the chance—I don't want to go through life with a grudge, but people are astonishing. *(Pause.)* After that one trip Edna didn't want to see me again.

(EDNA'S voice: "I can't give you more than 15 minutes a day.")

When you fasten onto a wild horse, you should know how to ride it. I don't want to degrade her. She's not here to defend herself. "Only man causes pain without any further object than doing so. No animal ever tortures for the sake of torturing." (Schopenhauer) *(Chuckles.)* What about cats? Don't they torment their prey? *(Laughs.)* Only psychotic cats that've been civilized do that.

SOUND: Screeching of a wild bird.

Edna married him. And only Keats was there.

"He did not rave, he did not stare aghast,
For all those visions were o'ergone, and past—"

(BROTHER'S voice: "Ninety percent of women will steal your soul.")

Yes. It's in their genes to do that. I don't blame her. I've a dangerous tendency to fantasize. It probably comes from all the alcohol I took when I was younger....The books I read are clarifying meaning comes from what I give to the outside world. That truly bothers me.

SOUND: Wind rises, blowing papers about.

(HE laughs nervously.)

Perhaps I should move to a big city. Egg and bacon dripping on a counter,

ROSARY HARTEL O'NEILL

cigarette butts gumming the floor. Find safety in anonymity.

(BROTHER'S voice: "It's a cruel craft.")

Joke time: Three little boys were concerned because they couldn't get any-one to play with them. They decided it was because they hadn't been bap-tized and didn't go to Sunday school. So they went to the nearest church. Only the janitor was there. One said, "Nobody will play with us. Won't you baptize us?" "Sure," said the janitor. He took them into the bathroom and dunked their heads in the toilet bowl, one at a time. Then he said, "Now go out and play." When they got outside, dripping wet, one of them asked, "What religion are we?" The oldest said, "We're not Katlick, because they pour water on you. We're not Baplist because they dunk all of you." The littlest said, "Didn't you smell that water?" "Yes. What do you think that means?" "That means we're Pisscopalians."

SOUND: Bells toll in the distance.

(To BROTHER.)

Father's house and the beach, this was our world. (Smiles, shirks off the wind.) I glimpse flashes of us. I saw a boy on the beach, the image of you, and I realized, no, you're grown up. And I spotted this man playing ball and God, he looked like Father.

SOUND: The bells toll louder.

"Ask not for whom the bell tolls. It tolls for thee." (John Donne) (Looks at the sky.) Why was I set adrift?

(BROTHER'S voice: "Don't think so much." Followed by FATHER's voice: "You don't work with your brains, you'll work with your back.")

Father was a silent partner. He didn't need long discussions. He loved life. (Lifts up a piece of cardboard.) I kept the sign he put by his hospital bed. "Don't quit." Father could determine health by looking into our eyes. Talking to him was a validation I was sane. (Pause.) His last words were:

(FATHER'S's voice with SAM'S voice: "I'm proud of you getting that professor's post.")

SOUND: Tolling bells fade into the sea.

(To MOTHER.)

I don't want a tea biscuit or cheese. Food pours in, while the appetite stops. *(Laughs. Cautiously.)* Thanks for the basket, Mother. I'm sorry you had to go...to your room. *(Chuckles.)* No, I'm not disputing why. *(Pause.)* Yes, I'll give you my full attention. I'll put down the pencil. No, I admire your facing issues. Say something. We don't live in a telepathic world—

(MOTHER'S voice: "You're self-absorbed.")

I feel bad I'm not with you, but Brother's there. I'd like to give you what you want: money, grandchildren. But I can't rise at five to write before I drive you about. I avoid taking lunch so I won't get sidetracked in the kitchen. *(Angrily.)* Maybe you should get a dog, some furry creature to chase you. Sorry. Don't cry. *(Pause.)*Don't. I wish I hadn't said that. Before we were all so damn responsible, people didn't expect so much. I like to please you, but...You keep trying to fashion me into something that works for you, not me. *(Pause.)* I can't...come home. We choose a path because it seems easier at the time, and the time becomes the life.

(MOTHER: "You're an egomaniac.")

(Paces angrily.) Did throwing my books out make you happy? I can't live in jolly discomfort, putting aside my "fancy dreams." Cling to every cent as if it could save me. *(Pause.)* Now you're giving me the silent treatment. I, well, I won't sanctify money. I'll dope, numb or kill myself—first. *(Pause.)* Eventually I'm going to be gone from here because soon these books won't be enough. *(Pause.)* Don't walk away, Mother. Don't leave while I'm speaking. I've a sore throat. *(Pause.)* Mother.

(MOTHER'S voice: "Vile. Filth.")

(To MOTHER.)

I won't stop. How dare I ponder new ideas when you're stuck in repetition?

(MOTHER'S voice: "You said you'd make time for me.")

You dump my books in the trash.

ROSARY HARTEL O'NEILL

(BROTHER'S voice: "Leave her be.")

(To BROTHER.)

It's confusing when the bad people become good, and the good people become bad. She's shown nothing but hatred for my calling. Tardiness with messages. Hiding mail. Throwing my writing out.

(BROTHER'S voice: "Calm down. Come inside.")

I don't want to see that house. I want to remember it when Father was there. Home was Father, more than anything else.

"Turning and turning in the widening gyre
The falcon cannot hear the falconer,
Things fall apart, the center cannot hold.
More anarchy is tossed upon the world." (William Butler Yeats)

(Screeching of seagulls. SAM is suddenly paralyzed. Screams.)

Oh God.

(To BROTHER.)

I'm afraid to move. I'd like to plan my life, but there's intransigence now. I'm in the synapse, the gap between.

"Midway along the journey of our life,
I woke to find myself in some dark woods,
For I had wandered off from the straight path." (Dante)

Don't touch. I need a suicide specialist. Some potion to release the soul.

Paris is a place that calls me. In Paris, I perceive my path as normal. You can find this enclave of writers who've chosen to make the sacrifices necessary to grow.

Maybe writing attracts people with a gene for insanity? Does manic depression birth literary creativity? If to survive, an artist has to put up with insecurity, neglect, ridicule, he will show the psychic effect of adverse conditions. In 1550, young Italian artists displayed savagery and madness, while in the Egyptian civilization or the Middle Ages, artists were pleasant and well adjusted.

(FATHER'S voice: "Suffering can be a challenge.")

I think if I keep questioning a door will eventually open and someone will say, "I know you've been knocking for a long time; I'd like to let you in."

(FATHER'S voice: "Writers are soothsayers paving the way.")

"But educated people draw little distinction between the trade of a poet or that of an embroiderer." (Pascal)

If I put all my personal soul in my work, people will see me as an alien. *(Pause)* Another joke? A couple, age 76, went to the doctor's office. The doctor asked, "What can I do for you?" The man said, "Will you watch us have sexual intercourse?"

The doctor looked puzzled but agreed. When the couple had finished, the doctor said, "There's nothing wrong with the way you have intercourse," and charged them $10.

This happened several weeks in a row. The couple would make an appointment, have intercourse, pay the doctor and leave. Finally the doctor asked, "What exactly are you trying to find out?"

The old man said, "We're not trying to find out anything. She is married and we can't go to her house. I'm married and we can't go to my house. The Inn charges $30. We do it here for $10 and get back $8 from the government for a doctor's visit."

(A woman's breathing and laughing. MARGARET'S voice: "Perhaps laughter releases the soul." FATHER'S voice: "Come along." SAM looks up, shocked.)

Father. Oh my God. It's Father and Cousin Margaret.

(COUSIN MARGARET'S voice: "Help! Help.")

Where are you, Margaret? I can't see. Don't go. I can't find you. You're fading.

SOUND: Sound of woman breathing.

Come back. I miss the sweetness of your body. Come back. I need your soft embrace.

(BROTHER'S voice: "Don't think about her.")

I must. Cousin Margaret!

(Echoing of "Cousin Margaret" on the breeze. HER laughter.)

"Come live with me and be my love,
And we will some new pleasures prove—" (John Donne)

(COUSIN MARGARET'S voice: "What do you like best about me?")
The names you call me…

(HER voice overlaps HIS: "Dear, dearest, precious.")

What else?

(MARGARET'S voice: "Your brilliant naiveté which comes from living in the world of dreams.")

With you, "I would be ignorant as the dawn—" (Yeats) I dreamed I can fly and I do. I can fly. I'd forgotten that. Up with a thought and quickly I'm off with these amazing powers—. I am a bird, flying up. I don't worry. I'm free. I land anywhere. I'm free.

SOUND: Sound of COUSIN MARGARET breathing.

My favorite thing is to watch you. You're beautiful, and even more intelligent. I'd be happy being engaged for a long time. I want us always to be touching. Everyone needs a guardian angel. When I walk into any crisis, I call forth how you would handle it.

"Who can doubt whether we are in the world for anything but love?" (Pascal)

SOUND: Sound of a heartbeat.

(BROTHER'S voice: "You're obsessed.")

Margaret carries my picture around and kisses the lips. She needs affection every day like people need food.

(MARGARET'S voice from an eerie distance: "Do you love me as much as the first day we kissed?")

(To MARGARET.)

Sure. Some couples don't set dates when they get engaged. I...I can't commit now.

(MOTHER'S voice: "She is using you, son.")

I know she cares. With Margaret, I've given up hopelessness.

(MOTHER'S voice: "It's a trap.")

I know your limitations. I don't expect you to be thoughtful. Margaret wants me to live free as a bird. *(Pause.)* I've decided to marry her.

(MOTHER'S voice: "First cousins can't marry.")

I knew you'd make me feel bad. I've my feet parked firmly and I'm holding to my course.

(MOTHER'S voice: "It's forbidden by the medical profession, the Church.")

We won't have children.

(MOTHER'S voice: "See someone else.")

I won't let her go, back off from...from planning the future. When Margaret thought I'd stopped loving her, her eyes went red and she told everyone she had a fever. I said, "Don't listen to Mother."

(MOTHER'S voice: "I wish Margaret loved you like I loved your father.")

(Angrily to MOTHER.)

Quiet.

(To COUSIN MARGARET. The Angelus drones in the distance.)

I walk about in circles. The point is not whether we marry, but we are growing apart.

(COUSIN MARGARET'S voice: "Sometimes I miss you. Sometimes I don't.")

(To COUSIN MARGARET.)

I don't know what Mother said to your parents, but you can't cut me off.

(To BROTHER.)

We showed Mother Margaret's ring. I said, "Mother, we're engaged." Mother looked away and said, "So what." I couldn't confront Mother. So Mother ignored Margaret. When Margaret said your mother has a mean streak, I defended her. "She loves her sons," I said. "She did worse to Brother's wife. Talk to her."

(MARGARET'S voice: "You choose your mother over me.")

"The ceremony of innocence is drowned;
The best lack all conviction, while the worst
Are full of passionate intensity." (Yeats)

(To BROTHER.)

I suppose if we had a definite wedding date, Mother's cruelty wouldn't bother Margaret.

(MARGARET'S voice: "She's perfected unkindness.")

(To MARGARET.)

Mother's taken a fall. I can't upset her.

(MARGARET'S voice: "She acts like a wife, making you hold her hand, sit by her.")

(To BROTHER.)

Margaret fears we'll have to live far away.

(COUSIN MARGARET'S voice: "She began removing her clothes in front of you—")

Mother comes from a big family. She had that weak spell.

(COUSIN MARGARET'S voice: "But even so, pulling up her nightgown to show you where she fell.")

I looked away.

(COUSIN MARGARET'S voice: "Wanting you to change her lingerie.")

I can't get involved in all this. I can't be forthright. So little time with you and you won't—

(To BROTHER.)

Cousin Margaret says no matter what she does, even if she sees her priest daily, she can't overcome her anxiety. I can't bear not seeing her. She won't elope.

"It is asked whether it is necessary to love. This should not be asked, it should be felt. We do not deliberate upon it, we are forced to it." (Pascal)

(COUSIN MARGARET'S voice: "There's an intimacy you won't share with me.")

(To MARGARET.)

Now you just wish to meditate and sit in the garden. What do you want me to do exactly? Disappear from your life?

(MARGARET'S voice: "My plants bloom for me as if they're my children.")

(To MARGARET.)

We're doing a tango. One step forward, two steps back.

(MARGARET'S voice: "I'm happy to putter here—")

And not talk.

(To COUSIN MARGARET.)

I don't want to marry someone uncertain. But— No, I won't take back the ring.

(MARGARET'S voice: "It doesn't mean we're engaged. There's no date.")

Wear it on your middle finger.

(BROTHER'S voice: "Her leaving was a brave gift because there would have been an explosion.")

(To COUSIN MARGARET.)
I reread your letter: "In order to honor our past relationship, you—

(COUSIN MARGARET'S voice over his:)

Release me from our engagement vows, and hope blessings will come my way."

(To COUSIN MARGARET.)

On what grounds are you leaving me?

"What the hammer? What the chain?
In what furnace was the brain?
What the anvil? What dread grasp
Dare its deadly terrors clasp?" (Blake)

SOUND: *Sound of erratic heartbeat.*

(BROTHER'S voice: "Margaret's a high fever.")

What? No . . .when?

(COUSIN MARGARET'S voice: "No safe haven till I meet God.")

(BROTHER'S voice: "A severe infection. It came on sudden, quick.")

(To BROTHER.)

Oh God. Hold on. I'm coming. Nothing will separate us. Hold on!

Heartbeat irregular, fading…

Margaret's arms are weeping from the injections. She can't eat because of the tubes down her throat. She is letting go of her old body. Sores all over her hands. When I asked her to let me know if she knew me, she made a violent gasp. Brother says often she is in another place outside her body. Margaret rallied, then failed. She doesn't want to get out of bed. First they decline badly and then they dive. They are letting Margaret die, weaning her off food, then her other systems will shut down.

"Suddenly I saw the cold and rook-delighting heaven,
But that seemed as though ice burned and was but the more ice." (Yeats)

Margaret can't squeeze my hand or say anything. *(Pause.)* She died. I stay in the present, and by doing so, I don't cry. Margaret was half there in her shell body. We are 98% energy. But now her 2% is gone.

SOUND: A funeral bell tolls.

I still wake up wanting to hold her. *(Looks around.)* There are hyacinths all over. She looks cold but peaceful. There's the sunshine dress from her mother. So fluffed, ribbed cotton.

(BROTHER'S voice: "We should leave.")

I like being in the same room as Margaret. Feel if I stand by, I can protect her. Look at the hand-embroidered pictures of the beatitudes overhead. Her face looks old. Her color is yellow. Couldn't they do something about that? Her hands are covered with a handkerchief; they are so discolored.

(BROTHER'S voice: "Her body is there but not her soul.")

Maybe my body is here, but not my soul.

(MOTHER'S voice: "No one dies of a broken heart.")

"Through me the way into the doleful city, Through me the way into eternal grief, through me the way among a race forsaken. ABANDON HOPE FOREVER YOU WHO ENTER. (Dante)

(SAM starts to drink. To BROTHER.)

ROSARY HARTEL O'NEILL

I take whiskey to get out of my brain, which would eat me, alive. "Man is but a reed, the feeblest thing in nature...A vapor, a drop of water suffice to kill him." (says Pascal)

I came far in my desire for intimacy, but I didn't make the final hurdle. Margaret abandoned me, and that's what I thought I was going to do. *(Pause.)* Death stalks us and wins. Joke time. "That was a terrible storm ye had down your way." "Twas surely. Our hen had her back to the wind and she laid the same egg five times." Or,

A ghost in the town of macroon,
One night found a ghoul in his room
They argued all night, as to which had the right,
To frighten the wits out of whom.

(BROTHER'S voice: "Don't blame yourself—")

I don't have to think of worst-case scenarios, they're here.

(Billowy scrim, vague faces, soft light, misty. All voices cry, "Come inside.")

(Turns away, looks deep into the sea.)

"I live my life in widening rings, which spread over earth and sky." (States Rilke)

(To MOTHER.)

There's a balance between how much insult you're willing to take and how much you're willing to protect your feelings. *(Pause.)* My major debate is when to put the pillow over your head. *(Laughs.)*

(MOTHER'S voice: "Don't start with your poor me.")

I see more than you. I've been to the extremity of experience. Been on the edge. Don't grab your head. You're not dying. What did you tell Margaret? What? Viper...No, I will not shut up. Pretending you need me while draining my life. No, I'll not be quiet. I'll scream and rage. Better yet, I'll slit my wrists in front of you. Lance a finger. Cut an eye out. You killed Margaret by turning me into a coward. A weepy Keats crouched in a thicket. Well, no more. I'll cut the umbilical cord. Pry my way out.

(Begins to pack. To BROTHER.)

I'm leaving for London, psychoanalysis, hospitalization, who cares what. If Mother's in a rage, I'll leave the range of fire. *(Pause.)* Was a time when the thought of going would have sent me into a frenzy.

(MOTHER calls out: "Don't leave.")

Now terror inspires me. Then again, maybe I'll get on the train and come right back.

(MOTHER cries: "We need you.")

(To BROTHER.)

I suckled at the tits of wolves and emerged with my humanity intact. Their behavior has contaminated me—

(MOTHER'S voice: "Oh, son. Don't scream.")

You're not on anyone's side. You exist for yourself. You know I'll drive a stake through your heart if you fuck with me. You've the nervous system of a rattlesnake. Drop you off naked in Antarctica, you'll survive.

(MOTHER'S voice: "Don't be angry, son.")

If I don't do what's right, what you want me to do, will I set something off?

(MOTHER'S voice: "You know I love you.")

You think this is the greatest place because you live here. In our family you get to hold the leash. I've got rid of so much I feel like I'm a dead person.

(MOTHER'S voice: "This is your home, son.")

No, it's not. It's a big house to have nobody in.

(MOTHER'S voice: "You're breaking my heart.")

The older I get, the easier it is to do things that are devastating. Every place I go there's something wrong with me. I've got to start getting used to liv-

ROSARY HARTEL O'NEILL

ing in my own chaos.

(MOTHER'S voice: "Sit by me.")

I knew at 9 years old that I'd never have the answers to your questions. I remember looking in the mirror saying, "You will never have the answers to her questions." So I comforted myself with Pascal's _Pensées_. "How happy is a life that begins with love and ends with ambition!"

(MOTHER'S voice: "Hold your mother's hand.")

(BROTHER'S voice: "You're making Mother cry.")

No. I just realized it's over for you, Brother, and me. Eventually it all goes away anyway. It's not if I leave, it's when. *(Pause.)* I'll move to Paris. Whenever I go to Paris, I feel loved. I guess the key is to leave, not to wait.

SOUND: Sound of wind rising. Voices call out: "Stay! Stay!"

So long, beach and sky. So long, wind and greystones—Father and— Margaret, Brother—forgive me.

(A whisper like a hoarse breeze. Lights dim. His FATHER'S image startles him.)

When the going gets rough, I want to yell, "Father." Should I go to the hospital? Get psychoanalyzed. I don't know. That's as close to a yes as I'm going to get. You don't have to be sick to die. I'll keep moving forward. And I'll keep my feet gripping for the next hold on the rock edge. If I do this religiously, nothing but stars await me now.

Maybe the heavens will open up and swallow me.

"Rest not! Life is sweeping by;
Go and dare before you die.
Something mighty and sublime,
Leave behind to conquer time." (Goethe)

THE END

Property

A PLAY IN
TWO ACTS

*First produced
in October 1999
in Thilisi,
Republic of Georgia.*

CAST OF CHARACTERS

IRENE SONIAT DUBONNET: Fifties. A landowner, she redefines the word style—in designer dresses, and flawless makeup. Irene is one of those striking women—nerves of steel, iron lungs, sharp as a tack—who has nothing to do but protect her grown children, and she watches them like a dog guards her bone.

ROOSTER DUBONNET: (Nicknamed Roo) Late twenties. A painter who has pushed himself beyond reasonable limits. He is critically ill from cancer. The disease gives him a distinct nonchalance, the charm of the damned.

BUNKY DUBONNET LEGERE: Early twenties, her grandson. He dresses like a rebel. His consuming interest is singing the blues. When he drinks, his personality changes into an exaggerated gaiety and a hair-trigger rage.

OOZIE RANSOM: Thirty to fifty. Companion to Irene. Oozie is always fixing herself—freshening her lipstick, puffing her hair, buffing her rings.

MONICA FALCON: Late twenties. A nurse, attractive, with a passion for things of the spirit. Her gentleness is matched by delicate features: fine skin, graceful hands, hair which tumbles around her face.

SETTING

The day room of a Garden District mansion, New Orleans, Louisiana.

TIME

Valentine's Day to Mardi Gras.
The not-too-distant past.

ACT i
SCENE i

(A spacious garden room. There is a luxuriously cushioned day bed with an empty bird cage like a Chinese house. Vivid landscape paintings are placed about. The effect is of a boy's dream, the actual furniture being less important than the wonder created. It is raining quietly, one of those late afternoon showers that New Orleans is famous for. ROOSTER DUBONNET, a young man, late twenties, dark-haired, gaunt, almost emaciated, lies in bed in silk pajamas. If HE were not so sick and pasty-looking, HE could be handsome with strong features, thick hair, and broad shoulders. Even so, there are kindness and nobility in his face.)

ROOSTER: I'm cold. Maybe the rain makes me that way.

(ROOSTER closes his eyes. MONICA FALON, a stunning nurse, twenty-eight, arrives. SHE pauses at the doorway, removing her cape. SHE is dressed simply but impeccably and holds a satchel under her arm.)

MONICA: Hello, hello…anyone there? I'm Monica Falcon, the new nurse.

ROOSTER: What? *(Calls out)* Ma.

MONICA: *(Puts a thermometer in his mouth)* Are you in pain?

ROOSTER: No. *(HE pulls out the thermometer, leans to an intercom.)*

MONICA: You sounded as if you were in pain.

ROOSTER: *(Into the intercom)* Ma, pick up.

MONICA: Everyone's gone.

ROOSTER: Unlikely. *(Into the intercom)* Pick up, I said.

MONICA: The house echoes quiet.

ROOSTER: *(Into the intercom)* Ma. They sent a woman.

MONICA: You've a wonderful house…

ROOSTER: *(Into the intercom)* I asked for a male nurse.

MONICA: It's like a hotel.

ROOSTER: (Into the intercom) You're not my guest. I'm not lying about half-dressed with a woman.

(MONICA checks about for lights.)

ROOSTER: (Cont.) Don't.

MONICA: Do you live in darkness?

ROOSTER: Best way to survive in the Garden District.

MONICA: (Looks at her feet) These shoes looked good before I walked through water.

ROOSTER: Click your heels and go back to Oz.

MONICA: (Opens a curtain.) We can catch the last rays of the sun.

ROOSTER: You're not staying.

(HE sits up, reaches for his robe, but is still weak and has to breathe a few moments. SHE looks out the window. HE reaches for the phone.)

MONICA: The light feels good. Cold bracing sunshine, right behind the rain. That'll keep you awake.

ROOSTER: (Into the receiver) Is this the Parker Agency?

MONICA: I love a bright afternoon sky.

ROOSTER: This is Rooster Dubonnet. I requested a male nurse.

MONICA: (Reaches for the phone) Give me that.

ROOSTER: (Stretches phone away, panting, talks into it) I'm not paying for this woman.

MONICA: What do you have against women?

ROOSTER: *(Into the phone)* I was nice to those rejects you sent. She can't be the only nurse who'll come.

MONICA: *(Takes out a blood pressure kit)* I'll take your blood pressure.

ROOSTER: *(Into the phone)* You said you had 200 nurses.
(Into the phone) I don't want this woman. *(Into the phone)* Tell her to leave.

MONICA: *(Takes phone, speaks into it)* Everybody's fine. *(Hangs up. To ROOSTER)* One, two, three…up.

(ROOSTER sits up, very weak, wraps his robe limply over his silk pajamas.)

ROOSTER: Stay away. I'm warning you.

(HE reaches for the phone, but SHE grabs it and puts it in her pocket.)

MONICA: I'll change those sheets.

(HE stumbles to his feet. HE pants for breath, totters, and grasps onto furniture. HE stops for a second. SHE watches him from the corner of her eyes and goes to make the bed.)

MONICA: You can do it?

ROOSTER: I can do it.

(HE presses a hand alarm, which blares. THEY struggle for the alarm.)

MONICA: What's that? Turn it off.

ROOSTER: Not likely.

MONICA: Give it over.

ROOSTER: No.

MONICA: *(Pulls alarm from his fist. SHE pushes it off.)* You think you can get rid of me?

ROOSTER: You're the roughest…

MONICA: My landlord's evicted me.

ROOSTER: Toughest…

MONICA: Called me at five a.m.

ROOSTER: This is not a hotel.

MONICA: I've no friends or relatives here.

ROOSTER: That's the first good news about you.

MONICA: Can you do it alone?

(HE walks, but stumbles. SHE calls out as HE moves cautiously along.)

ROOSTER: Uh-huh. If I push myself I can. I'll be right back.

(HE walks carefully. Reaching the window, HE calls out, "Police! Police!" then turns and sets off a strobe light siren. SHE runs over. THEY struggle for it.)

MONICA: You crazy…Out of my way! Stop. Nobody's going to bail me out.

(SHE turns the siren off. HE staggers to a chair, and leans over the back coughing.)

MONICA: (Cont.) Have you had anything to eat? Or drink?

ROOSTER: Not today.

MONICA: (Hands him some water) Take a few sips.

ROOSTER: No, thanks. Have you ever heard of the nurse who poisons the emperor? This emperor so feared assassination, he only ate ripe figs from a tree.

MONICA: Drink.

ROOSTER: In the night, his nurse injected them with poison.

MONICA: Just a little.

ROOSTER: In the morning, the emperor ate one and died.

(HE *pours water on a plant. SHE speaks continuously, overlapping him.*)

MONICA: Since you won't let me help you, may I ask you some questions?

ROOSTER: What's that?

MONICA: I'm studying astrology...on the side.

ROOSTER: It's amateur night in Dixie.

MONICA: I looked you up. You've got a tenth house, Pluto in Leo.

ROOSTER: Fortune tellers. They're everything I'm running from—

MONICA: Which means you're gifted...

ROOSTER: (*Breathing fast*) The whole specter of charlatans—

MONICA: At being able to...

ROOSTER: That haunt artists' history.

MONICA: Translate archetypal energy...

ROOSTER: I'm three times more likely to die from the flu...

MONICA: Through the power of the personal image...

ROOSTER: Than to speak to a student astrologer. Y'all are the psychos of the science profession.

MONICA: I know you're a famous artist from a well-to-do family...

ROOSTER: Why do people pursue me?

MONICA: May I ask you some questions? It would make my job easier.

ROOSTER: You haven't a job with me.

MONICA: You're so…

ROOSTER: Difficult? Some artists don't do interviews, and thank God they don't. I don't want to be the entertainment.

MONICA: And you're not.

(ROOSTER rises with effort, crosses to the bird cage, whistles "Dixie.")

ROOSTER: My parrot, Commander Butler, just flew in.

MONICA: Where?

ROOSTER: He died but sometimes he visits. He's my very special house ghost. The two things Butler does best are scream "Where's the maid?" and whistle "Dixie." Calling the maid is so passé.

MONICA: What's your diagnosis?

ROOSTER: *(Pause)* Are you from the South?

MONICA: Delaware.

ROOSTER: Y'all like to eat on paper plates in halls covered with graffiti. What do you have going for you?

MONICA: My husband was from Jackson.

ROOSTER: There's a touch of Mississippi in your family? What does Mr. Falcon do?

MONICA: My…I…Oh Lord…I mustn't let…Where're my Kleenex? You think I'd be here if I…

ROOSTER: Don't start the sadness machine.

MONICA: It happens frequently. It's not professional. Your bed is ready.

(Rain pours around the sides of the room. SHE removes the thermometer, writes something on her chart. HE pulls a sketch pad from behind a seat.)

ROOSTER: I've not stopped painting because I wanted to. This morning I said, I'm going to paint, if my energy holds out…Soon as it's warm and the sun's shining…

MONICA: Well?

ROOSTER: *(Rain begins whistling around. HE rubs the armrests)* My energy didn't hold out…Listen to that rain blowing round outside.

MONICA: It sounds neighborly.

ROOSTER: Coming right through the sun.

MONICA: I love to hear it when I'm inside.

ROOSTER: Oh, but it's cold walking into the rain. *(Begins to shiver)* Look at me shake? The thought of rain and I start to shiver.

MONICA: Try to nap. Would you like another blanket?

ROOSTER: *(HE lies back slowly; she covers him)* That does feel good.

MONICA: I told you.

(HE has closed his eyes and gone to sleep. MONICA watches over him as the lights are brought down.)

END OF SCENE 1

SCENE 2

(The lights come up. Lapse of time of only a few hours. We are still in the day room. IRENE DUBONNET enters in a smart contemporary cocktail suit with a hat and veil. SHE is holding a pistol and a purse. SHE yells off stage at her chauffeur, HUCK.)

IRENE: *(Looks about)* Huck! Put up the car. It's dark as a coffin. I've seen funerals that were less solemn than this!

MONICA: I'm the new nurse.

IRENE: Huck, take down the rifles. Let out the dogs. *(Points the gun)* It's a trick to scare off burglars. *(Puts the gun in her purse)* I keep guns 'cause I hunt doves. You can only kill ducks in Louisiana…I go to Mexico, shoot doves, and give them to the peasants. They've no meat, so I feel like a queen.

MONICA: Strange hat.

IRENE: *(Looks in the mirror, removes a veil)* I get red if I even think sun. I wear a veil if it's sunny at six o'clock. *(Glances out a window)* Whose rattle-trap car is that? I don't know anyone who drives a Chevy.

MONICA: Mine.

IRENE: My Cadillac's little. I'll trade it in, soon as one comes out I like. *(To MONICA)* You should park on the Avenue. I can't park there. Last time, somebody smashed my windshield, and my insurance doubled. New Orleans is the worst managed and most—

MONICA: Intoxicating city. Before I came South, I thought flowers were extravagant, now I find them necessary. You can buy any house you want in the Midwest but you can't have that big oak tree; for that you'll have to come to Louisiana. So I say, "If anybody lives in the upper Midwest…leave."

IRENE: Have you been downtown yet? They're laying off people. Where will you stay?

MONICA: I don't know.

IRENE: There's the servants' quarters in back.

MONICA: Thank you.

IRENE: *(Giving her the once-over)* You look like you just graduated from nursing school.

MONICA: I was twenty-eight yesterday.

IRENE: *(Looking back over her shoulder)* Ah, twenty-eight! *(Smiles)* Sit down. The chair for the nurse is over there. *(Pause)* What's your success rate with your patients?

MONICA: He's my first.

IRENE: Lord. I ought to send you back. You should always say it's your second. At least your second. *(SHE looks out the window at the dogs, yells)* Huck. Let out the dogs. Huck calls our house the dog spa 'cause dogs get the best treatment here. It's the Red Door of dog care.

MONICA: Tell me about your son.

IRENE: Roo's a fifth generation from the Garden District. Is it of any value, his rearing and education? This complicated system of breeding only understood by the sophisticated. Males here think as females in the fact they think a lot.

MONICA: They say he has been treated for a rare type of cancer.

IRENE: Don't say the C word! *(Pause)* He's stopped eating. A bite of lettuce, a tomato but no meat, no protein. He stirs his plate. It's this hypersensitivity artists carry.

MONICA: I'll make him eat.

IRENE: What'd he say to you?

MONICA: He fired me.

IRENE: In this house, I hire and fire. He was a chunky boy, like a chipmunk. Your job is to be sure he takes his medicine.

MONICA: May I see the doctor's notes?

IRENE: You can never read a doctor's handwriting. The men in my family were Jesuits or surgeons! The robe or the coat.

MONICA: What's the patient's history with cancer?

IRENE: He collapsed in Puerto Vallarta after painting seagulls on the beach.

MONICA: Maybe I should speak to the local doctor.

IRENE: We didn't use a local doctor. My son is a subtraction of his former self. Half of his friends are dead by their own hand, and the other half are only alive because they didn't succeed.

MONICA: How would you judge his condition?

IRENE: *(Agitated, feels her watch)* Roo is like no one I knew as a girl.

MONICA: You never knew painters?

IRENE: I made him transfer to law school. My late husband said why not let him take a crack at another art school.

MONICA: How marvelous.

IRENE: I learned one thing in this family. Watch art, don't be in it. People don't want enlightenment, they want entertainment.

MONICA: Why has Roo stopped painting?

IRENE: They say you always stop when you're the strongest.

MONICA: But you're his mother. Surely you see.

IRENE: I'm a secondary character in Roo's life. Most men are aliens…narcissistic, ruthless. Loving a gender they have been taught to devalue. What can we expect?

(IRENE exits to dogs barking. It is dark. ROOSTER is asleep.)

SOUND: The clock chimes.

LIGHTS: Shadows creep across the room.

(MONICA turns on Bach music [the Goldberg Variations, Three Part Invention, French Suites or Italian Suites], lights the lamp. ROOSTER wakes.)

ROOSTER: Have I been asleep long?

MONICA: Two hours.

ROOSTER: Why didn't you wake me? I'm embarrassed.

MONICA: Sleep's good for you.

ROOSTER: You should've waked me.

MONICA: Come see what we've got. Fresh strawberries. Happy Valentine's Day. (HE rises. Walks slowly to the table.)

ROOSTER: Valentine's? Is it?

MONICA: Cranberry juice?

ROOSTER: Not thirsty.

MONICA: Yogurt.

ROOSTER: Not hungry. (HE cries) I'd hoped I'd feel better.

MONICA: You look stronger.

ROOSTER: Maybe later I'll go out.

MONICA: You're unstrung?

ROOSTER: I've been weepy a lot lately. You think it's the weather?

MONICA: Perhaps. What'd you do all day long?

ROOSTER: I listened to the rain…Sage blue rain. It's beyond rich, it's beyond blue. Feels like living from drop to drop. Time starts to lose its shape, to cover you, and you feel its weight. You hear in the patter what your day was. You notice how the sounds glide, how they envelope each big old empty tree. Afterwards, you feel time like rain…like death.

MONICA: (Picks up ROO's photo lying face down) What's this?

ROOSTER: I played football. Quarterback at Jesuit. They used to say I was tough.

MONICA: Eat something.

ROOSTER: No, thanks. You know what bothers me most? The quiet...

MONICA: These strawberries smell good. If I cut one up, would you eat?

(HE nods. IRENE enters and sits ROOSTER up with a pillow.)

IRENE: You should be resting, son. I'm having Mother's mink made into pillows. Roo loved Mother.

ROOSTER: (Turning away) You didn't do that for me. I hate fur.

IRENE: Who told you to set the table?

MONICA: I wanted to help.

IRENE: Don't do anything till I tell you to. (To ROO) Guess what I lost today?

ROOSTER: Your looks?

IRENE: I pitched my cane in the Mississippi River. My eyes are failing—

MONICA: You're attractive.

IRENE: The worst is when I get lipstick on my teeth or rouge on my chin.

MONICA: Me too.

IRENE: Really. Dinner's late. Angela forgot to defrost the roast.

MONICA: Can I do something?

IRENE: Perhaps you can help in the kitchen.

ROOSTER: She's a nurse.

IRENE: (To MONICA) I expect you to clean, mop, and sweep. You're responsible for Roo's area.

ROOSTER: (Calls out) I can do it.

IRENE: *(Shivers)* Don't be foolish…It's spring in the South. But inside, it's pneumonia alley. *(ROOSTER has a twinge of pain)* I've got to wear a coat and keep the room at sixty degrees. So many layers. Makes me feel like a bird. I come prepared to shed.

MONICA: Snakes shed, birds molt.

IRENE: Don't you understand polite behavior? The phrase I prefer is "I agree."

ROOSTER: Oh-oh…a pain.

MONICA: *(To ROOSTER)* You need help?

ROOSTER: Just your hand.

IRENE: Is this some new-fangled therapy?

(BUNKY LEGERE, twenty, dressed in black leather, struts inside balancing mail and a book. Afternoon champagne makes him defiant.)

BUNKY: You look wonderful. You look like a Queen. If I were a stranger, I would propose.

IRENE: *(Looks BUNKY over)* Those boys from Jesuit. Once you take them out of khaki, they don't know how to dress.

BUNKY: I began with the jacket. Then I went for the whole look.

IRENE: There's something unsettling about having a mortician for a nephew.

MONICA: Nephew?

BUNKY: She doesn't like the word "grandson."

IRENE: Miss…Falcon. Bunky Legere. It's not short for anything grand like Beauregard. What's this?

BUNKY: *(Kisses her)* Valentines for you and Roo.

IRENE: I mailed myself ten from unknown admirers.

BUNKY: And Roo's got a candy heart from Monica Falcon.

MONICA: *(To ROO)* Let me feed you some.

ROOSTER: Chocolate-covered cranberries.

IRENE: Bunky, get them a fork and a plate.

BUNKY: Happy Valentine's. *(Distracts her with a gift)*

IRENE: *(Lifts book)* The Treasury of Clean Jokes for Seniors.

BUNKY: *(Reading)* What four things stand in the way of Southern progress? Winter, spring, summer, fall.

(BUNKY laughs with MONICA.)

IRENE: Now we make the child king. In the nineteenth century, the child wasn't noticed at all.

(Trying to lighten the mood, BUNKY plays "Goodnight, Irene" on the stereo. HE and IRENE dance. ROOSTER rises slowly, takes a step or two and grabs on to a chair.)

BUNKY: "Irene, goodnight. Irene, goodnight."

IRENE: "Goodnight, Irene. I'll see you in my dreams."

(BUNKY twirls and dips IRENE. MONICA and ROOSTER watch in silence.)

ROOSTER: He sure can move. Everyone wants to catch him in a bell jar. Want to dance, Monica?

(ROOSTER dances with MONICA…then he falls.)

MONICA: Need help?

ROOSTER: No.

(HE dances again, falls.)

IRENE: Huck! *(To ROOSTER)* Son, what's gotten into you?

BUNKY: He's not hurt, is he?

MONICA: Nothing's wrong with him. He fell but he got up.

IRENE: Bunky, go clean Roo up in the bathroom. *(BUNKY and ROO exit)* Roo was mean to me today, as usual. But I'll survive. *(SHE stops by the refrigerator)* My second old-fashioned. Two's my limit. That's not what you'd call lapping it up.

OOZIE: *(offstage)* Angela's come. Dinner's in half-hour.

(IRENE checks her watch.)

IRENE: That's Oozie! *(Explaining to MONICA)* I hired a companion. The daughter of my mother's housekeeper. Now she's taken over my third floor.

MONICA: When did Roo last go out?

IRENE: Sometimes he makes it to the slave quarters.*(Savors her drink)* Course he doesn't go lately.

MONICA: That must be hard for you…to see him get worse.

IRENE: I keep a cheery face.

MONICA: Because I imagine the thrill of his success…

IRENE: If I'm not optimistic, I don't come out.

MONICA: And watching him make great art.

IRENE: Can you hand me that swizzle stick?

(MONICA gives her the swizzle stick.)

MONICA: Giving such beauty to people.

IRENE: In his profession you're a failure unless you're a star.

MONICA: But Roo was making a name for himself.

IRENE: There were wonderful things said about him, true. And positive reviews.

MONICA: What led him home?

IRENE: (Worrying about her drink) More saccharine. (MONICA crosses for a packet. IRENE shrugs her shoulders) I don't understand his melancholy. I never had the luxury.

MONICA: Some people need to reflect.

IRENE: If I didn't have to see Roo but an hour a day, I could take it. This glass is leaky.

MONICA: I'll get another. How did his depression start?

IRENE: With mood swings. First I thought it was the temper he'd shown as a boy.

(IRENE checks the door to make sure no one is listening.)

MONICA: Then?

IRENE: He began painting less and less. He stopped doing everything. Before he was…

MONICA: Inspired.

IRENE: Up at dawn and off to work.

BUNKY: (offstage) Angela wants dinner now.

SOUND: Mendelsohn's "Andante Symphony no. 5" plays subdued.

IRENE: Nothing is done as it should be. Roo has always been special. (Irritated, waves her hand) Roo was born with a veil of skin over his face. A sixth sense. Nurse put it in a jar of formaldehyde.

GHOSTS OF NEW ORLEANS

MONICA: What did the doctors say...about his depression?

IRENE: They hit me with scientific terms for...the "C" word...but I walked out. Then they ran tests. They sent up these terminal statistics. The entire medical group is concerned.

MONICA: Mrs. Dubonnet, you're crying.

IRENE: I'm not crying. I've an allergy. If you're done, go help the cook.

MONICA: Roo's life's still before him. He'll get better. You'll see.

END OF SCENE 2

SCENE 3

(Lapse of only a few seconds. We are still in the day room. BUNKY appears in the doorway.)

BUNKY: Have y'all seen a purple pencil with the name of a funeral parlor on it?

IRENE: Why do you always ignore me?

(BUNKY searches about, paces to the liquor table, pours a drink. The following lines overlap.)

BUNKY: There's a party in parlor B before the parade tonight.

IRENE: Don't you have a paper to write?

BUNKY: My brain hurts.

IRENE: I'm trying to steer you in the right direction.

BUNKY: I'm not a car. If you want to steer something, buy a Ford. Having you on my case is like being pecked forever by a duck.

IRENE: Why do you want to study the blues? There's no future with—

BUNKY: I need to major in something I like.

(OOZIE RANSOM sweeps in with truffles and a box.)

OOZIE: Cousin Irene. Cousin Irene.

IRENE: You insist on calling me cousin.

OOZIE: "Plain Irene." Sounds disrespectful.

IRENE: You're not working in the kitchen. Take a vacation from personality and be bland for a while.

OOZIE: I'm looking for Roo to show him my dress.

IRENE: He's with Nurse du jour.

OOZIE: What do you think of my going-away suit? *(Twirling about)* It's Buck-a-roo blue. I'm getting a whole bedroom dyed this shade.

BUNKY: *(To OOZIE)* It looks very Renaissance.

OOZIE: *Fin de siecle.* My wedding's using a Victorian theme. *(Passes an invitation)* See my invitations. I hope I don't cry like when I read them for the first time. Look. *(Reads)* "Mrs. Peter Malter Dubonnet requests your presence at the marriage of her cousin."

IRENE: It doesn't say third cousin, or cousin-in-law.

OOZIE: Oh my God—a typo! It says Floozie, not Oozie. God.

IRENE: Efficiency's not the same as working with grace and creativity.

OOZIE: Floozie! That can't be. *(Puts invitation to her eyes)* No, it's my contacts. *(Reads)* "To Purvis Axelrod."

IRENE: Oozie Axelrod. Doesn't go together.

OOZIE: "Reception immediately following the ceremony, New Orleans Country Club." You have to be a member to entertain there. I told Purvis, "I don't want much for my engagement but I want it big and I want it real."

GHOSTS OF NEW ORLEANS

(Flashes her ring)

BUNKY: Don't wear that on any back streets.

OOZIE: He keeps saying, "Where have you been all my life?" I reply, "Well, for half of it, I wasn't born yet."

IRENE: It's easy to flutter like a virgin if your groom is eighty-one.

BUNKY: Poor Purvis is so homely…You have to tie a pork chop around his neck to get the dog to play with him…

(BUNKY exits.)

IRENE: The man looks like a corpse until he begins to move.

OOZIE: Purvis is young for his age. Been married three times but no children. I'm still intact.

IRENE: Please. You are at the most arrogant age. Old enough to think you know something, young enough to not know you don't.

OOZIE: Purvis won't let me do a thing. The only exercise I get is to switch on the ignition, to press the air conditioner, and to dial the car phone. Without cars and the weather, there'd be nothing to talk about.

IRENE: What business is Purvis in again?

OOZIE: Purvis is a third-generation screw manager! You know that! He's gone further faster than anybody!

IRENE: It's awkward to say he's in screws.

OOZIE: He runs the family business, "The House of Screws." Forty thousand feet of screws…There are fifty types, Italian screws, French screws. He's got a ranch paid for by the House of Screws. Rooms and rooms of furniture and *(Pronounces it wrong)* tester beds.

IRENE: *(Correcting her)* Tester. If you were a first cousin, you'd know. *(MONICA enters)* Monica, meet Oozie Ransom. A distant relative of my late husband on the black sheep side of the family.

OOZIE: I was born Elivira. But I didn't like it so I had it legally changed.

MONICA: Monica Falcon.

OOZIE: Falcon? I don't want to be eaten.

IRENE: Ha. Now Oozie's leaving. The last person who knew my Mama as a child.

OOZIE: We'll always be close.

IRENE: People say that when they're moving away. Why not buy the house next door?

OOZIE: I'll have eighty acres of Texas land and my own ranch, three blocks long. Purvis had the nerve to add on.

IRENE: A big house? At first, you do it, then it does you.

OOZIE: I found the right key and all the doors are opening. With one "I do," I'll go from tenant to landlord. I'll have three dogs: Quiche, Brandy, and Caesar, and look for people to do nothing with.

IRENE: I thought you liked it here?

OOZIE: Now I can enjoy the fruits of my labor, of all those years of hustling on tired feet, knowing the only excuse for not showing up for work was death. Mine. I'll learn to become soft in a house that's bigger than yours. The way to happiness I see is being a woman of property. With means, you can say things that cause flack. Property gives you courage. You can take that power and live it for the rest of your life.

IRENE: (Stumbles, then screams, as they exit) Why must Huck wax every step? Someone's going to trip and sue me for a million dollars. (to OOZIE) Go check on dinner.

OOZIE: I never wear a watch. I don't know the time.

(OOZIE and IRENE exit. ROOSTER enters with a scented candle. He wears a fresh shirt and slacks.)

GHOSTS OF NEW ORLEANS

MONICA: Let me take that.

ROOSTER: Walk with me. I feel better today. It's fresher.

MONICA: Keep inside. It's still damp and humid.

ROOSTER: I need rain, no sunlight.

MONICA: Is that so?

ROOSTER: Is it raining hard?

MONICA: A drizzle…

ROOSTER: It's going to be a wet night?

MONICA: Yes.

ROOSTER: No moon?

MONICA: No.

ROOSTER: A splendid sky, wonderful, dark with three stars.

MONICA: You like having company.

ROOSTER: I like having Monica.

(MONICA pours him water. Places it in his hand. HE holds hers.)

MONICA: Drink. *(HE takes one sip; SHE watches him)* You lived at home for a long while? With your mom? That's a hard…

ROOSTER: Not if you need money and time.

MONICA: What was your mom like…before?

ROOSTER: Mom's a bravura figure. When you're fifteen years old and you think you can do anything, Mom is someone who can help you think you can do that. How wonderful Paris is, she'd say, and we'd be off with a maid to pack and a teacher to explain the tour. We would stand for hours before

ROSARY HARTEL O'NEILL

the Renoirs at the Louvre. *(Breathing deeply)* While she studied the light and the shadow. Then we'd take a few days off and go to the Baltic Sea. The National Gallery in London. Perganon in Berlin. We'd ride in taxis above the crowd...stay at the Ritz. It was the white-glove approach to travel...breeding children who reacted to a European sensibility. *(Pause)* I'm her last child so I ride on the cusp of her extravagance. *(Rain whistles around the house. Rubs his hands together)* Listen to that rain.

MONICA: Why can't you paint here?

ROOSTER: Maybe it's the rain. It's full of emptiness. Cold blue in the morning, bright blue at noon and intense Italianate blue in late afternoon. The walls soak up the rain. There is vermilion in the shadows, violet in the gray. Like the sound of everything that's there, that I try to paint. When you are inside the rain, there's a luminosity. I want images that have the density of rain. Nature does it easily. When you try to copy it, it's gone. Rain's not easily captured. It's the pink lie, the last little thing that crawled out of Pandora's box with all her colors. If I could paint rain the way it is, thick and smelling of oak leaves, I could jumpstart death.

MONICA: Have you got a fever?

ROOSTER: I don't think so.

SOUND: Rain howls outside.

MONICA: Let me fluff your pillow.

ROOSTER: Thanks. Fix my blanket. *(SHE puts a blanket over ROO; HE squeezes her hand)* I'm afraid I'm going to die and never get off this bed.

MONICA: Listen to me. I'll take care of you.

(ROOSTER falls asleep. MONICA moves to a chair, sits, studying the report. BUNKY enters, chased by OOZIE and IRENE. The following lines overlap.)

BUNKY: My report card.

IRENE: Between the Valentines! All F's for absence.

OOZIE: Why didn't you have an ugly friend say you were sick?

BUNKY: I've never taken a test. I refuse to be tested!

IRENE: I'm not traumatized. Not after last week. When Bunky wore spandex to Fendie's. And got potatoes in his eyebrows.

OOZIE: How can he study, with girls out back till three a.m.?

IRENE: Beer cans lining the drive—

BUNKY: Like hell.

OOZIE: He gobbles aspirins.

BUNKY: Like hell!

IRENE: I could take a few exasperated screams, but to make "hell"—a part of the currency of conversation!

BUNKY: You know what I hate about you?

IRENE: The men in my family were scholars.

BUNKY: You hit the room like a nasty breeze. That's why I like the blues. Music pushes your spirits up. Ka—boom.

IRENE: He'll just keep singing until no one shows up.

OOZIE: Somewhere deep down music has put the bite on him.

BUNKY: *(Singing)* There's a crying Blues. A three o'clock moaning Blues. *(Hits a high note)* That's falsetto. The deceptive voice. Nameless artists taught me that. Great unknown figures. Their families erased them after they died. If you distill Blues to a drop, it'd be a prisoner with a guitar and a hot toddy. *(Sings solo song and dances to a rap)* Hot toddy in the cool rain. I love to sit in the rain and let the sounds come through the bones of my body like liquid music. Be there like the Mardi Gras Indians that come out to dance in the drizzle. I'd forget who I was and say, "Something is right with this picture."

END OF SCENE 3

SCENE 4

(Sometime later. ROOSTER enters in a sweater and slacks, holding flowers behind his back.)

ROOSTER: *(Hands MONICA roses)* Happy Mardi Gras. Do you know you've been here for thirty days?

MONICA: Roses?

ROOSTER: Read the card.

(SHE gives him back the roses. Overheated, HE follows her, drops the roses on a table, sits.)

MONICA: Thanks. Roses smell like dew.

(As MONICA passes him, HE takes her arm.)

ROOSTER: You're a Dresden shepherdess.

MONICA: Don't forget to take your medicine.

ROOSTER: Light just kisses your hair.

MONICA: The light kisses me. *(SHE puts a thermometer in his mouth)* That's nice. I studied you in my astrology class. I'll give you the bare bones of it.

ROOSTER: *(Removing the thermometer)* I'm not ready.

MONICA: You've come out of the womb wearing female clothes.

ROOSTER: Preposterous.

MONICA: You are to grow towards the territory of world teachers.

ROOSTER: Too big a role for me.

MONICA: That doesn't mean you're to become famous.

ROOSTER: Thank God.

MONICA: Your core assignment is to express the personal story through the universal medium. *(Shakes her head as she reads the thermometer)* Still this low-grade fever.

ROOSTER: I'm not taking on a personal assignment. *(Shudders)*

MONICA: You okay?

ROOSTER: Comes all of a sudden...

MONICA: Mind if I peek at these paintings? *(Picks up a painting)* This one looks like a holding place for heaven. *(Lifts another painting)* And this. My.

ROOSTER: A tree is naked.

MONICA: Is someone selling these?

ROOSTER: *(Puts away the paintings)* I contacted the first agent for money, the next three for revenge...the fourth agent said, "These are highly marketable paintings. I suggest you show them to someone else." The fifth agent said, "I wanted to like your paintings, but I don't." The sixth was the cruelest. "I like the birds, the atmosphere, but there's no substance to the work." The last agent was triumphant in his rejection. "Painting the South isn't fashionable," he said. They say Southerners will always paint the South, but I didn't think I would because I always felt like an outsider.

MONICA: But you were born here.

ROOSTER: I don't understand all the unspoken things you are just supposed to know. America's a young country, but the South feels old. *(HE has put up the paintings and sits exhausted)* Listen to that wind...

MONICA: Laughing like a loon at sunrise.

ROOSTER: I need a rainstorm every now and then. But I hate that rattling sound.

MONICA: I had a passion once...for someone.

ROOSTER: Your husband?

MONICA: I was totally prepared for his death. I'll never be as prepared as that…and then when it came…when they put him in the ground, I thought this man who dominated my life doesn't live anymore. He gave me my ideas.

(BUNKY bursts in.)

BUNKY: Uncle Roo…I've got to talk to you.

(MONICA starts to leave.)

ROOSTER: Where're you going?

MONICA: To get a vase.

(MONICA exits.)

BUNKY: For God's sake, don't talk to Angela. (Crosses for a drink) I don't know how to tell you…

ROOSTER: You're in love with the cook? Ma will die.

BUNKY: Women marry like birds flocking in winter. When one takes off, the others trail behind.

ROOSTER: Angela's a good chef. Marry her, you'll get fat.

BUNKY: No! If I can hold out, I'll be all right. Angela says, fine. Then she threatens to kill herself. She's collecting all the sleeping pills she can find in the house. I read about a capsule that gives you a cold for a day—like a virus—and then presto you die in your sleep. Your heart explodes. Gosh! She's three months pregnant.

ROOSTER: What? Congratulations. You're a father. Mom's a great-grand-mother.

BUNKY: Here's the test results. "Positive" has never had such a negative ring.

ROOSTER: There're several options.

BUNKY: Yes, one: an abortion. Two? I could marry her.

ROOSTER: There are many ways to make a woman miserable besides marriage.

BUNKY: Three? She might have the baby, and I could pay for it.

ROOSTER: Any way…you'll pay for it.

BUNKY: She'll probably abort the thing.

ROOSTER: No. This'll be a wealthy baby with a big inheritance. Rich babies don't die before they're born, but in a car wreck at fifteen. The first thing Ma will say when that baby opens its eyes is "I wonder when he'll be able to see Mardi Gras." I should order one of those little chair ladders for the parades. But poor Ma. Losing her companion, and her cook. Maybe we should have a double wedding. When will you announce the news?

(BUNKY refills his plastic cup, exits. OOZIE enters.)

OOZIE: Dinner is ready. *(Notices the flowers)* Gorgeous roses. Did Purvis send them? *(Reads card)* "I absolutely adore you." What a sweetie. *(Exits screaming)* Cousin Irene. See my flowers. Cousin Irene.

MONICA: I saw your show in Philadelphia.

ROOSTER: Unlikely.

MONICA: Two years ago. *(Smiles softly)* I can't paint, I can't write, but I can recognize quality.

ROOSTER: After Philadelphia I quit. Soon as I did, people said to me, "You look liberated." And it was true.

MONICA: Your life was easier.

ROOSTER: No one hated me anymore. I'd spent my whole life bullying people into hanging my paintings. Watch out, it's him again.

MONICA: But you started as a legend.

ROOSTER: Successful, but on a shallow incline.

MONICA: People said your name with reverence.

ROOSTER: Before they boiled me in a pot and ate me. Most people don't like my work.

MONICA: I'm sure it has a devastating effect because it's incredible. *(Picks up a portfolio)* And you do everything: oils, watercolors, pen and ink. Oh...my...sketches of me. Well?

ROOSTER: Horribly awkward, isn't it?

MONICA: You haven't done your best...your finest...

ROOSTER: My signature work?...

MONICA: When you start painting a lot, it will happen.

ROOSTER: In my last painting, I sought the perfect blue. I thought of myself as being inside the blue...

MONICA: *(Opening an envelope)* What's this?

ROOSTER: I won an award...a retreat for artists, but I don't need any more slaps from the museum people.

MONICA: You do nothing, and they give you an award.

ROOSTER: I'm sick. Maybe I'll die.

MONICA: You're living now.

(HE has a sudden cramp, staggers.)

ROOSTER: Something's wrong with me again...*(Holds on to the table)* I'm dizzy...I feel weak and all that...I'm...

MONICA: *(Trying to support him)* Breathe.

ROOSTER: It's nothing. (*HE stumbles to a chair, sits, grins until the pain dies down*) It's...gone.

MONICA: Lie down.

ROOSTER: How did this happen?

MONICA: It'll get better. It's simply hard now, after the treatment; trust me.

ROOSTER: That's what I believed. (*HE has another weak spell.*)

MONICA: Don't talk.

ROOSTER: I've been thinking about the place I'd like to live with you. It'll have eight rooms, a wraparound porch, and beautiful trees...a magnolia, a pecan, and an oak.

MONICA: I don't think I could live in the South. I'm not a real New Orleanian. My great-grandparents didn't live here and bank at the Whitney.

ROOSTER: It's okay to be a Northerner for a while. (*Pause*) I haven't had many women in my life. That's the truth. Work and pain...I don't want to die.

MONICA: You're not dying. You're living. (*HE relaxes and lies back on the bed*) You hear me? (*HE closes his eyes*) Sleep.

ROOSTER: I want to talk about my paintings so you'll understand...

MONICA: Rest.

ROOSTER: (*HE has a sudden chill.*) I'm scared I'll sleep and never wake up.

MONICA: My husband's name was Speed. He got that from playing football. He told me, "When I die, I want you to be there." We became closer through his disease. Suddenly, one afternoon he breathed a little moment and went away. It was just a breath, it was very calm. But you will not die. (*Pause*) Your life's your own, and you must do something with it. (*Pause*) Try and nap.

ROOSTER: Don't leave me if I sleep.

MONICA: I won't, unless you tell me to.

(HE closes his eyes. SHE watches for a moment.)

ROOSTER: *(Screaming)* Monica. Monica!

MONICA: What's wrong?

ROOSTER: I had a bad dream I was burning to death. I kept calling to you to save me.

MONICA: And did I?

ROOSTER: I don't know. I woke up. You don't think I'll die, do you?

MONICA: Probably not.

ROOSTER: Because I want to live till I'm old. If anything does happen to me, will you promise you'll take care of my paintings?

MONICA: Nothing is going to happen.

ROOSTER: If it does?

MONICA: Then don't worry. I'll always protect them.

ROOSTER: Same as if they were yours?

MONICA: Same as if they were mine.

ROOSTER: Is it hot in here?

MONICA: No, honey. It's cool as evening.

ROOSTER: Why am I so warm? I want you to make me push myself to paint, if you want to.

MONICA: I'd like to.

END OF SCENE 4

INTERMISSION

317

ACT II
SCENE 1

(The day room. Three weeks later. Six p.m.The afternoon is drawing to a close. Wagner's Lohengrin's Bridal Chorus plays on the stereo. A lighted lamp stands on the table. IRENE, in a Victorian "mother-of-the bride's" dress, is sitting reading a "Town and Country" magazine. OOZIE is dressed in Victorian wedding attire complete with tiara and veil. SHE stands at the back of the room for a moment with her hands clasping a nosegay. Then SHE comes back near the table, picks up a mirror and looks at her face.)

OOZIE: You like my dress?

IRENE: Pretty, but it's not soft enough for me.

OOZIE: I don't want to look frail like I'm living in a fairy tale.

IRENE: You don't.

OOZIE: I had my hair done. I liked it for about an hour.

IRENE: *(Looks at OOZIE'S hair)* Strange shade. Looks like chicken feathers.

OOZIE: It's my natural color so my hair's a restoration. Now I've passed the big four-oh.

IRENE: Big fifty, and you're pushed up too high!

OOZIE: Roo's the one you should yell at. *(Striding up and down the stage)* He's with that nurse. And what's more, she's not from here. She's an import.

IRENE: To think Roo was in "Life Magazine" at twenty as one of the red hot one hundred.

OOZIE: Maybe he can fix my photo with some of his painting talent.

IRENE: But if your photo's not to the paper on time...

OOZIE: I will not get the upper right-hand corner of the Living Section. I don't know if I'm frustrated or disappointed.

IRENE: You always have problems with distinctions. Frustrated is like an itch. Disappointed is like a tear.

OOZIE: Roo doesn't call, if he doesn't feel like it. He doesn't know they've invented South Central Bell?

IRENE: Never do anything for men thinking you're going to get what you want. When they conform, it means they are asleep. To be effective, one needs to expect catastrophe. This should be easy. I've watched so many boys in the Garden District acquire an unfeeling attitude. They stay at home but they aren't there except when they're tired, hungry, or broke. For entertainment, they torment their relatives. Women are by nature more sensitive than men. We've to curb ourselves to keep them. Acquire a short memory—Never look back. It's not their fault we're more intelligent. We provide amusement. We have for centuries. *(SOUND: The clock chimes. IRENE looks up.)* That clock's been in my family for a hundred years. The sun and moon on top change places. It made time important, once.

OOZIE: I'm going to get changed and drive myself somewhere nice. *(Starts to go, stops, and crosses to the phone, dials.)* Lord! I've no car. Purvis promised to lend me his.

IRENE: You drive a car until it smokes, and he won't let you do that to a Jaguar...

OOZIE: I hope his secretary's not using it.

IRENE: Already? These questionable generosities.

(IRENE returns to her "Town and Country," looking preoccupied. Awkward silence. OOZIE sits, yanks off her shoes, and sticks her feet out. Horrified.)

OOZIE: My feet hurt. I need a toe reduction. I just hate my toes. My second one's too long. Purvis is mad, because I've scheduled foot surgery. Purvis's got this back pain, so he can't...*(Rolls her hand.)* He has to use this "donut" pillow to sit down. During dinner, he'll push a button and shock himself. At the opera, he shoots up in his seat, then guzzles vodka. *(Looks for ROO. Holds up her ring)* This is a two-carat diamond. It's very nice, but Purvis gave his first wife a five-carat flawless one from Tiffany's! She kept it after the divorce.

GHOSTS OF NEW ORLEANS

IRENE: You can keep yours, too.

OOZIE: *(Crosses and brings IRENE her drink.)* I don't want to be a divorcee. I'm not marrying Purvis unless I get jewelry of equal value. They can put his back on ice, I don't care! Now we're engaged, he's blackmailing me into accepting inferior jewelry.

IRENE: You love him?

OOZIE: I don't know. My God. I don't think about it.

IRENE: It's time.

OOZIE: Love doesn't pull a lot of stroke. Purvis is not my dream man because he lies, steals, and cheats.

IRENE: Every man should have on his desk, "The truth stops here."

OOZIE: If only he would lie to other people and tell me the truth.

IRENE: Optimally, it should be that way, but it's not.

OOZIE: My job is to make him look good! What can I do?

IRENE: Nothing. They lie once, twice. Then lying becomes addictive.

OOZIE: *(Stuffs Kleenex in her armpits.)* I'm sweating like a pig!

IRENE: Ladies "moisten." They don't sweat!

OOZIE: This family treats me like a dog. Throw her a scrap. Toss her a bone! It's a cautiously staged attack. I've this awful pimple on my lip. Keeping myself intact is impossible. I've got to move in sections and reassemble once it's safe. If only your husband was alive…Pete was so easy, so good, so…

IRENE: Try not to talk so much, so we can live with each other.

OOZIE: Roo was born too late. You were too old. I told you.

IRENE: I was trying to hold the marriage together.

(BUNKY enters impatiently, hurries over to the liquor cart. HE pours a fistful of aspirins.)

IRENE: Another bird in flight. *(To BUNKY)* You didn't tell me, "Hello!"

BUNKY: I said "Hello" this morning when I saw you in the parlor.

IRENE: But is one hello a day enough? You get up looking for a drink?

BUNKY: I'm trying to kill this headache.

OOZIE: By mixing alcohol and aspirin!

BUNKY: I drink more when it rains. You, see, there's reality, and there's real reality, under everything else. If you get too much into real reality, you'll drink too. Salut.

(HE pours himself bourbon and a glass of water.)

IRENE: What did I tell you about men? I've nearly been ignored to death on some occasions.

(The phone rings. BUNKY hurries back in. OOZIE grabs the phone.)

OOZIE: *(Into phone)* Hello…What? *(To BUNKY)* Ocshner Fertility Clinic. They hung up.

BUNKY: I'm going to sit in the rain. I'm talked out.

OOZIE: Wait. Didn't I see you there? I was in a class, "Intimacy for Seniors."

BUNKY: Don't be crass.

OOZIE: Have you frozen parts of yourself for extra drinking money? Become a father so young?

BUNKY: I wasn't there.

OOZIE: Well, it must have a been a holograph of you!

BUNKY: Or your bifocal contacts.

(SOUND: A phone rings. BUNKY grasps it and whispers into the phone.)

BUNKY: Hello. It's sure? Yes…yes…Sometimes they make mistakes.

(BUNKY slips offstage with the phone. IRENE peers at the garden.)

OOZIE: Finally the king arrives.

(ROOSTER and MONICA enter the garden whispering.)

ROOSTER: Audubon's the most sensual park. Geese gliding in the ponds.

MONICA: Camellias. So big and light. Nature is such a big part of our days.

(ROOSTER and MONICA enter through the garden door.)

ROOSTER: Every time I go out I feel I can paint again. I'm a magnet for the color.

IRENE: I don't have to walk that long to feel good.

OOZIE: Close the door. *(Points to the door)* You're throwing the cooling system off whack.

ROOSTER: Attack of the lonely women.

OOZIE: Why can't you arrive on time?

IRENE: She's afraid she's losing her looks, and there wasn't much to begin with.

ROOSTER: That was a hit.

IRENE: It wasn't a hit. It was a home run.

OOZIE: Only someone heartless could fail to appreciate a good photo.

MONICA: Roo…has to rest.

IRENE: A pushy nurse.

MONICA: *(Exiting)* It's Roo's choice, isn't it?

OOZIE: *(To ROOSTER)* I'm placing myself at your mercy! I've had two premarital divorces.

IRENE: Just because you've been under the knife doesn't mean you're photogenic.

OOZIE: You're lazy. That's one of the deadly sins? Pride, covetousness, anger, gluttony, envy, sloth.

IRENE: You forgot lust. *(Exiting)*

OOZIE: Yes, well...This wedding has cost a fortune, but we will line up horse-drawn carriages and have invitations delivered on horseback! Still, it's hard to leave.

ROOSTER: It was a good place to live from zero to eight.

OOZIE: We'd sit in the dining room...

ROOSTER: Waiting for the swish of the door when Ma would go upstairs.

OOZIE: Yes, she was very busy with her facials, her manicures.

ROOSTER: You were always there with Dad.

OOZIE: And with you! You're my boy. My beauty boy. We'd go outside, watch the cars passing and you promised, "When I'm big, I'm going to buy you a yellow car and I want the license plate to say 'sunshine,' because you are my sunshine."

ROOSTER: I don't want to talk about the way it was.

OOZIE: OK. Good-bye, Saint Charles Avenue. Good-bye to the grandfather's clock chiming. And cut-glass front doors...Does anyone value New Orleans really?

ROOSTER: It could have been nice to live here...if we didn't have this cloud of uncertainty.

OOZIE: What uncertainty?

ROOSTER: When you and Dad were on the porch with that little light on, I'd go to the gallery and watch the streetcars clang by. And in her room Ma would sit up late, immobilized, the help grumbling in the kitchen. Dad and you. Just talk or fire. I strained to figure something of it. Perfectly lovely dinners we had. You on one side of Dad, and Mom on the other. Thank God we've a gallery to escape to.

OOZIE: You know? I wished you were mine.

ROOSTER: *(Points outside.)* Look, the rain's cooled it off. Ma's cutting some flowers. I look like her. I never realized before how overwhelming she is…so much love and yet somehow a lie inside it all. She'd start out enthusiastic about my art, then lose interest. And Dad, he came to my last show and yelled, "Good job, kid," from his wheelchair.

OOZIE: He was hard not to love. Can't you forgive me?

ROOSTER: Sometimes I think if Mama had the right loving, she'd be warmer…

OOZIE: Maybe. But soon I'll be your aunt of, with, by, and from the state of Texas.

(IRENE enters)

(OOZIE exits)

IRENE: Have you been tormenting Oozie?

ROOSTER: For God's sake. Sit.

IRENE: Little children have little problems. Big children have big ones.

ROOSTER: I'm right next to a change, but not yet in it.

IRENE: To be alive is the important thing.

ROOSTER: *(Struggles with himself)* Yesterday and again today, I told myself it's impossible…out of the question. Sit. Please.

IRENE: Is that it?

ROOSTER: *(HE puts his hand to his head)* I feel hope.

IRENE: Hope has been unfashionable for a long time.

ROOSTER: I thought I'd never concentrate again…Then The Hyde Museum hit me with phone calls—

IRENE: *(Interrupting)* Is this the good news?

ROOSTER: I got a grant. A year's retreat in North Carolina.

IRENE: Who knows where we'll be in a year.

ROOSTER: It's one of those rare miracle days that lift your mind.

IRENE: You don't know enough yet?

ROOSTER: I'm going to travel again. Paint my signature work. I can't do a miracle here because everybody knows about me. I'm the son of the son of the son.

IRENE: Yes. You belong to a family at the peak of perfectionism.

SOUND: We hear a parade passing.

IRENE: Let's watch the parade. I added up the years our family has been involved in Carnival, and it came to one hundred twenty-three. *(Points at the parade)* One day…I hope…you'll dress like a captain, in white velvet with a cap and plume. You'll ride horseback before the floats…then escort the queen in the grand march around the ballroom. *(Picks up a scepter and crown enshrined on a table.)* The Carnival Ball links the South with European culture. Your great-grandmother, grandmother, and I were queens—on Mardi Gras day. I practiced for months how to waft a scepter, to walk with a heavy train. When you're Queen of Rex, the doors of society swing open.

SOUND: Jazz band from the parade.

You used to love the romantic nostalgia. Remember when you costumed in Proteus ball—

ROOSTER: When I was ten.

IRENE: As the son of Paul Revere? I'd hoped you'd become active in the Carnival clubs.

ROOSTER: I need to separate myself...

IRENE: Your paintings will disappear, but Mardi Gras will survive. Quit New Orleans?

ROOSTER: I don't believe what I might paint here could be respected.

IRENE: I'll set up a place in the yard or rent a spot in the park.

ROOSTER: If I keep moving, my health will come back.

IRENE: Your immune system is shot.

ROOSTER: True...but in North Carolina I'll be supported to work...

IRENE: Baked by the sun, eaten by bugs. Who knows what will happen if...

ROOSTER: Ma, the amazing thing is that most of the time I'm not in pain. Some days I've more energy than others, and when I don't I nap.

IRENE: That's what you should do.

ROOSTER: But staying here, there's another kind of pain. When I was a boy, I was flattered you wanted my opinion. But now I can't be on the phone five minutes you don't scream, "Who's that?" If I compliment Monica or any other woman, you make these grim faces....Look, I know I was Dad's replacement.

IRENE: What a horrible—

ROOSTER: I'm not blaming you. I need to be out on my own, meet other artists, see and move–

ROSARY HARTEL O'NEILL

IRENE: I'll call up this retreat and say I forbid it.

ROOSTER: I don't need your permission. Until Dad died you never toler-ated girls around me. And when you did you'd slip this stab in like a hypo-dermic needle, and the poor girl wouldn't know she'd been inoculated. Or you'd let me invite her on a cruise, then refuse to seat her at your table so you could humiliate her. In Puerto Vallarta, when I finally had a girl and a commission, you created that awful scene before her parents and the people from the Guggenheim....

IRENE: Lies.

ROOSTER: But even that pain wasn't enough to make me rebel against you. I've been thinking a lot about you lately. I wake up and feel you in the room, whenever you come to visit. Look, I'm not going forever.

IRENE: How can you tell?

ROOSTER: I've got Louisiana on my driver's license and my birth certifi-cate is recorded here.

IRENE: This isn't the best time for me. My favorite dog died this morning. The Catahoula hound with one crystal eye and a white cross on her fore-head.

MONICA: *(Returning)* I heard about your dog.

IRENE: *(To ROO)* My old dog, Ophelia's, in mourning. I hope she doesn't drown herself by the willow tree.

(BUNKY enters, pursued by OOZIE. ROOSTER shows them an envelope.)

BUNKY: Somebody died?

ROOSTER: I won an art competition. A residency in North Carolina. On an estate for artists. They give you a cottage and a studio for work.

IRENE: If Roo starts obsessing on painting again, it'll be a catastrophe.

BUNKY: *(Turns on the stereo)* Let's do a happy dance. *(ROOSTER nods no.)* You dance the success of this person. The first rule is, "Never dance alone!"

(To IRENE) I'll practice on you. I want a report card.

IRENE: Dancing's not my preferred activity.

BUNKY: In Africa they say if you can walk you can sing, and if you can sing, you can dance. *(HE and IRENE dance.)*

(OOZIE spins by herself in delight. ROOSTER and MONICA observe. BUNKY swipes IRENE'S old-fashioned while she isn't looking.)

IRENE: Nobody needs family. My son wants to live in a Boy Scout cabin. North Carolina's bursting with nuclear waste. Before you eat their wild duck, you've got to get it tested for radioactivity.

OOZIE: Can you sell paintings there?

IRENE: I wouldn't go any place where you bring your own toilet paper.

BUNKY: Working without a net, it's exciting.

IRENE: Quiet. Roo was born stubborn, remained stubborn, and will die stubborn.

SOUND: *Music stops.*

(ALL sit. ROOSTER gets the painting.)

MONICA: Mrs. Dubonnet, this award's a great honor.

IRENE: How many artists applied, two?

ROOSTER: Here's the painting that won.

IRENE: It's easy to feel proud when you're not by yourself. *(Rings bell)* Where's Angela? I'm tired. Oozie and I made mint jelly all morning.

OOZIE: *(Serving crackers and jam)* Everyone's got to eat.

IRENE: Nobody needs art. Even the Statue of Liberty is not maintained. She's like a giant jigsaw puzzle. Three hundred copper sheets for skin. Only indigents and tourists brave the ferry...

SOUND: *A phone rings off stage.*

(BUNKY exits.)

MONICA: Roo's artwork was judged by an impartial panel.

IRENE: Who're soliciting my donation. The Hyde Museum's not my favorite charity. *(Reaches for her old-fashioned, but her glass is empty.)* Who's stealing my old-fashioneds? I've wealth but not leisure. *(To ROOSTER)* I'd like to prop your career up, but it'd mean a misallocation of funds. Sometime, I'll outline for you how the family foundation works.

ROOSTER: Don't spoil this.

MONICA: Your mom will be fine once she sees what this means—

IRENE: *(To ROOSTER)* You want money? Ask me.

ROOSTER: Just because you've closed the door to your own talent…

IRENE: What a dreadful thing to say. *(Rises to leave)* I've got to have eye surgery. I can't see a dang thing. *(IRENE slightly falls)*

MONICA: Mrs. Dubonnet?

IRENE: Don't let that woman touch me! Why must Huck overwax these floors? Someone's going to slip and sue me for a million dollars.

(IRENE walks out supported by OOZIE. MONICA watches them. BUNKY enters, chugging whiskey.)

BUNKY: Everybody's gone? Lucky me.

MONICA: *(Keeping her voice low)* Wha'd you want?

BUNKY: I'm drunk.

MONICA: I know.

BUNKY: I mean I'm real drunk. I'm so drunk I got mixed up and hollered for you in the bathroom.

MONICA: Stay away.

BUNKY: I'm hot. And sleepy.

MONICA: Go to bed.

BUNKY: The things you imply.

MONICA: No closer.

BUNKY: Men are weak, sweetheart. What can I do? And women tempt us, you know…

MONICA: Please go.

BUNKY: You don't have to love me. It can be worth your while…

MONICA: I'm not looking for fun.

BUNKY: *(Takes a few steps closer.)* One sweet dance…with a brother's hand…

MONICA: Oh God. Move.

BUNKY: Kiss me.

MONICA: No!

(MONICA hits BUNKY. HE storms about as if he'll beat her.)

BUNKY: Most girls like it.

END OF SCENE 1

ACT II
SCENE 2

(A week later. 6:00 p.m. Dusk. It's drizzling. OOZIE enters in her Victorian bridal gown, carrying a pearl rosary. ROOSTER enters in slacks and a gray turtleneck, takes out his camera. HE begins to photograph her, moving about easily with the camera.)

OOZIE: I bought you a rosary from Guatemala. Inside this crystal. You can see Our Lady.

ROOSTER: *(Referring to her pose)* Don't move.

OOZIE: I got it in the French Quarter. From that bead lady who spits at you. Irene's in her manic mode. I cried Friday night, Saturday night, and Sunday night.

ROOSTER: *(Sets down camera and moves inside the picture)* I'm getting in the frame.

OOZIE: She's so upset about you, she wants to put off my wedding. The heart doctor's doubling her pills! God knows what'll happen if you move to North Carolina…Somebody's got to stay here.

ROOSTER: She's too rich for the doctors to let her die.

OOZIE: You're her only son!

ROOSTER: At best, I'm excluded from any authoritative decision.

OOZIE: *(To ROOSTER)* Purvis's no comfort. *(Flabbergasted)* He'll postpone our wedding indefinitely to have it on her tab at the Country Club.

ROOSTER: Purvis is eighty-one, but his liver is a hundred and seven.

OOZIE: He wants to admit himself to a detox center, but they have to wait to put Purvis in, until his brother gets out!

ROOSTER: Hold that.

OOZIE: I said, "Don't mess with me, Purvis." He's going ahead with this ceremony if I've to drug his oatmeal to do so. I'll pull him out for the wedding, then put him back in.

ROOSTER: Whoa.

OOZIE: Say you'll stay here. If not, she'll punish me. A teeny lie. *(Touches his cheek)* Ah, there's that dimple. I swear you could sleep in that dimple. *(OOZIE strokes his arm, singing. ROO joins in.)* "The itzy bitzy spider climbed up the water spout. Down came the rain and washed the spider out. Out came the sun and dried up all the rain. And the itzy bitzy spider climbed up the spout again." *(THEY repeat the refrain, dancing and laughing.)*

OOZIE: Stay home till after my wedding. Irene's frightened of my marrying, and she's a right; she's no friends.

ROOSTER: You didn't bring much gaiety—

OOZIE: All my life I've dreamed of marriage. I tried on perfume I couldn't afford, avoiding the cleaners to get by. I was afraid to stand up and be a woman, so I kept my demands small. I said I didn't want anything, but I needed a lot.

ROOSTER: How ironic.

OOZIE: Maybe she didn't know about me and Pete. Hah. I hated your mother's guts. Hatred and love. The two go together.

(IRENE arrives in Victorian wedding attire and on a cane.)

IRENE: No dinner. Angela just sits in the kitchen, and when I ask her what's wrong, she cries. *(Pause)* Let's get these pictures over with. Angela puts mismatched socks in my bureau drawer. I've three maids, but no dinner.

ROOSTER: Everybody smile. *(Takes a photo.)*

IRENE: Roo'll put me in Metairie Cemetery next week!

ROOSTER: You feel bad?

IRENE: I shouldn't have thought it made much difference. Most sons care for their mothers. I don't take it personal you don't. If you take it personal, it's four old-fashioneds in the room at night.

(BUNKY enters. HE wears several thick ropes of Mardi Gras beads over Victorian attire. HE does a jig over to the liquor cart.)

SOUND: *A parade passing.*

BUNKY: Bacchus parade's passing. I caught some purple beads with gold babies. I love Mardi Gras. These lavish stupidities.

ROOSTER: Everybody line up.

(ROOSTER shoots various poses during the following sequence. Parade passes with fanfare.)

IRENE: Why take pictures when we don't know when the wedding's going to be? *(To BUNKY)* Stand by me. Grandpa loved Carnival. Three times he was king of a parade and ball. For me Carnival's the divine element in New Orleans. It's the part that connects us with history. Dancing at those balls with men in silver boots, velvet tunics, and plumed hats. Sitting in the roped-off section for wives. Mardi Gras. That dream machine where you fall in love with—

ROOSTER: Everybody smile. Say, "Carnival."

ALL: Carnival.

IRENE: A new dress a night.

BUNKY: Without Mardi Gras, life's just a drag.

IRENE: In the old days, Bunky, there were mule-drawn floats and flambeaux carriers tap-dancing for quarters. One caught on fire, and Grandpa threw his coat over him and smothered the flames. Still, there were fewer accidents since the mules moved slowly and the floats were smaller. Now the tractor, the fluorescent light, and two-tiered floats have changed that.

ROOSTER: *(Referring to the photo)* I think I've got it.

BUNKY: See that monstrous float!

OOZIE: It's going to get caught in an oak tree.

IRENE: Let's go get a better look.

(IRENE exits with OOZIE. BUNKY waits. HE empties the glass, takes a second.)

BUNKY: Uncle Roo, I hope this doesn't overload your brain.

ROOSTER: It won't take much.

BUNKY: I've downed enough booze to kill a small animal. Angela's just back from Oschner Clinic.

ROOSTER: And the baby?

BUNKY: It's fine. (Shrugs) Unfortunately. Don't look like that.

ROOSTER: You should grow up. What are you, twenty-one, twenty-two?

BUNKY: I can't bear thinking about it for long. *(Picks up another old-fashioned.)*

ROOSTER: Mama will kill you. She will be more upset about you than about me.

BUNKY: It's not funny. Angela is crying, and I can't stop her. I sat through her sob story, even though I was vaguely destroyed by it. And I made a fool of myself with Monica.

ROOSTER: Wha'd you do?

BUNKY: I wanted to kiss her, I think.

ROOSTER: What? Did you hurt her?

BUNKY: She hit me. The whole thing happened too quickly…

ROOSTER: You embarrassed her? You act like a zombie.

BUNKY: *(Sighs deeply)* I'm not thinking of anything. I can't think of any-thing. *(In a low voice)* I've given up thinking. Swear to God.

ROOSTER: Go to Angela. Support her.

BUNKY: After the parade. How bleak it is here. Darkness and rain and funeral gloom. Day after day throughout Carnival. Never a flash of sun. Remember how I loved the parades? I'd follow them halfway to Canal Street before I realized I was tired and would have to walk back. Move in step to the hard-charging sounds. Ground moving beneath my feet. The excitement of the parades comes from the toes through the body. Showers of trinkets from the floats. Running in the street yelling, "Throw me something, Mister." You see these floats, like beautiful swaying clouds. Soft big puffs moving down the street. You look up and you feel better. Hearing the sirens, and the rush of jazz. Watching the gypsies come in and out and the Indians. Just yesterday I was a school boy. Everything was so nice. So easy...so...Football games, homecoming and sweet-sixteen parties. Convertibles and girls and...

(BUNKY falls asleep. IRENE enters with OOZIE.)

IRENE: Angela's crying and dinner's not ready. Monica's somewhere watching the parades. A new era's hit this house. *(To ROOSTER)* I want to compliment you. That woman could con the whole family sequentially. Faded smocks. Hair in a desperate condition...

ROOSTER: Don't get started.

IRENE: Once working women hit thirty, they begin having that disheveled look.

ROOSTER: She's filled me with profound hope.

IRENE: Is there any sex in this? Maybe not, but it's all about it.

OOZIE: I tried the same thing at Roo's age—

IRENE: Cohabitate if you must, in one of those rabbit hutches in the dark parts of town. Wear Birkenstock sandals and look painfully thin. I can float above it. Soon all you'll have is the memory of money.

ROOSTER: Shut up.

IRENE: The situation's impossible. You know that line by Milton. "Chaos,

chaos, welcome to hell."

OOZIE: Calm down, honey.

IRENE: *(To ROO)* Don't expect me to support you two. I'd have to be really desperate or really…Dead!

OOZIE: *(Handing her a drink)* You'll feel better with a toddy.

IRENE: I called that cabin place. They don't have plumbing or electricity. I'll have to tell Monica.

ROOSTER: Don't you dare. Talk to her, go near her, accuse her.

IRENE: I'm trying to maintain a veneer of civilization. To smooth over something rough with—something refined.

ROOSTER: No, you're not.

IRENE: Fine. I've spent time checking up on this flea-bitten cabin place.

ROOSTER: Who asked you?

IRENE: You just want to go there to drink and screw this girl. You'll sing a different tune if your body…

ROOSTER: For God's sake I…

IRENE: *(Quiet)* What's the point of running off?

ROOSTER: *(IRENE walks over and strokes his hair.)* Oh, Ma. I yearn to travel…*(Pause)* Ma, you and I both know there's a difference between removing death and extending life. I'd like to postpone dying as long as possible.

IRENE: Don't use the D word.

ROOSTER: Everything changes in the shadow of…

IRENE: You don't know what—

ROOSTER: There's a special light that comes from a different state of being. It's almost blue-white. Colors I've seen in Florence and Rome around the cathedrals at night. You lose your edge. You merge with everything. And yet, you see sharper. The sun, the rain, you smell the grass when you go out in the garden. You can almost taste the green leafy trees. Light and color intensify. The purity at dawn, the stark reality at noon, and the romantic sunset, the final burst of red before blackness. Then there's twilight, the hour of gentleness, so mysterious, so sad. I don't know what color it is. I went outside to see, but it was silent. Nothing moved; then it turned dark. Time's going by so fast, it makes me mad....I want to go to North Carolina.

IRENE: Take my advice; say, "No." *(Pause)* Everything comes down to caution in the end—You haven't real choices. . .

ROOSTER: You've been so concerned.

IRENE: Where's it gotten me? Bunky's flunking out of college. And you'll have a relapse.

ROOSTER: Let me find out?

IRENE: You have to be cared for by someone.

ROOSTER: And that someone is you?

IRENE: The *grande famille* doesn't exist anymore.

ROOSTER: *(Directly to his MOTHER.)* Do you think this decision's nothing for me? I've been practicing how to talk to you. I look around the room, this nowhere space where I dream. I turn on the lights and tell myself not to feel, to think, that you'll want what's best for me. I look at the ornaments, the photographs, the relics of my youth. Books, paints, papers. Everywhere I look I find a feeling. Each object recalls a scene. When I gaze about, I'm a boy with idle dreams. I've stared through the memories. Opened the sealed doors of grief. Said good-bye to all the fantasies and let them evaporate like so much smoke. *(Pause)* I'm going to ask Monica to live with me.

IRENE: A man in your state can't co-habitate. It isn't feasible or proper.

ROOSTER: I'm almost out of my mind. Can't you see that?

IRENE: I can't believe you're doing this.

ROOSTER: I'm going to keep asking her till she says "yes." When I was a little boy, I decided that I was no good. I ran to this room, when I heard you and Dad fighting. I decided it was my fault. You rushed in here and I couldn't get you out, not even when I, oh God, pushed you and screamed, "Go on." So I slept in the chair and let you stay. I know you depend on me for someone to be close with. To do things for. You're important to me. Ma, needing to please you doesn't fade with age. Once you lower your expectations, you'll feel better.

IRENE: I've got...to tell you...I know you're capable of hearing this.

ROOSTER: Yes...?

IRENE: All this business about being exhausted...being unable to paint...all this isn't...the real problem. . .

ROOSTER: What?

IRENE: The sickness you've contracted...can't be cured.

ROOSTER: That's not true—

IRENE: Your body's...breaking down.

ROOSTER: You mustn't...say things like that.

IRENE: I don't...I don't want to. But it's a fact.

ROOSTER: Nothing's hopeless.

IRENE: I want you to stay home...near me, the doctors...

 ROOSTER: That's what I can't take. Lying here...till I become helpless. Monica!

IRENE: You can't count on her. She'll be off soon as she meets a richer artist with bigger rooms. I know these semi-pious types, feeding you illusions while they soak up your money. I wonder who she'll find to mooch off next.

ROOSTER: Don't speak to her. Accuse her.

IRENE: I told Doctor Ryan that you and your fly-by-night nurse might run off. If you don't quiet down, you will be hauled off to the hospital and she will be reported to the A.M.A. and lose her license.

ROOSTER: Out, out, out. Out, out, out!!

IRENE: Oozie! Oozie! Where did I put my drink?

(IRENE stumbles out.)

(ROOSTER collapses on the day bed and dims the lights. Moments later, MONICA enters, covered in strands of beads and in street attire.)

SOUND: *The Bacchus parade rumbles in the distance through a screaming crowd.*

MONICA: They're throwing doubloons by the handful. Showers of gold. This is the city where trees wear pearls. It's mighty dark. *(Turns up the lights)* Look, I've got six metallic beads and green ones with gold babies.

ROOSTER: I'm tired.

MONICA: Are you going to bed so early?

ROOSTER: I want to show the world I'm still autonomous.

(SHE quietly opens her satchel and takes his pulse)

MONICA: You're not turning down the award?

ROOSTER: *(Rips the device off his arm.)* I didn't say that.

MONICA: *(Hands him pills and water)* You don't want to worm your way through it?

ROOSTER: Mom's a study in cement, like she's mired in gray.

MONICA: When you're away a while, you'll love her again and miss this place.

(On the street there is a general hubbub, people yelling, the roar of a motor car.)

ROOSTER: There go the gypsies! Hah. Hah. The last of the gypsies. *(Tries to laugh again)* I'll throw them some beads. Hey y'all. Want to come in? Hey there. Throw me something.

MONICA: You're working yourself up—

ROOSTER: The last of the gypsies.

MONICA: Stop it.

ROOSTER: Give me those beads. *(Grabs at her beads)*

MONICA: You're cutting me.

ROOSTER: Hurry.

MONICA: Let me do it.

ROOSTER: Take them off.

MONICA: No, they won't unhook.

ROOSTER: I'll have to break them.

MONICA: Wait.

ROOSTER: Too late, they're gone. *(Heads for the door. SHE blocks him.)* Out my way.

MONICA: Where're you going?

ROOSTER: To find the gypsies.

MONICA: Not tonight.

(HE starts for the door)

ROOSTER: Out my way.

(HE trips, rushes back to the bed, throws himself down.)

ROOSTER: I'd like a knock-out injection. Monica?

MONICA: Yes?

ROOSTER: What're you doing?

MONICA: Watching you.

ROOSTER: How long do you plan to do that?

MONICA: Long as it takes.

ROOSTER: I can't stand being pent up. It gives me the jitters. You know Ma keeps a loaded gun by her bed. I never go in this house without screaming her name, because I'm afraid she might accidentally shoot me.

MONICA: She's a survivor. She can take care of herself.

ROOSTER: "To take care of someone" has a double meaning.

MONICA: How long can you keep losing chances? Little bits of life. Shreds of dreams. God wants success for you, but you must give something up? You can't hold God in one hand and her in the other.

ROOSTER: Dogs have been known to go crazy when their leash was cut. What if my body gives out, and I can't do the things you want?

MONICA: Pray for grace.

ROOSTER: You're not operating on a practical level. You think God can help all the time?

MONICA: Every second.

(HE kisses HER violently, desperately. SHE draws away.)

ROOSTER: There're so many things I take delight in. You mostly. Nice to be young. To see trees like lace against the sky. You've gorgeous eyes. Forest green. One day, I'm going to take you to Antoine's. Buy you whatever you want. As long as you wear green. Green for spring time. Green for Christmas. It's the kind of bartering a husband can do. *(Pause)* Marry me.

(IRENE enters and glares at ROOSTER.)

IRENE: Monica, I need you to help with supper. Roo, Bunky needs you. I promise I'll be polite.

MONICA: Sure.

(ROOSTER exits)

IRENE: It's interesting how few Yankees have mastered this culture, Monica. What're you doing?

MONICA: Bringing in the plates.

IRENE: Oozie will do that. You mustn't think I condemn all travel. I imagine there're some invalids who can improve. Most Southerners would rather live with security. Sit...here. Why do you keep pushing my son?

MONICA: He's improving.

IRENE: Roo feels safe in New Orleans; it's the opposite of the fractured feeling he gets back east—

MONICA: He'll do even better in the mountains.

IRENE: I'm not going to rescue him like we did when he fled to the beach. Called the seagulls our ancestors. Painted from can't see to can't see. Driven by some undisguised lamentation.

MONICA: He wants your blessing to go.

IRENE: And after that, what is next?

MONICA: Don't mock him.

IRENE: I lived with the boy all his life. He's mine to use. But this time I...I can't teaspoon him back to life. *(Pause)* What are you? You're certainly very sure of yourself, but I'm not convinced you've any education at all. Where

ROSARY HARTEL O'NEILL

are your degrees? You come here and set yourself up as some radical healer. You've no friends, no phone calls. You never go out with any normal men.

MONICA: I know you lost your husband recently. I lost mine too. I think you probably miss him more than you realize.

IRENE: I got the sparks between you and my son. My intuition is like radar. *(Pause)* How long were you at it before you knew you were on your way... A week? Using your eyes as a sexual organ and this hocus-pocus spirituality as a guise. Your extremity is awe-inspiring. You wouldn't be the first girl thrown from nursing—for hysterical excess.

MONICA: Oh, Mrs. Dubonnet.

IRENE: It's important to have a fairly fast start in medicine, and my comments could destroy you.

MONICA: You wouldn't do that...I'm trying to help...Roo is a good person and a fine painter. He needs to use his days well.

IRENE: Painting made him sick. And your nasty affair will make him worse. Go pack. You're fired. Do what I tell you to do, or I'll have you removed.

(Removes and raises her gun)

MONICA: God almighty.

IRENE: Tomorrow morning at daybreak. Huck will drive you to the airport.

MONICA: Wait...

IRENE: Get out. *(Calls)* Oozie. Come here. Oozie.

(OOZIE hurries in with food)

OOZIE: Angela's gone. But dinner's ready.

IRENE: Oozie, Miss Falcon is leaving.

OOZIE: With Roo?

IRENE: Have Huck dump all the paintings. The garbage man will pick them up.

OOZIE: The garbage man?—

IRENE: I paid for them, and they belong to me.

MONICA: No, they belong to the creator.

IRENE: Get out!

MONICA: Each painting a little piece of his heart.

OOZIE: An old-fashioned?

IRENE: Get out.

MONICA: I'm not leaving.

(BUNKY comes in.)

BUNKY: (Rushing up) It's Bunky. Put down the gun.

IRENE: No! Never!

OOZIE: Get back.

(THEY struggle. IRENE shoots wildly at the ceiling. OOZIE collapses.)

OOZIE: She hit me. My arm. My leg! No, my shoulder. It's inside me, burning.

MONICA: For God's sake. She's still breathing.

IRENE: (To OOZIE) I'll make it up to you. We'll have a party at the Boston Club.

OOZIE: I don't feel a thing.

IRENE: She can't die. She's getting married.

END OF SCENE 2

ACT II
SCENE 3

(One week later. Five p.m., OOZIE'S wedding day. Light rain. IRENE crosses the stage slowly on BUNKY'S arm. Both are dressed in Victorian wedding attire as in the previous scene but they also wear coats and gloves.)

IRENE: *(Yells.)* Huck, take down the guns and lock the gates. *(To BUNKY)* Thanks for walking me.

BUNKY: *(Takes a silver bell from his pocket)* Want a wedding bell?

IRENE: You shouldn't have stolen so many. When I looked at Oozie all decked out, my feet gave way. She looked pretty. Happy. It was all so depressing.

BUNKY: Thank God she took off that sling.

IRENE: *(Pauses to catch her breath)* Wait. Let me dry your face; you're damp.

BUNKY: Drizzle.

(SHE dries his face with her handkerchief.)

IRENE: I'm changing my will. Roo's hurt me so. Arriving with that woman.

(THEY exit. ROOSTER enters. HE wears a jacket over slacks from the previous scene. HE looks weaker and drained. ROOSTER calls to his mother.)

ROOSTER: Ma. I wanted to say good-bye. Hey, Ma? Don't forget. I'm still your son.

IRENE: *(Returning to the doorway with BUNKY)* I haven't a son. Who's this stranger? *(Exits.)*

BUNKY: *(Calls back before exiting)* Try her after her nap.

ROOSTER: *(To BUNKY)* Right.

(MONICA enters in a lovely dress, accented in green. Some combination from the previous scene's attire is possible. ROOSTER glances at the garden.)

ROOSTER: The sun's already fading through the oak trees.

MONICA: *(Looks at her watch)* You've three hours before the plane.

ROOSTER: Yes.

MONICA: The next hour's mine.

ROOSTER: All of it?

MONICA: Every minute.

ROOSTER: I've never been this tired in all my life. Never.

MONICA: Come. Sit. *(Hands him some water.)* Rest a minute.

ROOSTER: I see more when I close my eyes.

MONICA: You do?

ROOSTER: If I shut my eyes, I see you.

MONICA: What about me?

ROOSTER: I plotted out our relationship, and I thought it was going to be real sexy. Every time I came near, you looked off to the side, and then you left.

MONICA: I didn't want to ruin anything.

ROOSTER: I felt ashamed because I'd wake up in these hot sweats and you acted like a nun. I'd such sexy ideas in such an utterly nonsexy place.

MONICA: Did you—well.

ROSARY HARTEL O'NEILL

ROOSTER: You knew it. Huh?

MONICA: Every morning when I saw myself in your eyes, it reminded me I wasn't buried with my husband.

ROOSTER: You never told me?

MONICA: You kept me going. The last year with my husband was a battle I lost every day and started the next. My husband wanted to die. He couldn't stand getting weak. He was strong before. Raced motorcycles for the thrill. He didn't want anyone to see that he couldn't walk, so I'd help him down to his motorcycle, and he'd drive it to the mailbox. The bike roaring beneath his thin legs. He'd come back to the stairs, exhausted and sit. And when no one was looking, he'd ease himself up one step at a time. I smiled from the window—so attentive to what he was doing, merged with his courage. But finally the world of matter faded away, and he gave up, and I gave up. I keep thinking of my husband lying inside his casket. When I went to choose the coffin, I was so broke I couldn't pay much. Now I'm glad I did. The lids of the better caskets fit so well. I ran my fingers over the smooth gold trim. I thought about rain leaking in the casket, and I went and bought an expensive airtight one. You think when people look at a casket, they know how much it costs?

ROOSTER: I doubt it. I want to remember this place…in case I don't see it again. My father sat right here with the evening paper. He didn't read the obituaries. Most of his friends were dead by fifty-five. At night he came to this room and drank. Southerners mark rooms by events, not years. This is the room where my father died. Dad was an alcoholic, but he'd a cat called Christmas. Its ears had been burnt in a fire. Every night that cat waited for Dad at the garage. And he'd walk it under his umbrella to this room. When Dad died, Christmas got in here and tore the room apart. Wadded the drapes. Knocked everything on the floor. Howled. Tonight, I feel like Christmas.

MONICA: It's started to rain again.

ROOSTER: New Orleans is saying good-bye.

MONICA: She's crying because she loves you so.

ROOSTER: (Pause) I asked you to come with me, and you never responded.

347

GHOSTS OF NEW ORLEANS

MONICA: You'll soon be working nonstop, free of concerns.

ROOSTER: Look, I won't be here tomorrow. Have you forgotten?

MONICA: Yes, I'd forgotten. It actually slipped my mind for a moment.

ROOSTER: You like rings?

MONICA: What are you doing?

ROOSTER: I'm putting one on your finger.

MONICA: It's a fine diamond. Someday, somebody will be happy with it.

ROOSTER: Fight again. I'll be on your side. I'm going to live. Come with me. *(HE kisses her.)*

MONICA: *(The rain begins to pour again.)* The best rain doesn't have warning. It is merciful. *(They exit together.)*

(IRENE enters. Plays "Irene Goodnight" on the gramophone and looks out sadly.)

END OF PLAY

ROSARY HARTEL O'NEILL

Photo: Harold Baquet
Pictured: Maria Mason,
Barret O'Brien.

ABOUT THE AUTHOR

ROSARY HARTEL O'NEILL is the author of fourteen plays produced internationally by invitation of the American embassy in Paris, Bonn, Tibilisi, Georgia, Budapest, Hungary, London and Moscow. Her play UNCLE VICTOR was chosen Best New American Drama by the Cort Theater, Hollywood, and celebrated in the Chekhov Now Festival in New York. BLACKJACK was selected for Alice's Fourth Floor Best New Play Series. She was founding artistic director at Southern Rep Theater from 1987 to 2002. She has been playwright-in-residence at the Sorbonne University, Paris; Tulane University, New Orleans; Defiance College, Ohio, the University of Bonn, Germany and Visiting Scholar at Cornell.

Other fellowships include the Virginia Center for the Creative Arts (VCCA) Playwrighting Fellowship to Wiepersdorf, Germany, and two fellowships to the Playwriting Center, Sewanee University. She also received a play invitation to the Actors Centre, London, as well as residences in playwriting at the VCCA, Ragsdale, Dorset Arts Colony, Byrdcliff Arts Colony, and the Mary Anderson Center.

She was chosen outstanding artist in Paris and awarded a Fulbright to Paris for her play WISHING ACES. She was a finalist in the Faulkner Competition for New American Writers; a finalist for outstanding artist for the state of Louisiana 2002; and a finalist in the Ireland Tyrone Guthrie Residency in playwriting with the VCCA 2002. She was awarded a Senior Fulbright research specialist in drama to Europe, 2001-2006, and received first invitations to the Conservatoire Nationale du Drame (leading acting-training center in Paris) and the Conservatoire Nationale de la Danse (leading dance-training center outside Paris).

Recent professional achievements include: DEGAS IN NEW ORLEANS, which was invited to the New End Theatre (a heralded theater for contemporary plays) in London and featured in the Best New American Play Oktoberfest of the Ensemble Studio Theatre (a leading theater for new work) in New York City and in the Reading Series of the Abingdon Theatre, New York. She is playwright-in-residence at the National Arts Club, where much of her recent work has been developed. *Author photo by DC Larue.*

Praise for Rosary Hartel O'Neill

Rosary Hartel O'Neill has been a blessing to our New Orleans' theater community since 1986. We had long since lost our only Equity house. Rosary's sheer determination and drive to create a venue for Southern actors to work in their region, on Southern themes that other theatres could only hope to capture the essence, resulted in the formation of Southern Rep Theatre, which raised the professional bar for all theatre in our area.

Rosary writes with a flair that speaks to the pathos, struggles and isolation of an artist, told through the steely humor and vulnerability of her characters. It is with great honor that I have watched as these plays also reached audience members in Moscow and Paris. Rosary's theatre, her characters, and the people whose lives she touches, is only part of her legacy. The other part is the Rosary Hartel O'Neill SPIRIT and VISION that radiates through and gives things the Rosary touch."

Diana Boylston
Director, Producer, Teacher and Casting Director in
NY and New Orleans for Voice acting and Acting

"Rosary O'Neill's body of work consistently reveals a deep understanding of the human condition, and even better, an abiding affection for the personalities she brings so vividly to life."

Rexanne Becnel
Novelist

"Rosary O'Neill is a talented, multi-faceted teacher and writer whose works are provocative and original. Her plays based in the Deep South literally transport the reader and audience member to that part of the country."

Nancy Gall-Clayton
Kentucky playwright.

PRAISE FOR ROSARY HARTEL O'NEILL

"Aside from grace and charm, Rosary, you have a great literary talent I admire deeply. This great quality exists not just in your many superb plays but in the way you created the Southern Repertory Theatre of New Orleans over many years and brought it to its superb final home in Canal Place. How fortunate that lately you have moved your high talents on to New York and your country home in Rhinecliff."

Robert Kornfeld
Co-chair, Literary Committee of The National Arts Club

"After four years at the National Endowment for the Arts my time as the Executive Director of the Division of the Arts for the State of Louisiana would have been a real let-down had I not discovered the wonderful New Orleans Playwright, Rosary O'Neill, and been afforded a front row seat on the premieres of WISHING ACES and SOLITAIRE. Louisiana has produced another playwright in the mode of Tennessee Williams. Her plays leave you with a satisfaction equal to that of a great dinner at Antoine's!"

Emma Hale Burnett
Former Executive Director, Division of the Arts, State of Louisiana

"A great Southern writer with a rare sense of the dramatic and historical. She brings back another century with her wondrous plays in old New Orleans. A gifted, strong, and successful playwright."

Cheryl Downey, Executive Director
Costume Designers Guild, IATSE 892

"Rosary has the uncanny ability to conjure up New Orleans — the smells, the air, the heat, the inhabitants — in some kind of inspired poetic fever. She is a devoted chronicler of the past and present Southern United States."

Julie McKee
Playwright, Teacher of Playwriting at HB Studios

353
GHOSTS OF NEW ORLEANS

For more information about the work of Rosary O'Neill,
visit her web site at:
www.rosaryoneill.com

PRODUCTIONS AND PUBLISHING

FOR PLAYS:
ENGLISH LANGUAGE RIGHTS
Samuel French, Inc.
45 W. 25th St., 2nd Floor
New York, NY 10010
212.206.8990

FOREIGN LANGUAGE RIGHTS
The Marton Agency, Inc.
1 Union Square W. / Suite 815
New York, NY 10003-3303
212.255.1908

FOR NOVELS:
Edythea Ginis Selman Literary Agency
14 Washington Square Place
New York, NY 10003
212.473.1874

ISBN 142515665-7

9 781425 156657